Frances Partridge was [...]
Bloomsbury, in 1900, or [...]
architect. She was educated at Newnham College,
Cambridge, where she read English and Moral
Sciences. In 1933 she married Ralph Partridge, who
died in 1960. In addition to translating many books
from French and Spanish and helping her husband to
edit *The Greville Memoirs*, she is the author of
Memories and five other published volumes of diaries,
A Pacifist's War, *Everything to Lose*, *Hanging On*,
Good Company and *Life Regained*.

Other People

DIARIES
September 1963–December 1966

FRANCES PARTRIDGE

PHOENIX

A PHOENIX PAPERBACK

First published in Great Britain
by HarperCollins Publishers in 1993
This paperback edition published in 1999 by Phoenix,
a division of Orion Books Ltd,
Orion House, 5 Upper St Martin's Lane,
London WC2H 9EA

A CIP catalogue record for this book
is available from the British Library.

ISBN: 0 75380 109 4

Printed and bound in Great Britain by
The Guernsey Press Co. Ltd, Guernsey, C.I.

List of Illustrations

All photographs supplied by the author.

Foreword

The last volume of my published diaries, *Hanging On*, covered a period of about three years starting from the death of my husband Ralph on November 30th, 1960 – a time during which I was making desperate attempts to establish some sort of *modus vivendi* out of the ashes of an extremely close and warm married life. It was a question, too, (by my own choice) of leaving Ham Spray House in Wiltshire, where I had been surrounded by the country and surroundings I loved, for the stark loneliness of a London flat. By the end of the book in the middle of August less than three years later I had to some extent come to terms with my new life, largely thanks to the incredible kindness and support of my friends. Our only son Burgo had settled happily – also in London – with a young, beautiful and charming wife Henrietta Garnett, and the birth of their child Sophie on August 9th, 1963 made a *coda* to the book and seemed to give me a fresh interest in the future. I believed that a spell of reasonably calm and contented life lay before me. I was wrong. On September 7th out of the sky came death and disaster. Without any warning Burgo was struck dead by a heart attack while telephoning his friend Peter Jenkins.[1] His condition had not been suspected and Henrietta and I were told that nothing could have been done even if it had. I was too stunned and shattered to write anything in my diary except a bleak statement of the facts, adding 'I have utterly lost heart: I want no more of this cruel life.'

A few weeks later Henrietta (who had been incredibly brave) took two-months-old Sophie, and was whisked away to stay with her parents David ('Bunny') and Angelica Garnett in their house in France, while I went on dumbly preparing to carry out a previously made plan to go with Raymond Mortimer to Apulia. I don't think I was even capable of realizing at the time what a heroic act of friendship he showed me in going ahead with it. I made a deliberate but unsuccessful decision to live in the present.

[1] The political journalist.

1

Dramatis Personae

BRENAN, GERALD, writer and hispanologist. He had been one of Ralph's greatest friends ever since they were together in the First War, despite rows caused by his making love to Ralph's first wife Dora Carrington and to disagreements over the Second War. He was at this time living in Churriana in southern Spain. He was married to Gamel Woolsey, American poetess, and had one daughter.

CAMPBELL, ROBIN and SUSAN. Cyril Connolly had introduced us to Robin in 1948, when he was living near us at Stokke with his second wife, Mary (now DUNN). He had lost a leg and won a DSO in the war. After his divorce from Mary he married Susan Benson, writer of cookery and garden books, and himself joined the Arts Council. Robin and Susan had two sons, William and Arthur.

CARRINGTON, NOEL and CATHARINE, Dora Carrington's youngest brother and his wife (née Alexander). Ralph had been at Oxford with Noel, who became a publisher and designer, and died in 1989. They were country neighbours in reach of Ham Spray. Of their three children we saw most of Joanna.

CECIL, LORD DAVID and his family. We had known David's wife Rachel, daughter of our old friends Desmond and Molly MacCarthy, since she was a schoolgirl, and travelled with her before and after her marriage. Their children were Jonathan (actor), Hugh and Laura. The whole family were very kind to me after Ralph's death and I often stayed with them.

COCHEMÉ, JOAN, painter, especially of children's portraits, and a faithful friend for many years. She hastened to be with me when Burgo died. Her husband was Jacques Cochemé, biologist, native of Mauritius, and at this time a member of the Food and Agriculture Organization in Rome, where they were living in the Sixties.

DUNN, LADY MARY. Our warm friendship began in 1948 when she was living (and actively farming the land) at Stokke with her second husband Robin Campbell. After their divorce she made an unhappy match with Charlie McCabe, columnist of a San Franciscan newspaper. At the opening of this volume she was legally McCabe and dividing her time between Stokke and San Francisco. The situation is complicated by the fact that her first husband, Sir Philip Dunn ('the Tycoon') lived not far away in Wiltshire. Philip and Mary had two daughters, Serena and Nell, friends and contemporaries of Burgo's. They eventually remarried.

GARNETT, DAVID, and family. Only son of Edward and Constance Garnett, the eminent translator from Russian, David was generally known as 'Bunny'. He married my sister Ray in 1921, the year that I was taken on as assistant in his bookshop, Birrell and Garnett. He was thus my boss, brother-in-law, and a great friend for life. When his first book *Lady into Fox* won the Hawthornden Prize he left the shop to write over twenty more. Ray died of cancer in 1940, and in 1942 Bunny married Angelica, daughter of Duncan Grant and Vanessa Bell. He had two sons by Ray (Richard and William) and four daughters by Angelica; Burgo married the second, Henrietta, in 1962; the others were Amaryllis, and the twins – Fanny and Nerissa.

GATHORNE-HARDY, JONATHAN (Jonny) and SABRINA. The popular nephew of Lady Anne Hill and Eddie Gathorne-Hardy was at the time married to Sabrina Tennant, daughter of Virginia, Marchioness of Bath and David Tennant, creator of the Gargoyle Club, and was launching a career as a writer.

GOODMAN, CELIA, one of the well-known Paget twins, who used as girls to make glamorous appearances at concerts and Glyndebourne. Her sister Mamaine married Arthur Koestler and died at only thirty-seven. Celia's husband was Arthur Goodman, who had spent a gruelling time in a Japanese prison in the war and was now working in Shell, and they had two young children. I had only met Celia a few years before this book begins.

GOWING, LAWRENCE, painter of the Euston Road Group, had married in 1952 my 'best friend' Julia Strachey. She was eighteen years his senior, a gifted but very unproductive writer, an original, eccentric and at times difficult character.

4

HENDERSON, SIR NICHOLAS (Nicko) and LADY (MARY). Ralph and I had been friends of Nicko's parents, and he had come to swim in our pool as a boy. After he married Mary they came often to Ham Spray. He joined the Foreign Service when he was refused by the RAF on medical grounds. They had one daughter, Alexandra.

HILL, HEYWOOD and LADY ANNE (née Gathorne-Hardy). Our friendship began in about 1938, when they were both working in the famous bookshop in Curzon Street created by Heywood, and which still bears his name. When Heywood joined the army in the war, Anne kept the shop going with the help of Nancy Mitford. In the early Sixties the Hills were living in Richmond with their two grown-up daughters, Harriet and Lucy. Anne had four brothers, of whom the second, Eddie, had long been a friend of ours and a visitor to Ham Spray.

JACKSON, JANETTA (née Woolley, now Parladé). Ralph and I met her as a very attractive girl of fourteen, in Spain at the start of the Civil War. Young enough to be our daughter, she became instead one of our closest friends, and figures prominently in all my diaries. At the start of this one her marriages to Robert Kee and Derek Jackson had both ended in divorce and she was living with her children in Montpelier Square, but spending a lot of time in Spain. Her three daughters were Nicolette (Nicky) Loutit, Georgiana (Georgie) Kee and Rose Jackson.

JEBB, JULIAN, grandson of Hilaire Belloc, to whose small house in Sussex he sometimes invited his friends. Always interested in opera, theatre and cinema, in 1963 he was a journalist heading towards television. An excellent mimic and raconteur, and an affectionate friend.

KEE, ROBERT, Oxford friend of Nicko Henderson, who brought him to Ham Spray soon after his release from prison camp in Germany, where he spent three years after being shot down while a bomber pilot in the RAF. He very quickly became one of our greatest friends, and before long married another – Janetta. They both figure prominently in my earlier diaries, but the marriage became stormy, and by 1963 they had parted and Robert was married to Cynthia Judah. He had one daughter, Georgie, by Janetta, and a son and daughter, Alexander and Sarah, by Cynthia. He is a writer of novels and history – in particular of Irish history – and has also appeared in many television programmes.

KNOLLYS, EARDLEY, one of the three original owners of Long Crichel House, he was still living there in the Sixties, but had just decided to give up working for the National Trust in favour of his new love – painting.

MCCABE, LADY MARY *see* DUNN, LADY MARY

MORTIMER, RAYMOND, writer on art and literature, at one time literary editor of the *New Statesman*, then for many years top book reviewer on the *Sunday Times*. Our neighbour when Ralph and I lived in Bloomsbury, he became a close friend of us both, coming often to Ham Spray and travelling with us by car in France. He joined his three friends at Long Crichel House soon after the inauguration. Travel and reading were his greatest pleasures.

PARLADÉ, JAIME, eldest son of a prominent Andalusian family. Ralph and I met him in the Fifties in Marbella, where he owned an antique shop, which afterwards developed into a decorating and architectural business. He is now married to Janetta.

PENROSE, LIONEL and MARGARET, and their extremely clever family. Lionel was an FRS and Galton Professor of Genetics; his wife Margaret had been my friend at Bedales School, Newnham College and ever since; Oliver and Roger are distinguished mathematicians; Jonathan was British Chess Champion for ten years; Shirley is a clinical geneticist. All addicted to chess and music.

PHILLIPS, 'MAGOUCHE' (now FIELDING). American by birth, her first husband, the famous Armenian painter Arshile Gorky, gave her her unusual name. After his death she married Jack Phillips. Later she came to Europe and lived in France, Italy and London with her four daughters (Maro and Natasha Gorky, Antonia and Susannah Phillips), in all of which places she made a great many friends. I got to know her through Mary Dunn and Janetta.

PHIPPS, LADY (FRANCES), widow of the diplomat Sir Eric Phipps; she had been ambassadress at Berlin and Paris. She and I made friends late in our lives but had quickly become intimate, agreeing on such subjects as politics, war and peace, sharing many tastes in books, opera, and even for driving Minis. She was a talented amateur painter.

SACKVILLE-WEST, EDWARD (Eddy) had become fifth Baron Sackville at the age of sixty, on the death of his father in 1962. His musical talent had already appeared at Eton, and after Oxford he became a music critic, as well as novelist, biographer and poet. One of the three original owners of Long Crichel House, he still spent half the year there even after buying Cooleville House, County Tipperary.

SHAWE-TAYLOR, DESMOND one of the three original owners of Long Crichel House. Writer on music and other subjects, in the Sixties, he was music critic for the *Sunday Times*.

STONE, REYNOLDS and his family. We first met them as country neighbours during the war, and acquaintance became friendship later when they lived at their romantic rectory at Litton Cheney, Dorset. Reynolds was a brilliant engraver on wood and stone, painter of trees and designer; Janet is a professional portrait photographer. They had four children: Edward, Humphrey, Phillida and Emma.

STRACHEY, ISOBEL, first wife of John (Lytton's nephew who had intervened in the Bussy inheritance), but long since divorced. Her only child Charlotte had been a great friend of Burgo's since childhood and was now married to Peter Jenkins. Isobel had published several novels and stories and was a dearly loved crony of mine.

STRACHEY, JAMES and ALIX (née Sargant Florence). James was Lytton's youngest brother. Both were practising psychoanalysts of long standing and James had translated the entire works of Freud in twenty-three volumes, indexed by me. Ralph and I felt towards them as though they were blood relations.

STRACHEY, JULIA *see* GOWING

TENNANT, GEORGIA, daughter of David Tennant, creator of the Gargoyle Club and Virginia, Marchioness of Bath. I first met her staying with Janetta in Alpbach, Austria in the summer of 1961, and took a great fancy to her, which built up into a firm friendship. A delightful and intelligent girl, who was at the time in a state of indecision as to what she should do with her life.

WEST, KITTY, the painter Katharine Church. She had married Anthony West, son of Rebecca West and H. G. Wells, who had left her and made a life in America. She was living in a charming little Dorset cottage to which she had added a big studio, and had also opened a gallery and craft shop in Blandford.

Houses

CRICHEL (as Long Crichel House, near Wimborne, Dorset is affectionately known to its intimates). At the end of the Second War three bachelor friends decided to look for a country house where they could gather for weekends and holidays, and invite their friends to stay. There were two music critics, Edward (Eddy) Sackville-West and Desmond Shawe-Taylor, and Eardley Knollys, representative of the National Trust and later painter. They soon found what they wanted – a charming Georgian stone house, formerly a rectory, with three good-sized living-rooms and a plentiful number of bedrooms. Great thought and care were given to the decorations and furnishings; the garden had a well-kept croquet lawn, several statues, and a terrace sheltered from the wind by glass sides and with a floor decorated by the owners with their initials in mosaic. Two sets of what were then called 'radiograms' of the highest quality, quantities of books, a series of resident staff and one or two dogs completed a ménage where conversation, music and croquet thrived. A few years later Raymond joined the original three as a resident 'Crichel boy'. In 1949 Ralph and I spent the first of many greatly enjoyed visits there. Only one of the original four, Desmond, survives to entertain at Crichel, but the house has never been without hosts to keep alive its unique atmosphere.

HILTON HALL, near Huntingdon, was acquired by my sister Ray from a legacy and is still inhabited by her elder son Richard and his wife Jane. She and Bunny fell in love with it from a photograph in a newspaper. It is indeed a very beautiful, stately but not large, Queen Anne house, and until Richard's day had been very little modernized. It still has panelled walls, flagged stone floors and a fine staircase of dark carved wood; in the Sixties it was one of the coldest houses I ever slept in. All Bunny's children, by Ray and Angelica, were brought up there and loved it dearly.

9

STOKKE near Great Bedwyn, Wiltshire. Robin and Mary Campbell were living in this rambling, Virginia-creeper covered house when we first got to know them, along with Mary's daughters by her first marriage and Robin's two sons by his. Mary was farming the surrounding land. The large garden was somewhat unkempt, except for Robin's rockery. Indoors the atmosphere was lively and semi-bohemian: youthful feet might be heard echoing along the upstairs passages in a game of cocky-olly, while downstairs in the long L-shaped living-room their elders sat round the big stove talking and laughing with visiting writers and painters or an occasional philosopher or millionaire.

1963—4

September 21st: Rome

Among many devastating emotions and events of my last days in London, first came my increasing love and admiration for Henrietta, and the bitter-sweet taste of all she told me of the happiness she and Burgo had had together; next Bunny's arrival, rosy and amiable, but not saying *one* word of regret for Burgo, only talking about settlements and arrangements; the tremendous kindness and solid support of Robert Kee, Julian Jebb, Joan Cochemé and many others; my visit from Rosamond Lehmann, and her hopeless woolly attempt to interest me in the spirit world.

Yesterday morning Raymond and I left London and flew here smoothly. The struggle to make my tired muscles of courage and composure respond to my will resulted in great physical fatigue, like the useless effort to use one's legs after running down a mountain.

The warm golden light enveloped us as we got out of the aeroplane; so did the incredible, magnificent beauty when we walked later up to the Capitol. I have woken early in a small austere room in the Hotel Minerva, to the deafening clash of street noise.

That same afternoon Raymond and I travelled in a train lined with red plush to Bari, and after being first rejected – '*completo*' – were taken in by a comfortable hotel on the edge of the sea.

September 22nd: Bari

The old town of Bari is charmingly pretty; a network of alleys and tunnels, brightly painted, with birds and flowers hanging outside, old women sitting on kitchen chairs knitting, and countless scrimmaging children. The two churches were noble Byzantine-style buildings with shallow rounded apses – their silvery stone in strange contrast to the white, pink and blue of the streets. Our sightseeing

11

however has almost immediately got confused in my mind – Mola, Monopoli . . . What did we see in which? Where was a doorway with two columns supported by wistful cows? Where a font carried by putti? Where a bishop's chair weighing down the crushed heads of two lions? Mixed in with all this sightseeing came the business of getting our hired car from the garage (an eggshell-green Fiat) and the awful angst of trying to remember how to start it and then drive it. I had not bargained with the novelty of a lefthand drive and almost at once scraped very slightly against another car, but towards the end of our journey I began to relax. Raymond can't drive, so I'm glad to be able to repay him for all he has done for me, all the paying of bills as well as planning of sightseeing, for his sweetness too and benignity to everyone.

We had decided to make for the extraordinary region of the Selva which is covered with small beehive shaped houses called *trulli*, the domes generally grey, the rest freshly whitewashed, and the domes smartly finished with a little cup and ball of white. Rising everywhere among groves of olives and vines, they looked quite fantastic and often very pretty; sometimes like collections of tents.

In our little car we clambered up and up through the *trulli* and the olives, high above the plain, and here at last stood our destination, the Villa Paradiso. It was obviously a summer haunt and lunch place, not a soul there but us. Very soon its queerness began to emerge. The rooms *looked* fine – but when Raymond put his attaché-case on a table it collapsed at once. The light above my bed would only stay on if you held the switch up in the air. As I was looking forward to an evening read I asked for it to be mended. Two youths took the switch apart and put it together again over and over, giving themselves electric shocks, for three quarters of an hour. Then '*sarebbe meglio*', I contrived to say, '*di darmi una altra camera*'. They went to fetch the *padrone* who was simply furious. 'Change your room?' he yelled at me. 'Why?' '*Perche sono "cansada" e vorrei riposarmi?*' I said relapsing into part-Spanish. '*Zanzara??*' they all cried in astonishment. (It means 'mosquito'.) I bethought myself of '*stanca*' at last, and grudgingly a new room (there were obviously dozens) was provided. I was lying quietly on the double-bed when half of *it* collapsed! I slept that night on the other half.

Our dinner was niggardly and bad, and the only red wine available had a label with 'Happy Drink' on it. We dared not try it.

Tuesday was a longer driving day, about 120 kilometres, and at the end of it getting into Lecce (which proved to be a large, populous

12

animated town crowded with cars and jay-walkers and one-way streets) about finished me off. But I think perhaps it more effectively numbed the aching nerve of the source of my pain than any other day hitherto has done. We have got so far away that the navel-string attaching us to normal life is stretched as thin as silk.

I am driving the Fiat with more confidence, the sky is royal blue, the sweat streams down my back. On to Martina Franca where every street and every building was pretty – a perfect marvel. And so on here to Lecce. Trouble again getting in, but our old-fashioned hotel is quiet and sympathetic. I was too tired to take in the town at first, but after two days of wandering about among its golden baroque churches it begins to grow on me.

September 26th

Our last day at Lecce. Last night, over a plate of inedibly tough meat in a restaurant, Raymond and I tried to hack out our plans. As I rather feared, he may want me to drive longer distances than I like. I said four hours in any one day would be too much, that I was feeling feebler than I'd thought. (This is true. I've had several migraines.) He was angelic and said of course I mustn't, but it means cutting out a good many of the desirable sights and this distresses me as well as him.

September 27th: Gallipoli, 6 p.m.

Lying on my bed in the first of these disgusting Jolly hotels I have yet sampled. It is a monk's cell, smelling strongly of stale tobacco. Apparently no one who is not part of a married couple is allowed to have a bath in these marvellous modern hotels: they have no private shower even and public bathrooms do not exist. Worst of all it is miles outside the town and on a noisy crossroads. We arrived here early on a golden afternoon and I would have loved to walk round the town after a brief rest but felt too nervously exhausted to set out again at once. The driving *is* exacting: and poor Raymond is hopelessly bad at map-reading, inclined to ask me (in a mild voice while other drivers hoot) which I think is the way, and not realizing that the one thing the driver needs is to be firmly directed. However he is angelically good-tempered and never minds asking the way of strangers. Because we went astray more than once and tried to take a road which stopped suddenly with the cheerful notice *Pericolo di*

13

morte, it turned into quite a long day's drive. I feel discouraged this evening. Can I do it? That's the question that at present occupies my mind to the exclusion of anything else. I have my dear glass of whisky beside me this evening and hope with its help to get sufficient strength to drive us into the unknown streets of the town for our dinner.

But I mustn't forget the great visual pleasure and beauty that today has provided: Ótranto's splendid church with a vast twelfth-century mosaic (an enormous tree and hundreds of grotesque animals and figures) stretching all over its floor. The sea in the harbour in stripes of turquoise and navy flecked with white. Our lovely drive along the Adriatic coast towards the southernmost point, by a fine road bordered with trees and rocks, looking down through olives to the blue sea and little havens full of blue and green fishing boats.

Raymond has been incredibly kind. He went out reconnoitring while I lay fuming and unrelaxed on my bed, and when dinner-time came we drove in to a little fish restaurant floating like an ark in the port, ate red mullet and drank a lot of mild rosé wine, then walked slowly through the pretty little old town, illuminated and *en fête*, with strings of girls and dashing young men, old women sitting beaming, while small children reeled along intoxicated with their gala toys.

September 29th: Táranto, 7 a.m.

From my quiet little bedroom I see and hear nothing but sea and sky and the chug of fishing-boat engines. None the less I woke about five this morning, to the usual doubts – can I do it? etc. Must try and glean an afternoon rest. Yesterday was very hot. Found my first batch of letters, fifteen or so – the most human being two from Joan. They twanged on the painful strings of reality.

7 p.m. (same day), Altamura, in a much less quiet bedroom, with a glass of whisky by my side and feeling pretty desperate. There is a fortnight more of this 'holiday' and I'm wondering if I can survive it. What a hollow mockery it is! True there is constant visual beauty, a flicker of interest here and there, amusement even, but it all lies like scum on the surface of a stagnant pool of heartbreak. And if I don't let myself plumb those dark depths, I'm haunted by the fear of shock – the dreadful moments of realization: that huge white face pressed so suddenly and menacingly into one's own. I should get out of this

14

world, this life. It's the only rational thing – I know it. Yet either
cowardice or some obstinate clinging to life may well prevent me.
I've no confidence in anything any more, when such savage
backhanders may come at one any moment. I'm pretty nearly in a
state of persecution-mania. Well, what use is it anatomizing my
melancholy?

October 1st: Andria

At Castel del Monte (a pink octagonal castle) I felt too weak to visit
it. Instead I let Raymond go alone; went to have a drink in a café and
rushed to be sick. We'd hoped to stay in that strange place (there
were a few rooms) but none were left, so on to this rather
meaningless town of Andria we came. Alas, I had all afternoon been
aware of a flu-like ache in my legs. I now began to feel boiling hot. I
swallowed some aspirins, but when dear Raymond poked his
solicitous face in about six-thirty I had no doubt I'd 'got something'.
Raymond's thermometer showed a temperature of 102° and he
insisted on getting a doctor, a nice young Italian who gave me some
pills which strangely enough seem to have worked, and today I feel
almost normal but am still quite happy to stay in bed. I'm terribly
upset at bringing this distress on Raymond, and don't know how to
make it up to him and become a more lively travelling companion.
To tell the truth the driving had quite tired me out and I'm glad to
take a total rest in bed.

At Castel del Monte I found a mass of the only pretty autumn
flower I've seen – the yellow crocus-like Sternbergia.

October 2nd

Woke at 4.40 a.m. and didn't sleep again. However I am marvellously recovered, got up and packed without effort, and found myself
with positive pleasure at the wheel of the trusty little car. We spun
across a flat plain with saline marshes and long greyish marquees of
extracted salt, to Manfredonia on the Heel of Italy.

October 4th: Manfredonia

Two peaceful days of eating, sleeping and reading have been almost
serene, and brought a feeling of intimacy and affection between
Raymond and me – not that it wasn't there already. I think we

understand each other better and for my part I love him more warmly than ever.

A few letters from England met us here: Bunny's is the one I wake in the night and think about. Henrietta and Sophie have returned to England already and he says their visit was a great success. Henrietta 'came more alive' – as if she had not been frantically and frighteningly alive in London – and this was partly because he had left the parcel containing her pills behind. Then comes a cheerful description of their life, visitors and the meals they cook.

I feel somehow in spite of all that is endearing in Bunny a certain ruthless selfishness and lack of sensitivity. He simply can't begin to imagine the nature of the shock Henrietta experienced if he thinks she could have got through it without pills.

Also there is something irksome to me in the way he cheerfully throws the responsibility on me for helping this poor eighteen-year-old girl deal with lawyers, flats, clearing-up, finding somewhere to live and all the rest of it, and gets back to collecting and purging his snails and cooking them with lots of butter and garlic.

October 5th: Hotel Jolly, Caserta

Well of course in the end I wrote to Bunny letting out something of what his letter had made me feel. As for the Garnett lack of responsibility towards Henrietta, I put in rather a sly dig, saying that I was very sorry they couldn't persuade her to stay longer in France but that I supposed they 'couldn't be very worried about her or one of them would have gone back with her to help'. It's really rather monstrous of me, because I'm trading on Bunny's affection and good opinion of me – but I did somehow want to give a clue to the fact that I personally was done for, in need of support myself, and that I felt it was their turn to take a hand. Why in heaven's name don't they *want* to?

October 6th: Caserta

Raymond and I got our excursion to Monte Saint Angelo. A strange and rewarding expedition. We foolishly took the 'old road' up the three thousand feet to the town, and it soon lost all pretence at a surface and tossed us between pot-holes, slabs of living rock and dusty white runnels worked by the rain. I am glad we took it, as our approach to the town along the very summit of the ridge was dramatic in the extreme, while below (whenever I could snatch a glance) the wide sweep of the bay dropped quickly down and away, the sea became aquamarine and only faintly rippled and Manfredonia a white blur. Triumph – there we were at the top and it was suddenly cold. A fierce town, full of barbarous little boys pretending to throw stones at the car, attaching themselves to us and badgering us: the rapacious cynical atmosphere of all pilgrimage places. The pilgrimage church was extraordinary too. One descended about eighty steps to find it hollowed out inside a prehistoric cave. This morning, brilliant once more, we took the train to this place and after lunch went to see the Royal Palace – Italy's Versailles. The palace was the most pompous and splendiferous building – surely the wretched little Bourbon kings must have felt dwarfed rather than aggrandized by these vast wide staircases, enormously tall rooms decorated with gilt, and huge statues and complicated inter-arching corridors.

October 8th: Naples

We have been in Naples two days in a comfortable, expensive, sympathetic hotel on the port. I like it, but it is almost too vast, and the streets are congested with hooting streams of crawling cars. Its liveliness is almost crushing. There are organ-grinding musicians touring the restaurants round the port, swooning tenors bellowing into one's ears, and the inevitable brides in faintly bluish muslin are everywhere, attended by slightly hysterical wedding parties lasting for hours.

Yesterday we went to look at the huge and magnificent gallery at Capodimonte: superb Masaccios and Bellinis and Botticellis; a whole room full of Titians; Greco and Goya.

October 10th

I'm counting the days till we get home. I wish we could go tomorrow. I'm conscious of the character of the town, but I never want to see it again as long as I live. See Naples, yes, and then die.

October 11th: Ravello

However today has been a better day. We got up early and took a bus to Amalfi and Ravello. It was without exception the most sensational

17

road I've ever travelled on and I would rather have been in a small private car than in this immensely long monster driven full lick and with bravura by our young and dashing chauffeur. We swirled round corners, lingered by overhanging cliffs, leaned over narrow parapets, and far below was the blue sea and a series of fantastically picturesque villages with their ports full of fishing-boats. Amalfi was hot and summery and people were bathing; I would have quite liked to stay there but on and up we came to this windy but charming village. The hotel is comfortable, has sunny terraces and (I do really believe) eatable food.

October 13th

Delicious weather all day. Thankfully I have sat and soaked up sun, realizing that this is the only day in all this holiday that I have been able to do so. After lunch today I went and sat in the sun again – it's only possible till about three – rather than lying indoors on my bed. Raymond looked almost pained at such independence, and I was pounced on by a friendly elderly American lady with a passion for Piero della Francesca.

October 14th

This evening, DV, will see us back in London. With all its commitments, sources of worry, faces of friends, piles of letters. On the whole I am anxious to get back, though the last three days have provided the dazzling, hot, balmy weather we have missed for so long. We took a taxi all the way back from Ravello, stopping at Pompeii for over two hours and no extravagance was more worthwhile; we saw the best, and compared to Herculaneum which is a livid mummy, Pompeii is pretty and has weeds springing everywhere, its paved streets intact, much more like a living town. The casts of people and dogs caught by the lava left me unmoved. The obscene paintings were shut away behind hatches, only shown to men – '*non va bene per le donne*'. Far the most striking thing was the painted room in the Villa dei Misteri with beautifully preserved strange, emotionally charged figures, large and boldly painted on a shining crimson ground.

So here we are back at Naples, not knowing quite what to do with our remaining time, for we have picked its bones pretty thoroughly. I must say that Raymond's natural sweetness makes him accept eagerly any suggestion I make, rather than at once seeing its drawbacks as some would. Slept badly thinking of how to get astride once more that infinitely intractable horse my LIFE, of all the 'things to do today' in London, wondering about Henrietta and Sophie, and what I'll find, and whether anything has happened in my absence (births, deaths) and about Janetta and Joan.

And I do hope the gush of London swirling round me will restore me a little to life and thought. It's really not fair to inflict poor kind Raymond with my dazed stupidity.

October 16th

I'm back. Infinite kindness and thoughtfulness of friends – Joan and Janetta especially. Henrietta and Sophie to lunch yesterday – Sophie's eyes are becoming black as night and she has a distinct look of Burgo. My friends' anxious faces looking to see whether love for the two of them is going to pin me to life.

October 18th

Days of trying to straighten things for Henrietta and talks to the footling Mr Bye of Craig's[1] firm (Oh good*bye* Mr Bye – 'By the by, Mr Bye' – 'Well I'll do that by and by, Mr Bye' – 'I hereby enclose' and so forth); talks to Bunny, to Craig, to David Galloway (Burgo's executor) have to some extent clarified the position. When I wake in the night it is the faces of Henrietta and Sophie that rise instantly before me and I start to turn over ways and means of helping without interfering.

I had a lovely evening with Janetta.

The sky is pure blue and the sun has developed a midsummer strength. I am lying on my bed at 4 p.m. trying to fight off despair. I'm not sure that I *can* stand much more of this. I have no libido to put into anything. It suddenly seems to me an act of insane folly to try to go on; it strikes me as illogical, irrational, even uncharacteristic behaviour, which I'm unable to justify and feel positively apologetic for. I am like a trailer that has broken loose and is rattling down hill out of control.

[1] Macfarlane, family solicitor and great friend.

October 20th: Cooleville House, Ireland[1]

Every word that I wrote last was true, but of course it is not logic nor rational processes that hold one to life, but only blind instinct. Talked a little to Janetta on these lines.

If anything could bring peace, relaxation, anodyne, it is this sweet and soft green country, whose flavour is on one's lips from the first moment of getting to the Aer Lingus station. Enjoyed my solitary flight. We were in clouds most of the way, but approaching Cork I saw a pale lake of blue opening ahead and on landing found myself in the middle of gentle all-pervading afternoon sunlight. A beautiful drive through this mellow evening glow, lying dazzling bright on the unexpectedly broad rivers, and lighting up the mixed colours of the already 'turning' trees. Recognition with pleasure – of the little fields tufted with rough grass and thistles, the groups of children on the empty roads, the lack of hurry, the absence of angst. It is like settling into a soft and especially comfortable armchair.

Found Julian and Eddy Sackville snugged in over the fire in the fine red room. It's a great comfort to find Julian here – three's company, two's none, or rather I want a rest from pseudo-marriage, and I am always afraid of 'paining' Eddy. It is enormously comfortable here in an old-fashioned way, food delicious. A horsefaced breezy middle-aged spinster came to dinner and I toppled into bed exhausted and slept soundly.

October 21st: Wexford

After lunch we drove to Wexford for two nights of the Opera festival, and I am lying in bed after the first of them – *Don Pasquale*. Lord, I find it cold though, and everyone else says how warm it is. I put the eiderdown from the second bed on top of me and slept in my dressing gown. The efforts of the Irish to please are most touching – there is a bowl of fruit in my bedroom. When I came in last night a complimentary packet containing two chocolates to bring 'sweet dreams' lay on each pillow – that which was assumed to be male flavoured with rum, the female one with orange. In a further attempt to make two people out of me they had wrapped my dressing gown round a hot-water bottle in one bed and my nightgown in the other. I was very glad of both, and plan to go out and buy woolly vests or a very thick Irish sweater.

[1] Staying with Eddy Sackville.

This is a friendly little festival – the weather so very unfestive (blowing and raining), the theatre a good way short of full, but the performance professional and lively.

I said I shouldn't see my Italian journey in perspective till I got home and it was true. Now I see that it was not a 'failure', that it was a salvage operation carried out more or less successfully and entirely thanks to Raymond's kindness and patience. My God, the electric fire has gone out! Time to get up.

October 23rd

Back at Cooleville. A gentle theatrical light begins to shine from under the hanging roof of dark clouds – the quiet and peace exuded by mile after mile of green damp surrounding country invades my bedroom. I do find it soothing here. Yesterday we left Wexford fairly early on a brilliant morning – but by the time we had got back here it was raining and I only went out to pad round the garden and pick dripping flowers. Scrabble in the evening – amusing set-to between Eddy and Julian (claws beneath velvet pads) over the rules. The talk is chiefly about people, anecdotic, superficial, but easy and often funny. Julian remarked *à propos* of imitating people (which he does brilliantly) that he could do me very easily and often did. I was astonished. It is part of one's view of one's hidden, anonymous identity that there's nothing to imitate.

Suddenly there are only two whole days left and I mean to get all I can out of them and not worry unduly about what awaits me in London. I am reading a French book for Gollancz, which gives me the semblance of work to do, and whether it is – as I suspect – that I have in every way weakened and given up, I seem to require less exacting tasks to get my teeth into, though at the back of my mind stirs the need to get something else soon. I had a shock at receiving a letter from *The Times*, asking me to write an obituary of Raymond for their files – unreasonable but outraged indignation.

Julian and I spent a morning reading in Eddy's new plant- and window-lined conservatory, oval in shape, both of us lying on long garden chairs. Julian was supposed to be reading a book for review, but I looked up and saw his eyes fixed, wide open and sad, over the top of his book. He is too vulnerable ever to be really happy.

October 26th

Back, oh back in rat-race London: speeding up of heartbeats and breathing, restlessness, times of near insanity.

I find it less and less reasonable or practicable to make the effort not to seem sunk in gloom, yet I would be prepared to guess that I do on the whole succeed in creating a false impression except to near and dear friends like Janetta; I'm constantly and painfully aware of being monstrously deformed by affliction, someone to be avoided by all: this makes me long to creep away into my hole and hide my head, and attain oblivion – the temporary one of sleep if I can't have the final one of death.

Ireland was a poultice on my pain, a sweet draught of illusion, thankfully lapped up – but one of the things I find hardest to deal with is that I cannot leave any empty space in my waking day, for fear of the desperate thoughts and feelings that crowd in. They can force the barrier of some delightful passive occupation like driving or walking in beautiful country which makes me prefer to it some footling activity like playing Scrabble. Scrabbling through my life somehow is what I seem to be doing, but God only knows what is the point of it.

Last night I dined with Janetta, Julian and Georgia Tennant and felt I was a grim skeleton at the board. Julian got fussed and over-talked himself; Georgia was inscrutable, and I wondered what had passed between her and Janetta since I last saw Janetta who looked rather sad and exhausted.

November 1st

I padded out in pouring rain and lunched with Heywood Hill, and in the evening Richard Garnett came for a drink and I went to my medical orchestra. The feeling of deformity by affliction still oppresses me. It is as if I was a pilot whose face had been horrifyingly mashed about in the war. Is one to force people to accept me, when they would much rather forget I exist?

Doctor Dicks[1] came beaming up to say he saw Burgo was a father. Oh dear – how to spare people and myself embarrassment? I wince and shrivel for hours ahead over such possibilities. And I have nothing funny or interesting to contribute to the general pool – just

[1] A member of the Medical Orchestra I belonged to. I played the second violin, and our weekly rehearsals were one of my greatest joys.

22

dark thoughts, or fierce rebarbative conclusions summing up my dislike of the Universe. I am very clearly aware of my slow subsidence into the bog.

I lay on my bed most of the afternoon reading Ottoline Morrell's Memoirs and finding her uncongenial; she was fundamentally a silly woman, who thought with her heart not her head; her enthusiasms were fuzzy and sentimental – 'I love heaths and wide open country, Milton, loveliness and Mozart' is the sort of thing she says. Her editor Bob Gathorne-Hardy treats her respectfully like royalty, and quotes her feeble remarks just as those of the Queen are set down. I must say she and her husband Philip did back some writers and painters, but the only thing I really respect her for is her pacifism.

November 3rd

A beautiful autumn morning, sunlight lying gently on the dewy grass and lighting up the red brick faces of the comfortable little stockbrokers' weekend houses I see under the branches of the huge cedar outside my window: I'm staying at the Goodmans in Crondall near Farnham, and this time Arthur, the father of the family, is here, and Wilfred Blunt,[1] as well as Celia and the two children and the crazy old Polish female retainer. Last night a writer, Sir John Verney, and his tall rheumatic wife came to dinner. Everyone is civilized, well read, interested in ideas. We talked of criticism. Like every other value statement, saying someone is 'too critical' or 'too uncritical' is purely relative. How to find a balance, even accepting that it must be relative and pragmatical, that's to say it must work? Criticize but don't condemn, remembering one's own fallibility the whole time? On the other side of the picture I dislike smug failure to observe the seamy side, the unspeakable horror of life as well as its excitement and beauty, in fact lack of irony and cynicism. Then, in my mood of self-questioning, I ask myself just why irony and cynicism should be so important? Because a view of life that doesn't contain them is like a picture with no shadows or depth – flat and meaningless.

November 8th

Pearly beauty of a November morning, especially crossing the Thames, from a train to Dorset and the Stones.

1 Writer and botanist, brother of Anthony.

I've had some pretty bad dips into the suicide well lately, though I usually emerge more or less sane after a night's sleep. Deep loneliness, a pitch-black night of it, invades me at times. Sometimes my mask seems to be effective, but I almost despise myself for it. I despise myself also for the *sheer cowardice* that prevents my killing myself. If there was a foolproof easy way, I believe I'd take it at once.

But I'll try and think of other people now.

November 15th: Crichel

I feel a need to stocktake. What has been on the credit side? The great beauty of that South Dorset landscape, kindness of the Stones and thoughtful cosseting provided by Janet, interesting conversation with Reynolds, walks in steep little valleys, smaller than they looked so that sheep on the far side seemed like cows, the pleasure of seeing Kitty West happy with her new shop at Blandford, and driving to London with her. Then in a quiet week I would single out going to *Don Carlos* with Duncan Grant and dining afterwards with Eardley Knollys and Edward Le Bas[1] at the Ivy; calling on poor old Clive Bell, ill again and looking thin and pale; going to my orchestra.

Eardley and I came here (to Crichel) last night and found Desmond Shawe-Taylor, Eddy, Raymond and Cressida Ridley.[2]

Still stocktaking when I woke this morning about exactly what my position in the world was. I now have no one who belongs to me, who loves me and cares what happens to me for some instinctive reason – as Ralph and Burgo and I suppose M.A.M.[3] long ago did. I must face the fact therefore that I shall only receive affection according to my deserts and if I contribute to other people's happiness. I can do this a bit I think by taking an interest in their lives which is entirely genuine. But I easily lose any confidence I ever had in my ability to be good company or a social asset.

This morning's light on the situation was to face me with a fork in the road and a signpost pointing each way. *Make up your mind*, a voice said in my brain: If you decide to die, go to the London Library and study forensic medicine, do everything to ensure success and a neat get-away.

---

[1] The painter.
[2] Daughter of Lady Violet Bonham Carter.
[3] My mother.

But if you decide to live, you must realize that no one is backing you instinctively any more. You are, and ever will be alone, to fight toothache, illness, worry, the approach of death and every other problem *entirely alone*. This may sound ungrateful for the vast and bottomless kindness of Janetta, Joan, Raymond and others. But I don't think it is – it's only realism.

Last night we talked about Shakespeare's Sonnets and who Mr W.H. was. I agreed with Cressida. Then Desmond Shawe-Taylor put on records of *Manon*. Again I agreed with Cressida – that it was rubbish.

November 16th

Yesterday passed pleasantly along. I went for a walk in the morning with Cressida and found her very easy to talk to and friendly. We talked mainly about her life – a recent journey to Turkey with her son Adam, her archeological plans. She has built up her strength of character on intelligence and force of will. The day was exquisitely still, sweet-scented and golden; Moses pranced in the woods near us but returned always at the first call.

Music in the evening – Schubert's *Schwanengesang*, already heard in Ireland. Cressida's knowledge of music and its technique and confidence in her judgement are impressive.

November 18th

I came down in my Mini to Lord's Wood yesterday morning – and I have been talking and laughing to James and Alix Strachey about everything in the world but what obsesses me; they have not mentioned Burgo; not even as ordinary non-analytical people do with accurate instinctiveness have they opened that subject. But I love them both and have been able to forget myself with them.

I walked with Alix on the Common yesterday afternoon, in delicious still weather with a smell of damp bracken. Her latest obsession is a strange one – to cut herself a path through the bracken and brambles so that she can make a circular tour away from the other houses. As we walked she talked about it lovingly just like a child. James and I talked largely of the disposal of the relics of 51 Gordon Square[1] and La Souco,[2] almost all of the contents of which

---

[1] The home of Lady Strachey and her family, including Lytton.
[2] French house where her daughter Dorothy Bussy and her family lived.

seem to be enormously valuable. Sotheby's for instance think the correspondence between Dorothy Bussy and André Gide may fetch £8000!! It's amazing, I can't believe it. The complication is that Pippa long ago told Marjorie[1] to burn it, as it too plainly revealed Dorothy's being in love with Gide. Marjorie pretended she had done so, but gave it to a friend to hide.[2] Now Pippa is blind she will not see if the sale is reported in the papers, but James with characteristic Strachey *folie de grandeur* thinks it may be on the wireless, and plans to disconnect Pippa's transistor at the time! There is a graver danger that some friend may read of it in the papers and report it to her, for she is bright as a button still.

Last night came the extraordinary news of the assassination of President Kennedy. After his excellent speech about international understanding to the American universities I fear this may make nuclear war more likely.

Poor Alix began to suffer with her false teeth last night and removed some of them, which gave her a rather terrifying witchlike appearance. What a strange being she is! She does *The Times* crossword in her chair each evening, incredibly slowly. She spends her time ordering horrible cheap goods from a Manchester mail-order place – boots made of cardboard and 25/– cardigans. This is the result of total psychoanalysis! Yet she is a first-class human being with a first-class brain. I asked at breakfast this morning how long a complete analysis lasted – 'two to ten years', was the answer, 'but of course before this a person can often become viable and start working or living a more or less normal life'.

November 24th

Alix's character fascinates me; at the age of over seventy she is still a tomboy. She has even taken to wood-chopping, and apart from the clearing of her explorer's path on the common she has hacked down an immense number of thorn trees to beautify the view from the back of their wood. She took me to a point whence we could gaze on the sloping field where they had grown, on our afternoon walk yesterday, and explained with loving care the tools she had bought for the purpose, and how long each tree had taken to chop down. This peculiar activity has given her a new lease of life and made her

[1] Lady Strachey's unmarried daughters.
[2] It was later published.

26

look and seem more robust. It is James now who lurks indoors and never goes out. He works hard at translating Freud and all the correspondence involved in it, as well as going constantly to Putney to see Pippa and Marjorie in their nursing home and busying himself (most enjoyably it's plain) disposing of the Strachey relics. Alix prepares the meals from tins and slowly puts on a plastic apron and holds the plates under the tap after each course: she spends long hours in front of the telly, talks about it a great deal, reads Westerns and Dostoevsky – or so it was yesterday.

Their quality of being so gloriously themselves endlessly delights me. 'Everything is what it is and not another thing.' Fearing that I might drink up their whisky I brought them the half bottle I got at the airport as a present – but not a drop have I had from it, nor has anyone else! Last night we listened to and looked at many programmes about Kennedy. I am appalled by the face of the new President, Lyndon Johnson, with his coarse elephant ears and squashy unpleasant mouth. It's dreadful that any possible prop of the world's peace has been withdrawn, and I went gloomily to bed.

As a substitute to work and also with a view to clearing my decks, I have lately been re-reading Ralph's letters and typing out anything I thought might interest Michael Holroyd, Lytton's biographer. Pretty bad evening – why mince words? *Horrible* evening, my mind slipping its gears, unable to settle to anything, or read, sick with despair.

November 28th

Two things have combined to hoist me about three millimetres above the ocean bed. A dinner party I gave to Julia Gowing, Raymond and Adrian Daintrey[1] last night was a great success and I felt the ghost of a returning power to function as a social being; and also – much more important – it looks as if I have a new job, thanks to the kindness of Eardley and Raymond and my own rather deft treatment of the tip they gave, which Gollancz has snapped up and it alters my outlook considerably.

I have been meanwhile spending my days ploughing through old letters and spending my evenings sociably: with Eddy to *Attila* at Sadler's Wells and supper afterwards with Desmond and Jack Rathbone.[2] I can't quite take Jack's 'How ARE you? Are you

1   Painter.
2   He and Desmond shared a London house.

WELL?' No, of course I'm not, you ass. Nor can I really take early Verdi straight to my heart and I think it affectation to pretend it's as good as middle or late.

November 29th

Yesterday, after lunch with the Japps,[1] Henrietta and Sophie, I drove the last two to the clinic for poor Sophie to be jabbed with various plagues. For quite a half hour I sat in the womb-heated hall where mothers bent over babies of all sizes and toddlers roamed about, crooning over large public teddy bears, tugged at each other's hair with poker-faced hatred and made other more friendly contacts. Some were quite hideous, though dressed with spotless, loving care. I felt proud of Sophie's noble round head, thoughtful intelligent eyes and general look of distinction. But I am half-terrified of getting too fond of her.

December 8th

At David and Rachel Cecil's, Oxford, in their new little doll's house – an improvement on the last, though every word can be heard through its thin walls. Walked with David and Rachel in the Parks yesterday afternoon – very cold, quite still. Coming home we saw a colossal orange sun sinking into the blue haze. The night was bitter and I'm not surprised to see the trees closely coated in frost this morning.

There were three young men at dinner last night – Hugh Cecil and his friend David Tweedie drove down from London and are still here; Simon Whistler spent the evening. He is the son of Lawrence Whistler[2] and his first wife Jill Furze, a very beautiful woman who died giving birth to the second child. Lawrence took her sister Teresa to live with him and look after the two children and later married her. She too, according to David and Rachel, is beautiful, intelligent and remarkable. There were two more children. This boy Simon was charming and good-looking, but more than that. He stood out from the three as being an interesting character, with a certain unusual, quite unpompous intensity. He's a professional musician and plays the viola in an orchestra at Amsterdam; age twenty-three. He took

[1] Darsie (painter) and his Spanish wife Lucila.
[2] Glass-engraver and artist.

David aside to his study after dinner and asked him about a book his father has written (not published yet) about the dead wife, his mother; did he think Teresa – his stepmother and aunt – would mind? The book is deeply emotional, 'sentimental', Rachel hinted, and intimate. Simon too had read it, and been moved to tears, though he was only four when his mother died and he could hardly remember her.

David and Rachel's interest and sympathy with everyone are remarkable – it's not true that absorption in your own family leads to shutters being drawn over the rest of the world, if anything the reverse is.

December 9th

Something of a talking marathon, but enjoyable. Thinking to find the house deserted at churchtime, I descended to the drawing-room and was at once involved with David, at home because of a cold. 'Do I talk too much? Rachel says I do – nicely of course – and that I shout people down.' The boys left in the morning and David went out to lunch. Left alone with Rachel I asked her about her religion and the subject came up again after dinner. Quite interesting, though there were areas which seemed almost indecent to probe. Rachel may have thought for a moment that my adversities had made me feel the need of religion and that David might convert me. I don't think it even flashed into my head that I could unconvert them. How could an omnipotent and beneficent God allow the world to be so cruel and beastly? was my chief question. Rachel would have liked to deny the evil but couldn't, and obviously hadn't thought much about it – her faith was incredibly simple, a hot-water bottle tightly clutched against her person. When I put my question to David later, he surprised me a little by his genuine fervour – I'd thought his answer might be more conventional. Also by his admission that God must be personal. (Murmurs of dissent from Rachel here. Hadn't they discussed it, or did she know from her experience of Desmond[1] how ludicrous this seemed to the irreligious?) David said: 'Not that he has a nose and all the rest of it of course – but since *I* know *him*, he (being greater) *must* be able to know me, mustn't he?' Unlike Rachel he at once admitted the evil and suffering in the world, and was even prepared to say it outweighed the good. So far as I could make out,

[1] MacCarthy, her father.

his explanation was that 'men now suffer as Christ suffered.' Their consolation must be that they are like him returning good (in the form of courage, or – even more – acceptance) for evil. I had said that I saw no good coming out of concentration camps – only more hatred and bitterness and wars. Because of this prevalence of evil in the world, David seemed to be informed by his faith of a necessary 'transcendent and eternal world of good'. I thought I detected that he felt this must exist because it would be so awful if it didn't. His faith first came to him in a religious experience lasting several hours in a hotel in Naples when he had been ill, but he had had others since. He sets great value on the rituals of religion and particularly on taking the sacrament. Of their children Jonathan mildly accepts religion, Hugh had a painful crisis in his belief at eighteen and, though David thinks him the most naturally religious of the three, does not go to church. David suggested that he might go on going, and see what happened, but Hugh said the ritual made him supremely uncomfortable. Rachel dreamily 'hoped he would return to the fold'. Laura discusses belief with her agnostic friends.

I'm glad to have explored this shut-away region and am interested in what I discovered there. I don't think it was resented and no fur flew.

December 11th

Putty-coloured weather and putty-coloured frame of mind. Janetta and I went to the Shostakovich opera last night. I enjoyed it and also the great sweetness and kindness of her company. Henrietta and her lodger Vivien were giving a party afterwards and had invited me to come. I couldn't make up my mind but felt a gentle pressure from Janetta not to go. We looked in afterwards at a little club she belongs to in Leicester Square and were joined by Julian who had been at the Cadogan Square party and described it in glowing terms – the beauty and youth of the guests, the touching welcoming faces of the hostesses, the lively dancing. But as I drove away from Leicester Square I was in tears of sorrow that Burgo wasn't there, and thinking agonizingly of that other glorious party so short a while ago to celebrate their wedding.

December 17th

I float so low in the water that the weight of a dead leaf submerges me. Janetta was coming to lunch today – the last chance of seeing her before she goes to Spain? but she rang up to say she'd forgotten she was lunching with Rose MacLaren. Well and good. As I am frankly killing time at the moment I went by myself to the twelve-thirty showing of Garbo in *Ninotchka*. Perhaps that wasn't lowering but coming out into the so-called daylight was, and brushing past figures with drab pinched faces, and having a sandwich and a Bovril in an awful café where everyone looked as though they were just going to drown themselves and the waitresses worse – expressionless, gone under. Now I'm back at my flat, feeling almost unequal to going to see Janetta at six as she asked me.

My present mood of desperation – and I have to face it – is about as bad as any I've experienced and makes me cantankerous and difficult. I don't want to be with anyone, yet I dread being alone. I *must* make an effort – oh how tired those words make me feel! I must force myself to do something not time-killing.

December 23rd

I spent a large part of today with Henrietta and Sophie, and now at quarter to five I am in charge and Sophie is beginning to cry fretfully and suck her thumb. I have found this contact with my 'family' delightful, exhausting and harassing. A very good no-barrier feeling between me and Henrietta. The day was completely filled – there was only just time to hoist the innumerable baby appurtenances up to her flat before I dashed off for a drink with the Japps and supper with Isobel Strachey.

Boxing Day

Gordon House, Lambourn with the Gowings for Christmas, as I was last, but the circumstances are very different. Lawrence and Jenny[1] are here. Christmas Day was totally ignored. In the afternoon Julia and I had a long and delicious walk, with the rolling spaces all round us disappearing in faint iridescent colours to the horizon, the winter trees standing with squiggly black twigs against the pale sky. The to-do about yesterday's turkey was terrific. It must be cooked *à la Gaylord Hauser* exactly twenty-three minutes to the pound, not a minute more or less. Therefore it must go on soon after eight. I was surprised to come down at nine and find the oven not yet turned on

[1] Wallis, later Gowing.

nor breakfast preparations begun. A mistake had been made in the sum and it had to go in an hour later. There followed a complicated scheme by which the egg-boiler was to go off every quarter of an hour and shifts were to be allocated for basting the bird. After much discussion Mrs Rose turned up and took over the entire lunch. The preparations for last night's dinner – two veg and cold ham occupied Jenny and Julia at full pitch for several hours. I have said I'll do lunch by myself today as this seems the easiest way of helping. Otherwise one runs into Julia's rules. Again no one was down by nine this morning, so I began to make breakfast, and had put the eggs in the saucepan, when Julia came and took them out, dropped one and broke it. It was against the house rules to put eggs in before water!

While she was getting the tea this afternoon Julia dashed into the television room and said: 'This is very egotistic but I must say what's in my mind. If only I had been able never to cook a meal since I wrote *Cheerful Weather for the Wedding*, I should have written any number of books. I had heaps of ideas. Young writers ought to have a grant so that they don't have to cook.' 'Well that would need a full-time servant to look after each one of them,' I said, thinking how little help the presence of Mrs Rose every day from ten till two seemed to Julia.

December 27th

So one more Christmas has blown past our ears almost unnoticed by mine. The good manners preserved by the triangle in this house are immaculate – yet there are storms beneath the surface.

I have been working at my new translation with tonic effect. I think I shall enjoy it. I work in the Oak Room, Lawrence in his studio, while Jenny sits in the telly room. Julia is upstairs, but I would say no work has got done there for one reason or another. House Rules are that drinks are served in the telly room and conversation can be held there. The Oak Room, as well as work room for me, is 'for the silent reading of good books'. No conversation is allowed in it, as it disturbs Julia in the room above!

December 30th: Combe (with the Hendersons)

Lawrence[1] is so annoyed by the fact that John Strachey has queered his sale of all Simon Bussy's pictures to the Marlborough Gallery by

[1] For the complications concerning the Bussy inheritance see *Hanging On*.

buying them himself for the same sum, that he got Julia to ring up James over Christmas and (under the cover of wishing him a Merry Christmas) suggest his making an offer of £10 more – i.e. £1510. Answer came back: 'Nothing can be done about it.' And of course it would be hopeless setting a sort of family auction in progress.

I came here yesterday morning, and the Hobsons[1] and Stewarts[2] lunched here. I asked Anthony Hobson if he as a Sotheby man had anything to do with the sale of the Bussy pictures. 'Everything'. In fact he it was who told John Strachey they were worth more and wrote to Craig to the same effect. Fascinating . . . He was very anxious to meet Lawrence, and he and Julia were invited to lunch – perhaps just as well they didn't come.

We had a social day yesterday – after the huge lunch, a short walk, then to dinner with the Jellicoes[3] at Tidcombe.

---

[1] Anthony and Tanya.
[2] Sir Michael (diplomat) and his wife.
[3] George and Philippa (Earl and Countess).

1964

January 1st: 16 West Halkin Street

A nice evening here last night, with Clive, Little Barbara Bagenal[1] and Kitty. It was a good idea to have Kitty, she was lively and friendly to both and stayed on after they'd gone, leaving just before the death of old 1963. I was in bed reading when the eerie sound of the jangling bells struck my ear – more like the distant baying of hounds or yelling of a crowd at a football match than any sound of rejoicing. Why rejoice indeed at the passage of time? I can only hope that 1964 won't be as bad as last year, it could hardly be worse. I dreamt of both Ralph and Burgo together last night, back in the anxieties of Burgo's adolescence, and awoke to stare into the deep black hole of their joint absence.

January 3rd

In the train to Saxmundham, where I've been invited for the weekend by Heywood, Anne and the Old Countess,[2] out of sheer kindness I know very well, because I wrote Anne a letter apologizing for being bad company when they dined here and admitting to desperate depression. I feel compunction now, and am full of resolves not to exude damp gloom over them all.

I have been harrowed to the marrow over poor dear Henrietta gallantly conducting her move today. Thank heavens I've been able to help her in one or two practical ways, such as getting someone to clear away her bottles and sweep out the flat. I wish I was much younger and more lively and could help her with physical work.

I have collected the old family stamp album and mean to sell it for her if I can. Otherwise I await confirmation that Gerald Brenan

---

[1] The companion of Clive Bell's last years, always called 'Little'.
[2] Of Cranbrook, Anne's mother.

would like to have me before I make up my mind about Spain. This is just plotting my position, and dull as possible. Thought shortage has been notable lately.

January 14th

The Gowings' crisis has intensified. Julia came here in a state of tremulous agitation which drove her eventually to see Craig and ask about a divorce. I feel great reluctance to leave her without my feeble support at this juncture.

Tomorrow I am to lunch at the Savoy with Victor Gollancz and a famous South American lady called Victoria Ocampo, whose autobiography I may have to translate.

January 20th: Crichel

I suppose my most important event last week was lunching with Victor Gollancz and Victoria Ocampo (literary queen of Latin America) at the Savoy. I liked her – a full-blooded, intelligent, blue-haired, warm-hearted Spaniard. I *may* translate her autobiography, and we sat until four-thirty on a sofa in the Savoy, discussing the problems of translation and the inadequacies of Bunny's translation of her last book from the French. Our table near the great window overlooking the river had an amazing view. After soup, and roast beef and Yorkshire pudding, Señora Ocampo declared she'd heard about something called semolina pudding and would like to try it. A row of waiters with real looks of perturbation on their faces hovered before her. There was none. Then I saw on the trolley a bread-and-butter pudding and asked her if she had ever tried that very English confection? She tried it, we had coffee and were thinking of departing, when the Greek chorus of waiters reappeared like birds on a twig and still with anxious expressions, bearing a small specially made semolina pudding. It's much to her credit that she tried that too.

It has set me up to feel I have gone a peg upwards in the translation world and I do believe Victoria Ocampo might help me to work. I've long wanted to get in touch with her.

January 22nd

I have rounded a bend of sorts, but the state of apathy in which at times I trudge on horrifies me – the way I deliberately force myself not to think (in a certain positive way at least) about Ralph and Burgo. Rather than be reduced to unutterable selfishness, I sink myself in the lives of other people, Mary,[1] Julia in particular, and listen to their problems with obsessional concentration. At the same time I continue to notice with surprise the complete egotism of suffering. Julia always makes a heroic effort to ask me about my life, work, state of mind; they don't exist for Mary. As I lay in bed before dropping off last night I pondered over the inordinate difference between Mary's way of thinking and mine – but it doesn't impair our mutual affection.

Fog has settled over England; dense enough to smell and taste and bring a foretaste of panic. Working day yesterday. I rang Gollancz to clarify my position; his secretary promised to let me know in a day or two. I doubt if she will. Meanwhile Weidenfeld rang up to ask me to do two books. Long talk on the telephone (very nice) with Julian. I am reading *Henry VI* in preparation for next week – what an extraordinary play!

February 2nd

Yesterday I should have been setting off to Spain, but I had no regrets, as old London burgeoned into charm, smelt of earth and twigs and roots and lay under a quilted blue sky. My window-box has green shoots springing up all over it. Henrietta brought Sophie to lunch yesterday and she too is sprouting strongly. Everyone everywhere looked renewed and hopeful. They needed it – in the brief fog ten days ago there were an appalling number of car crashes, and screams have gone up in Parliament and newspapers about the tigerish savagery of drivers. It's true enough: one sees them everywhere shaking fists, shouting with impatience, pressing forward at the traffic lights. Told they are tigers, they behave even more like them. Steeling myself to go out in eggshell Mini into this ferocious jungle has become more than ever an effort, yet I find it important to do so.

Last week I spent three days going with Eddy, Desmond, Eardley, Mattei Radev[2] and Julian to the *Wars of the Roses* – four Shakespeare plays crammed into three. One night I gave them all supper here. The plays exercised an obsessional magnetism, spread-

[1] Then McCabe, now Dunn.
[2] Eardley's Bulgarian friend.

ing themselves over the whole three days, drowning them in the abrupt virile music of the verse, the clang of stage swords on armour, and the sense of being back in time and forging through history. Each morning I reached for my blue volume of Shakespeare and read a bit of what we'd heard or were to hear. Fairly lively argument and disagreement between the six of us; my views were nearest to Julian's. Crumpled family trees of the York and Lancaster family emerged from every pocket.

February 14th

Janetta is back. That is the most important event on my human level. After *Aida*, Julian and I went to Montpelier Square – where were Eddy, Jonny Gathorne-Hardy and Sabrina, Magouche,[1] Mary, Diana Cooper and Lord Norwich, Patrick Kinross and a few others. Oh yes, Billa Harrod to whom I talked for some time. It's not 'my world' but I was fairly at home there, and then the door opened and in came the dear brown face of Janetta. Very nice to see her. On the telephone this morning, she said how 'everyone she'd wanted to see' was in that room and I realized the lack of overlap between her and me. They were smoking hashish apparently, though I noticed no difference in those who'd had some (Julian for instance). On the telephone also she'd said that Robert and I 'were the only people who were cross with her for not coming back earlier' – this according to Georgie,[2] whom I've not once seen.

February 16th: Stokke[3]

Conversation with Mary this weekend has aroused my old admiration for her vitality and appetite for life. Questioned by us all about life in San Francisco or America in general, her answers were extremely to the point, rivettingly graphic. Drink is what is wrong, according to her – the hard long working day of males and the pattern of social life arranges for everyone to be thoroughly drunk long before they sit down to dinner. And other features of the pattern – marital jealousy and what it boggles at – seem equally uncivilized.

---

1   Phillips, now Fielding.
2   Robert and Janetta's daughter.
3   Mary's house in Wiltshire, while she was in San Francisco with her husband Charlie McCabe, had been lent to Magouche Phillips.

Our party consists in Magouche and two smaller girls, Lizzie Spender, the Norwiches. John Julius Norwich is intelligent, responsive and thoughtful. Anne his wife intrigues me. Very pretty, with a long swanlike neck, a little head poised on top, curly brown hair, blue eyes and a wild rose complexion, she is a passionate abstract painter, 'quite uneducated' as her husband says, but thinks for herself a lot, is 'high-minded', and 'likes expressing her views'. Disarmingly, she described herself at lunch as 'an intense woman'. So she is, but I rather like her.

Yesterday Magouche led the Norwiches, me and Susu[1] out for an energetic striding walk. It was a pale, misty afternoon, nothing but white and grey, and three-thirty when we set out. Down by the pumping-station, nature suddenly put on a striking display for us. The canal spreads out there into a sort of lagoon and floating on it were about thirty pure white swans, perfectly still on the equally still water which reflected their every feather like a metal plate. Some Corot trees bent gracefully from the bank. We started along the towpath towards Bedwyn and suddenly a string of them was flying overhead with a deafening, yet soft, creaking of wings. This they repeated several times, once frighteningly low until – putting up huge Walt Disney feet – they landed on the canal. Two more were drifting along with upfurled wings looking exactly like china swans into which flowers like forget-me-nots are stuffed. Darkness began to fall and I didn't want to go to tea with Lord Bruntisfield in Bedwyn so I struck up by a short cut towards Stokke. Huge ruts, pools of water, invisible barbed wire, inexplicable confusion of a forest landscape in the dusk. I walked on and on, zigzagging now this way now that, wondering if I wouldn't circle for ever in the forest; I almost panicked. It rained and then snowed! I hobbled home at ten past six, cut myself a hunk of bread and butter, poured a whisky and sat for a while blessedly alone in Mary's 'broodery'.

February 19th

Sad, I lie in bed looking out at the pale grey shapes of Halkin Street and thinking of the very different greyness of the swan lagoon. Kees, Jonny and Sabrina, Henrietta to dinner last night. It seemed to me a trifle sticky and pointless. Dinner all right, conversation less so. I thought of Julia who, when I rang up to tell her what nice things had

[1] Her youngest daughter, Susannah.

been said about her last dinner party, after purring a bit said: 'Never again, my dear – it's an appalling business having to do the whole thing, and wait on everyone. The conversation is the difficulty. No, I'm going to lead a hermit's life in future.' So perhaps should I. At the moment my appetite for my life is nonexistent and it stands before me like a huge greyish plateful of cooling skilly. Am nearly at the end of my translation, and I feel I might perhaps benefit from taking my head out of dictionaries and doing some THINKING.

Sad is now matched by Bad, for back has come flooding possessive longing for oblivion, dislike of my own disapproving, anxious character, hatred for the sparrows chirping vulgarly as they bite into the plants in my window-boxes, and for the cold grey day outside – yet I must go out into it I think.

February 22nd: Stokke

Mary called for me early in her blue Mini and we drove down to Stokke together, where I now sit over the fire while she snoozes. From the garden comes the familiar aggressive Ham Spray noise of birds mobbing an owl. I'm very content to be alone with Mary – even little brown Honey[1] has accepted me as a familiar in the house. How strange it is that this form of settling in to other people's houses is one of the things I have found easiest to adapt myself to in my widowed life. Hosts should be two; to be a guest it is almost easier to be one.

Last night Janetta and I went to a Janáček opera at Sadler's Wells – exciting, electric, very well put on.

March 4th

Baby-sitting for Henrietta, listening to the crooning and sleepy mooing of Sophie in her crib next door, and feeling shamefully unsuited to carry the weight of her existence even for so short a time. The gestures with which she idly slapped her bottle or pointed her well-developed ballet dancer's toes while drinking from it delight me. Next week Henrietta goes off to Spain for a couple of weeks leaving Sophie with Angelica.

I've not written for a week and feel I must plot the graph of these days. I realized with quite a shock that I have grown to love London, almost to be 'in love' with it as though it were a person, to feel proud

[1] Her dachshund.

39

to belong to it (be a 'member of the wedding'), and I appreciate its various moods. Yet it's a short cry from the feeling of loneliness, crushing impersonality, restlessness and noise to this other – almost new – delight in the tall, pale houses and taller, black trees, the sparkling lights, the new clarity I seem to see in the air, and the signs of spring – twittering, green shoots, earthen smells.

Just after I wrote last I had a desperate call from Julia, summoned her round and spent long hours talking over her situation. Since then they have decided to tell the world about the divorce, and I got her in her desperation to say she'd come to Italy with me, perhaps even at once. Later the date was fixed – April 9th, and I wrote to ask Joan Cochemé to take rooms in a *pensione* in Rome she had found. Yesterday there were signs of wavering on Julia's part and I shan't be surprised if she doesn't come, indeed I pressed her not to feel tied as I would go anyway. I'm going to pay her ticket and if possible her *pensione* also. What worries me a little is that while patting herself on the back for 'facing up to reality' she contrives to be miles from it – or at least one leg is up in the air if the other rests on *terra firma*.

March 5th

I broached to Isobel last night the possibility of coming with me should Julia fail. She charmingly said she'd be delighted to come, had never been to Rome, and was prepared to do so at the last minute.

Henrietta left for Spain yesterday. She and darling little Sophie were here last week for lunch and who should turn up but Denis Wirth Miller[1] also. He had had yet another scene with Francis Bacon, who fired some home truths at him ('tactless, insensitive, lazy'). Of Bacon's new boy-friend, a burglar, he said: 'He's very good at cracking safes and that's a *creative activity*.' I didn't take this up at the moment but it has been rolling unpalatably round my head like a marble.

March 17th

Last night Julia announced in somewhat regal style that Rome was 'on', and she came to dinner to talk about it. But the cloud of fuss she put up has I fear somewhat taken the heart out of the whole project. J: 'I couldn't go by jet aeroplane'. F: 'Why ever not?' J: 'Not sure

[1] Painter.

40

why. Is it because it's too dangerous?' Catching an aeroplane at nine-thirty was impossible – she must defrost her fridge and then 'my make-up takes me two hours.' It's gloriously funny in a way, but it has given me a foretaste of what the smallest arrangements will be like.

April 9th: Rome

HERE we are. Six p.m. – a delightful *pensione* found for us by kind Joan Cochemé, and I lie on my bed relaxed, preparing to take a swig of my aeroplane whisky, and *thinking of Julia*. I should really have kept a record of all the fantastic fuss that has exercised her these last weeks. When we were discussing aeroplanes I forgot to say that I mentioned the Alitalia line by which we have come. 'What's that?' she asked suspiciously. 'Not one of these charter planes?' I assured her it was the regular Italian line. Over the Easter weekend an Alitalia plane crashed and I fully thought that would finish her, but I rather doubt if she ever heard of it, for she never reads the papers. But two days ago she rang up to ask whether we could find out the exact measurement under the seat for her hand baggage. To catch the five-to-one plane she got up at six-thirty, and I must say that the journey went without a hitch, although there's not a moment when she isn't dreading the next contingency and planning how to deal with it. At present it is the fact that there certainly won't be enough coffee for breakfast. Joan looked at me in consternation when we were alone briefly. I feel strong and able to face anything at the moment but I know there are great hulking reefs ahead. Also I do want time to myself, or alone with Joan sometimes. My resolves are three: to remember Julia is desperately unhappy, to treat her fuss merely as exaggerated farce and even enjoy it as such, and to be as adaptable as possible.

The limpid, pure blue sky of Rome greeted us in full glory and so did the magnificent regal personality of this noble town. I'm sure I shan't feel short of things to do while I'm here. My room has a tiled floor, ugly modern furniture, a table, a desk, and a window looking out onto Judas trees. I've been working very hard, was typing an index for James until seven-thirty last night, so I shall be glad to rest for a little while. If only I don't run short of material.

April 11th

Sitting up in bed, seven-twenty a.m. The Aventino, where our *pensione* is, charms me with its beauty, tranquillity, Judas trees in flower, drifting clerics. One could have no more delightful eyrie from which to try and become a member of the Roman wedding – but it's going to be difficult with my poor panic-stricken, half-crazed companion by my side.

She does think it beautiful, appreciates the architecture but fear makes it only possible for her to enjoy it briefly. What can I do for her? In her situation of being hedged round by multiple terrors her only 'defence mechanism' is fuss, fuss, FUSSISSIMO. 'Are you sure this is the way?' she asks me of a road already known by heart, 'don't you think we came in the other way last time? How do you *know*? How can you tell it isn't the other bridge? Are you sure this is the Corso? But *how* do you know?' And she will ask a policeman, or not one but three. What must it be like to be encompassed by such dreads? Her hair rinse might fade, they might not give her enough coffee for breakfast, we might be poisoned by the water, forget the number of the bus, and so forth. She is terrified of crossing the road (almost refused like a horse) and won't go up in Joan's lift – preferring to walk up five floors. Being late, forgetting the name of the street we are going to: everything scares her. As for 'taking a chance' ever, it's out of the question.

I'm trying to think of her as an invalid. I sometimes really think she is going off her head. Her memory is so weak, either from drugs or other things, that she asks me the same question ten times over, and I answer hollowly, knowing it will be dished up again in five minutes time. She has brought a ready reckoner given her by the bank to convert lire to sterling, yet she asks me over and over and over what 1000 lire is worth, and when changing money the other day she again asked the clerk the value of every separate note. I'm filled with embarrassment often, and ashamed of my embarrassment of course.

I made a little headway I think yesterday by getting her to recognize that her fears were not rational, that they were in fact phobias, and suggested treating them by the method of thinking 'What shall I do if the worst comes to the worst?' told me by an agoraphobic friend. I found that one of her chief fears about buses is that she can't remember the name of where she wants to go. Nor can she in fact. Getting into a bus in front of me, she panicked totally – the word Aventino is too much to remember.

6.20 p.m. I don't know how I could have written so heartlessly about trying to enjoy Julia's farcical eccentricities. They are a great deal more than a joke – a desperate tragedy which bids fair to sink me too. This morning, however, went smoothly. We walked gently along to the Villa Farnesina (Julia's idea) never losing the way once. I led her straight to the door; there wasn't another soul in the place. Later we sat on a wall of huge, pale stones looking down at the grey, sliding Tiber talking about Adrian Daintrey, and then explored the island. 'Was I sure this was the *right* island?' she asked. I assured her there *was* only one. We went on to a trattoria recommended by Daintrey, and there over a good and cheap meal Julia spoke almost in tears of her feeling that she might have to go home. The impact of Rome was too much for her, she was terrified all the time. I told her she must of course go if she wanted to, *at once*, and I think talking relieved her. I'm really afraid of a complete breakdown, a crisis. How too can I conduct my own life I wonder? I only like to leave her for a short time, and she takes no joy in her surroundings whatever.

April 12th

A gulp of the true pleasure of being abroad. Wandering out this mid-morning along the via di Sabina, which contains three churches, I found a wedding going on in one and became one of the congregation, watching the solemn little pair as they knelt before the altar banked with white flowers. All up the aisle were bunches of white roses connected by tulle swags. Sightseers prowled, as I did, unheeded. An elderly and very plain spinster – German? – in thick lisle stockings peered avidly at the symbolic representation of what she herself had never experienced – union with a man. I watched just as eagerly, following all the ritual; the priest took a swig of something, bride and groom did likewise, photographers flashed away unashamedly, and with deadly solemn and dreary expressions the couple advanced down the aisle. Outside – beams, and formal pecks from all friends, male and female.

Last night Joan telephoned and came to see me, we had an hour or so's talk and then saw each other home through the public gardens. It was a relief to share my worries a little with her. This morning I found Julia in a mood of valiant realism. A nightmare had brought her phobias psychoanalytically to the surface. She now feels that Rome was the best place for her to come, even though it has been hard for her. All at once she was her fascinating original self again, not confused and groping but trying to explain that the mythical figures on the Villa Farnesina, Raphael's Galatea and the rest, had acted violently on her emotions as symbols of what lay beneath the surface of her life. My line will be to convince her that she is someone who has just suffered a drastic surgical operation when in a very weak physical state. She said she would like to stay in her room and write about her mythical experiences.

April 13th

Ay de mi, I cannot sleep for thinking of poor Julia, and woke this morning – not to sleep again – before five. Such an in-turned uninterested apathetic travelling companion is quite outside my experience. I think with amazement of Eardley, Raymond, Janetta, and my darling Ralph. Yesterday we passed a soothing day which I hoped would be more to her taste. The sky had cleared to a palish blue and kind Joan asked us to lunch on her terrace. 'Oh, on the terrace?' 'Yes, she thought you might like to bring a hat.' 'Oh I don't think I want to sit in the *sun*. Well I must think what clothes to put on for the smuts – must keep something for best.'

Lunch was prettily laid out and delicious, and nothing could have been nicer than to look down from so high up at the town, the crawling cars reduced to gently buzzing insects. After lunch Julia said she would 'read her Conrad', was established in a *chaise-longue* and lay there with eyes closed apparently asleep for about two hours, while the rest of us washed up and chattered. About four o'clock Joan and I set out for the Janiculum – would Julia or Elizabeth[1] like to come too? Elizabeth (a handsome girl now, and sane – at the moment almost my favourite quality) said she wanted to finish making a dress. Julia said 'she was too weary' and indeed she looked it. So Joan and I went off by bus to a pretty public garden at the top of the hill where we walked among the Sunday crowds, enlaced lovers, tiny boys dressed as men in peaked caps, and bouncing children. Then to the church of San Pietro in Montorio with its dear little Bramante *tempietto*. Joan would have liked to walk further, but I felt we should return to Julia and sure enough she said to me rather accusingly later that she had had another bad patch after tea – a wave, of exactly what I don't know. We dined in the hotel, and I felt I should almost die of sitting opposite this shut, obsessional face and

[1] Joan's step-daughter.

knowing that she was suffering my presence and all her surroundings as best she could.

At the moment, I can't help it, I hope she will go home, and I think she should have a course of treatment in a nursing home. Selfish feelings well up in me to the effect that I too need some sort of holiday and that to look after someone in her state is nothing like one.

I try to get her to say what she'd like to do because I know anything I suggest will be found fault with. But when the moment comes to study the guidebooks and decide, she can't face it. So desperately I lay Rome's wares before her and try to interest her in one or another.

April 14th

Triumph! Julia has by some form of conjuring trick pulled herself suddenly together. What an extraordinary character! It happened on Monday night – apparently she lay 'thinking out her problems until one o'clock'.

Now there is the miracle. After facing her facts she began yesterday as a new woman. Luckily it was a marvellous day. She said firmly that she wanted to go sightseeing, and as it was Monday and the museums were all shut we set off for St Peter's. Twice on the way she asked me '*Where* is it we're going?' When writing a postcard on St Peter's roof she wanted to know what our *pensione* was called. But the change in her all yesterday was heroic and stupendous – in the late afternoon she even ventured out in a bus to the Capitol by herself. I'm simply delighted at these signs of recovery, and also full of admiration for the effort she made. In a way she really enjoyed her visit to St Peter's, thrust her tentacles into the rich sensorial stuff surrounding us, and had comments to make thereon. Phew! – I breathe again, or so it seems. We dined with Joan and Elizabeth, and this morning there has been no decline at all: we spent long hours walking across the Borghese Gardens and looking at the pictures in the Gallery. Late home to lunch.

April 16th

Julia's new look has been magnificently sustained and I am filled with admiration for her courage and determination. What's more her effort has, I'm sure, had a therapeutic effect, she does for a time forget her troubles and focus on the things that surround her. In her epic wrestling match with her devil in the watches of the night she did achieve a real victory. On Tuesday night we made our way through the darkened streets to the Piazza Navona and dined in a restaurant there.

The Piazza Navona was looking marvellously beautiful, dignified and far from crowded. The fountains were bathed in light and the turquoise water spouted forth. Julia was at her best – inspecting Bernini's creation from every angle and commenting on it all. It's particularly the animals she likes – 'Do look at that dear old lion – he's got such a *scholarly* expression,' she'll say. She has got herself, wrenched herself, back into her normal position of being a fascinating companion.

Our expedition to Tivoli and the Villa d'Este was a great success with us all; we moved slowly down through the painted rooms and terraced fountains and ate our picnic lunch at Hadrian's Villa, lying in the lush grass. Picked wild flowers – a blue anchusa, a vetch with black velvet wings – and wandered peacefully through the ruins. Dinner at the Cochemés. Cochemé[1] (back from Cairo with another scientist from the Food and Agriculture Organization) was there. It was delightful to hear the scientists talking about their subject – locusts – and how I envied them their rapturous, flashing-eyed absorption. Cochemé described watching a baby locust hatch out in the warm sand, force its way to the surface, take a vigorous but tentative HOP, fall on its nose and start again. One of their objects, he said, was to 'induce sexual maturity earlier in locusts'; I can't imagine why, as they are trying to exterminate them.

April 17th

Such golden goodness is being revealed in Julia, since she took the plunge! What's more my heart has been rejoiced to hear her laugh very heartily and with abandon several times, and it strikes me this is something that has been missing for a long while. She has been wonderful company lately, sympathetic, understanding, brave about her fears, avid for sights.

Coming back from this morning's sightseeing (the Gesù and the Doria palace), I told Julia how much I admired the way she had dealt with her phobias, and heard from her how at twenty-five she had been faced with a really awful attack of panic, dread of the universe, inability to understand the relationship of mind to matter or

[1] Joan's husband, a French Mauritian and biologist.

anything else – 'I think it has a name, something like "panic fear".' It had taken her months, but she'd gone down to the roots of it and taken it apart leaf by leaf. Her passage through life is a triumph of equilibrium, for I think she's well aware of the dark streaks in her character.

April 19th

This evening's sightseeing was a great success. We went to two sights Julia had seen before and liked, I never – churches by Borromini and Bernini near the Quirinale (I also took her to Sant' Andrea). Everything went well and all sights were enjoyed. Santa Maria della Vittória, much disapproved by Baedeker, is the sexiest little church I ever was in. Incredibly richly encrusted within with gilt and various coloured marbles, it leads up to an altar which is simply an illuminated vagina surrounded by radiating gilt beams. On the left is a very finished gleaming white statue by Bernini of Santa Teresa swooning backwards on the brink of an orgasm, while a pretty angel with a charming teasing smile raises an arrow to penetrate her. All the commentators, whether favourable or unfavourable, have hardly been able to overlook the obvious sexual symbolism.

Perhaps the clue to Julia is that she can't get over people not being exactly like her. What's more she thinks they oughtn't to be different.

April 22nd

One is always right when one senses a crack in the human crust, through which passions will soon shoot volcanically upwards. They did, yesterday evening, but no harm I believe has been done – even perhaps the air is cleared. We had, after the usual siesta, a successful excursion to Santa Maria della Pace yesterday afternoon. I know that the number of things I have to repeat twenty times in answer to the same question does exacerbate me ('the cloister is by Bramante. No, not Pietro da Cortona – Bramante'); also, the problems she expected me to give the answer to from my head, which she doesn't in the least want to know and won't remember for more than one second. ('What would the date of the Etruscan statue be, do you happen to know?' 'I suppose you don't happen to remember where the 95 bus stops, do you?') She has also a way of putting the most naïve posers like, who is Auden and what is the Légion d'honneur. The last amazed Cochemé.

Then in our return bus she began once more complaining of the lack of 'smartness' of Italian girls, and I replied that that was what I hated about 'smartness' – the present fashion in no way suited the Italian's special form of beauty: their thick gleaming black straight hair did not look at its best backcombed into a bird's nest, nor their strong figures in short straight frocks and suits. So, we reached a set-to about smartness, the act of aggression I fear being mine. The concept of smartness, so I maintained, cut right across the criteria of taste and originality and prevented clothes being (what they ought to be) a language expressing personality. Instead of this, I said, warming to my work, all personalities of whatever sort or kind were crushed into identical iron corsets. 'Ah', said Julia in a voice trembling with emotion, 'but that's just the fascination of it. The poet's genius is all the better for having to submit to the rules of the sonnet form.' (A good point.) F: 'But not to the modish deb vocabulary of the fashion of the moment.' Calm came after the storm and Julia said she wanted me to realize that she took smartness as a game, not quite seriously. All the same I don't feel this is true; it is an armour protecting her against the outside world, and she clings to it with suitable desperation.

April 23rd

I was rather afraid Julia had suffered some wave of despair yesterday, but in the afternoon we had an excellent expedition to San Clemente. Beside arranging to discover the way, which I'm not particularly good at, there is this encyclopedic information Julia expects me to have ready for her, and sometimes I get quite anxious as I mug up a subject for her to examine me – will I remember the dates or the names of the artists or the popes they portray?

In the evening we met Jim Lees-Milne, went with him to a neighbouring trattoria and had a pleasant evening.

April 25th

How can I make Julia enjoy her last few days, and not feel the whole thing was a big mistake? Her mind is at present preoccupied with the journey home and I think she's looking forward to going. Will she think of the whole thing with horror? I resolve to exert my utmost from now through these five days to sympathize and support her, for she's probably got a tough situation to face on her return. Today we tackled the Vatican museum rooms, meaning to look at the Pinacoteca, but after the immense walk outside the huge sloping walls and then inside the building itself the crush in the Raphael rooms was unbearable – just a dense sea of bobbing heads, a sort of human brawn, and a voice shouting 'Keep to the right!' We backed hastily away and went to see the Pinturicchios and the splendid primitives in the Pinacoteca.

Dined with the Cochemés and had a livelier evening than usual owing to an argument about Free Will and Determinism. Joan declared that she was a determinist and Julia that she couldn't conceive of anyone not intuitively being aware of free will – both of which was like a Conservative saying he simply couldn't conceive of anyone being a Socialist and expecting you to take that for an argument. I produced my traditional defence of determinism, and Julia challenged me rather aggressively to say what determinism was and so I jolly well did tell her. Julia put up some fascinating skirmish movements with remarks like 'Well, that famous scientist (whose name I forget) whose book I gave you to read and you said you liked, seemed to have a sort of hunch that there was free will.' Everything was, however, perfectly friendly, and Julia came away saying 'Well, we put up a fine Punch and Judy show for them, didn't we?'

But *now* – careful, gentle, sympathetic: I must be endlessly patient with her, and that is no easy task, for I realize that Julia has not these last weeks given me as a person a single thought, other than conceiving me as a banister to hold on to. I wish I'd been a better one. In my own defence I must record that it's these moments of irritation that I set down, but that I have really striven and struggled to contain my exasperation with her and a good deal of the time with considerable success. Alas I am not a serene and placid character. This morning I said to her that I felt perhaps it would have been better for her if we'd gone to some quiet sunny spot like Ravello. So I now think it would – but not for me, nor do I know how she would have passed the time though it takes her very little to do that. Almost her sole indoor activity while here, other than reading a few pages of Conrad, has been 'writing her notes'. This consists in trying to jot down the names of the sights seen each day.

However, today has passed in perfect serenity and amity, and Julia has made obvious efforts to remember that I too am a human being. Santa Prasséde and Santa Maria Maggiore this morning; my pocket (or rather my basket) was picked in a crowded bus.

April 28th

At dinner last night Julia talked of Eardley and his enormous and happy enthusiasm for his painting – 'I'm afraid', (this is always a bad beginning with Julia), 'I think it's sheer self-indulgence, like Rosamond's writing. I feel the temptation to give way to writing like Rosamond about Debenham and Freebody luxury and hot towel rails, but I don't let myself do it. Janetta has this very extraordinary and to me incomprehensible idea that you can write as a bird sings and not do anything to it, correct it, or go over it. I'm afraid I think all good writing involves agony and pain.' Quite a discussion followed, Julia doing everything to prove that a serious writer's task was well nigh impossible. J: 'But I don't know about other writers' technique – I never talk to writers about their writing. I don't know any writers.' F: 'But almost everyone you know is a writer.' J: 'Well, name a few.' I did. 'You may not think them good writers', I said forestalling her, 'but they're intelligent people.' J: 'Well, of course it would be nice talking to V.S.P.[1] about writing, but it would mean asking him and Dorothy to dinner and I can't face that.' This was embroidered as a comic theme. Later she said she hadn't got any friends, which I really believe is true, and then that there was no time (to talk to writers) 'what with having lunch' at which I couldn't help laughing.

I'm left feeling that she all the time thinks of herself as a special case, and doesn't really see that it's absurd to feel she's handicapped by 'having to have lunch'. Yet there are very odd, rather touching little moves made towards people. After our first evening with Jim Lees-Milne she showed no interest in him. After our dinner with both him and Alvilde she liked him, but thought Alvilde 'unfriendly', one of her commonest phrases. Last night she was busy writing her a note to say how we had enjoyed the evening and hoping she would ring her up and have a drink when Alvilde was in London. 'I hope to get Jim,' she said, 'I rather liked him.'

For all my preoccupation with Julia I've not ceased to be sharply, disturbingly, excitingly aware of Rome's character and grandeur. It keeps me bubbling and simmering – could being married to a marvellously beautiful woman be in the same way a perpetual agitation? But it could be one who wears hideous clothes, as Rome wears cars. Last night returning quite late, it was a pleasure to see the

[1] Pritchett.

50

angles between the narrow cobbled floor of the Via Lata, which leads past the Doria palace, and its stupendous walls, clear of any obstacle – so that the street had the design and proportion its architects intended.

P.M. Very good morning at the Thermae – sunny weather outside and in. A little difficult to find something for this afternoon. Julia said she would like to see the Bramante *tempietto*, but 'the effort of getting there is too great.' Anything in the Colosseum direction is 'too like Bournemouth'. (!) What she wants is some delightfully beautiful little church in the 'bulge'. Ah well.

April 29th

In the end we ventured forth into the 'bulge' of the Tiber and looked at three little churches. Agostino, Luigi, Antonio – two with Caravaggios, one a Raphael. Julia is anxious always for 'great names' of artists and architects. We gave dinner to the Cochemé family in the Piazza Navona in the evening, and that went really very well. Julia took great trouble to be pleasant to Joan, so much so that I marvel that she really can feel such antipathy as she makes out towards her. The dog's wagging tail should surely alter its state of emotion. Today is the last day together for Julia and me. I wonder how our strange alliance will look in retrospect and what stories she will tell of me in London. She's made a noticeable effort to treat me as a human being lately.

9.30. Obsessional fuss has returned to swamp Julia. To see her scuffling in her bag over the dinner table to find her bill with her newly done ('hopeless my dear') hair-do like a Skye terrier hanging over clawing front paws, was really tragic. What heavy weather she makes for herself! Once again she began to retrace the network of circumstances in which she enchains herself. 'Well you see I couldn't bring a note-case because the one I have is stuffed with things like cleaner's tickets.' F: 'Couldn't you empty them into a drawer and bring the note-case away with you?' J: 'You don't suppose I've got a drawer in my flat, what with all Lawrence's dirty clothes and paint rags and huge boots?' It transpires that she's carried all her English money about everywhere as well as her Italian – an envelope of notes, a purse of coins. 'Well what do *you* do?' she asked. F: 'Put all my English money, passport, travellers cheques, and air ticket into my small suitcase and lock it.' 'What, all the English money loose?' F: 'Why yes.' J: 'Oh I couldn't possibly bear that. I like everything neat and in its right place.' F: 'Well, you could put it in an envelope inside the case if you wanted to.' And so on *ad infinitum*.

She complains of the cold – no one else does. The trees are out in full spring greenery, roses bloom and scent the air in the corner of our square, the ground is becoming dotted with the fallen flowers of the acacias and the Judas trees.

Last evening at the *pensione*. As usual one is sad to see the last of the tenor-voiced waiter; the old couple (the Riccis) who live here, and whose little grandson delights me by his eager interest in everything, and his passion for conducting the telly music; little fat Robertina (a Mrs Molesworth child) the spoiled house baby; and the sallow Pakistani from FAO (who has left two wives and eight children in Pakistan, so Cochemé says). An odd bit of my life has come to an end.

May 2nd

After seeing Julia off to her aeroplane, I returned to the hotel, packed my things, and Cochemé kindly came to transport me to my temporary nest in Elizabeth's room – a little ocean-going cabin in their flat. Yesterday, a national holiday, Cochemé took us on a fine long drive into the country. His first objective was Monte Cassino – I dreaded the unutterable gloom of places destroyed in the war, particularly the shame of it being done by us, and murmured, 'But surely there's nothing left of it?' 'Oh I think it's been entirely rebuilt on the old plan,' said Cochemé. The tour was then to take in several little places on the sea and finally Anzio! There's no question but that the interest of their war history was what drew him to these places. Nothing to be done but submit, and off we went along the *autostrada*. Fate luckily intervened and it being a national holiday, five million other carloads had had the same idea. Near the top of the rocky pinnacle on which Monte Cassino was perched we all came to a standstill and it was clear that the monastery, parking space and everything was jammed. We turned and retreated, with on my part an enormous sense of escape. Cochemé is very male, very much a man of action, and he always wants to look at some scene connected with male activities, if he's not engaged in them.

May 6th: Siena

Sudden arrival of Raymond in Rome two days ago, and I came here with him last night, after a complicated but successful day seeing Tarquinia. This was after several days' soothing spoiling by Joan in the river-side flat, looking out after dark from the terrace at the Tiber glittering along in one direction in the light of the street-lamps while the stream of red rear lights of cars flowed down the other. Above stood the peaceful block of the Aventino with its dark trees and churches, looking like home. Above again, the intensely rich deep indigo sky. One would never be tired of looking at it, any more than the downs at Ham Spray, but grow to love it more.

Tarquinia was extraordinary, both beautiful and interesting. We descended the stairs into about eight little funeral compartments, along with a serious Italian couple and the guide, and found ourselves surrounded with lively brilliant paintings of leopards, dancing girls, musicians, horses, all drawn in with a sure, fine, bold line and then brightly coloured. No sense of individual artists, though they covered several centuries in time. Small not very interesting obscenities. Why this lack of individuality? Is it that one can't read it, any more than the expressions on a Chinaman's face? How much do we miss by this?

Our journey by train from Tarquinia to Siena was lovely. I've never seen Italian scenery spread with this variety of glorious fresh greens, sprinkled with flowers. I couldn't read my interesting book but sat gazing out of the window, over-stimulated. The great pleasure to be got from natural beauty when combined with its man-made elements of tree-planting and house-building is surely very close to that got from painting and architecture. It feels the same – how exactly does it differ?

May 7th

A lovely day yesterday, soaking in the Sienese richness of the Pinacoteca, in the afternoon to the Duomo. In the evening almost exactly the same flavour of pure, ecstatic, devout richness was produced by a concert we went to in an extraordinary room in the Palazzo Chigi. Four unlikely looking men – they might have been dentists or criminals – got into a close knot together and sang motets by Palestrina most beautifully.

Raymond is serene, and benign, delightful company. We get on very well. I must have been pretty difficult on our last sad journey I now realize.

May 11th: Assisi

My bedroom window reaches to the floor and looks straight out at the beautiful, hazy plain. Slept better and feel ready to start again gulping in the floods and floods and floods of sensation that Italy provides. We spent four days in Siena, and its remarkable personality, its impressive, grand, rich, splendid stand-offishness is stamped on my mind as a print is related to its film. We got to know it, saw almost all there was to see, poked in the little churches, where there was a single Sano di Pietro or Matteo di Giovanni, walked on the fringes where spring-like farmland and strong aromatic smells took over from the last houses of the town. Still getting on without a hitch with Raymond.

May 13th: Assisi

I can't believe that the day after tomorrow I'll be surrounded by cream stucco, grey pavements, the telephone, all my 'things' and a pile of bills. It has grown really hot the last day or two so that one fears it a little and plans to creep into the shade. This is our last day here and we have taken the train to a dear little town called Spello, with Roman remains and Pinturicchio frescoes, and back again here.

Walking into the huge church, you are overwhelmed by all the frescoes brilliantly decorating its walls – the Giottos in the upper church, Simone Martinis and Lorenzettis in the lower. I've been driven frantic by the fact that the Franciscan friars refuse to put any lighting in the lower church but a glowworm glint here and there, so that one strains one's eyes almost in vain into the obscurity. When I asked one of them if it was possible to have more light he angrily said no it wasn't. They don't *want* us to see these masterpieces (Lorenzetti's *The Descent from the Cross*, Martini's *St Martin*), they don't *want* anyone to have such voluptuous pleasure, they don't *want* it themselves. The odour of sanctity is dense, stubborn and stifling. A nun stood in a rattling bus, reading her missal, a friar in the crypt where St Francis is buried obviously liked being in glum near-darkness; another tourist came up and protested because Raymond and I were discussing the frescoes in spite of the *silenzio* notice.

I can't think of any place where religion has expressed itself in the past with more brilliant, creative gaiety and now exudes such suffocating inhibitory negativism.

But Nature reflects or echoes the brilliance and gaiety of Giotto and Lorenzetti. The weather seems set fair, the gardens at Spello were full of huge roses. I dream of sightseeing.

Yesterday afternoon I woke from a nap just in time to save myself having to fly an aeroplane solo. 'I *suppose* it's all right?' I thought. Well, it's what I have to do, so I imagine the dream wish was trying to convey that it was normal.

Yesterday we ran into the head of the Victoria and Albert looking at the Giottos, and brought him back for a drink. A nice, dry museum product.

May 20th: West Halkin Street

Arriving with Raymond by air on Whit Friday I walked into the dead cube of air contained by my sitting-room. One piece of ivy and two twigs stood in my Spanish jug; my heart sank like a stone. The weather radiant, as hot as Rome. Janetta in Majorca, everyone I rang up was 'away for Whitsun', except Margaret Penrose who was just going. 'Why don't you come too?' she kindly asked and I did. The feeling of dreadful unreality and loneliness, which hit me like a blast of hot air when I opened the door of my flat was dissipated by finding myself at the steering wheel of my friendly Mini spinning off into the blue-and-green, Bank-holiday-jolly countryside on Saturday.

The Penroses' National Trust show house has a cardboard appearance but is immensely livable in, like a stage set which has had a lot of use. Margaret is rapidly becoming as round as a football; she rolls about the house with a 'cheerful bumpy sound'. There was a bearded anthropologist and his wife, a mental nurse, on Saturday night and next night a medical student girl friend of Shirley's.[1] These very intelligent girls giggled like any others about young men and parties when left together. Lots of fascinating talk, much of it scientific; ramshackle croquet, a walk with Margaret. Lionel has found that one in every hundred babies born to a mother over forty is

[1] Lionel and Margaret's daughter.

a Mongolian imbecile and one in every forty-five if she's over forty-five. Surely this should be widely publicized?

The Penroses lead a good life, and this is one of only many possible good lives; their lack of visual feeling or sensual appreciation makes no matter at all – they're fully engaged thinking, enjoying and radiating warmth to their friends, interest in the world and humanity.

May 21st

I've been driving about London in a daze, landing beyond my destinations in unknown surroundings – all because of thinking of Julia. Thinking of her kept me awake till four last night in spite of a lot of pills (which I'd been trying to wean myself from). Oh dear, oh dear, oh dear, oh *dear*. I fear she's beyond my aid. After two warm letters thanking me cordially for the Roman holiday she asked me to dinner (a 'quiet bite') last night, and I went round feeling eager to know how things were going.

I rang the downstairs bell and started up the stairs. Before I got to Julia's door she had emerged and stood poised like a fashion model at the top. It was as if she had been bewitched by some extraordinary spell and she gave me a quite unexpectedly frosty reception. Instead of the usual Hallo, and welcoming smile, this time there she stood, every gesture studied, in a neat black dress, with a bright pink scarf carefully arranged round her neck. 'I say, my dear, you're looking very elegant,' I said. 'Is it a dinner party?' 'Oh no, very much not so,' said Julia. But the grizzly thing, the wounding, chilling thing was that I felt her dislike and disapproval hitting me like a wave, implicit in her cold eyes and her mask-like face. There followed a grand display of her social manner. 'Do sit down.' Head tilted back, a scornful *grande dame* expression. A great many 'Oh reelly?s' and the symbolical sniff. I made a bid to get a note of relaxation and intimacy into the conversation, but it was so futile that I literally felt like bursting into tears. My saying I'd seen Bunny who had been to the Bussy sale, and preparing to tell her about it, met with: 'Oh well, I'm really not in the least interested.' We drank our whisky, I feeling more and more desperate, and she then insisted on taking me out to eat an expensive meal at Lyons' Grill and refusing to let me pay my share. Throughout her manner was artificial in the extreme, like someone going through a part in a play, and we left at nine-thirty. Ten minutes later I saw as we stood on her doorstep that she expected me to go home and not come in. A little later I was tossing and turning in bed, thinking how much she must have hated the Roman holiday, looked back on it as a nightmare and borne a strong grudge against me for taking her. I'm left quite uncertain what was the explanation. But I'm very sure that she feels no affection at all for me at present and a great deal of dislike, also that I can't bear this remote withering formality from someone I've known since she was eight. The result of my nightly tossing is that I've decided to keep silent and apart until such time as she makes a move in my direction.

This has been extraordinarily upsetting; I don't know how it will end.

Earlier yesterday I lunched with Isobel and went on to visit Bunny on his barge on the Thames. I was giving a slight picture of Julia's timidity in Rome when (beaming and rubicund) Bunny said: 'Well, I see you've come round to the view that there's some point in courage.' Interesting talk about Rupert Brooke – his dazzling looks, his excellent conversation, gaiety and intelligence, narcissism. I asked if he had been a homosexual, and he thought ambivalent. He had broken with Noel Olivier when she fell in love with James and he with her. He was extremely jealous. Lytton became his anti-Christ, why I can't quite understand, and then he turned against all intellectuals and unconventionality and became the pet of Churchill and the Asquiths, a war hero. 'But take it all in all, would you say, you *liked* him?' I asked Bunny. B: 'If the impossible were to happen and he were to ring up and ask me to go and see him now, I should be off like a shot.' Did Bunny think him a good poet? Yes.

May 29th: Hilton

I live on two levels at the moment. Underneath is the sad grey lumbering tide, my longing for the end of it all. On top (I can say with truth) I am enjoying being here at Hilton during a hot beautiful weekend; and there's no inconsistency. Also I believe that the subterranean flood is unguessed at by my companions. Yet it's there all the time, the first thing I wake to when I become conscious in the morning.

Have enjoyed things I've done with both Bunny and Angelica separately but am saddened by the sudden new feeling of their being two quite disconnected people. Bunny told me something of this and it's evidently true – not on his side but on hers: those grey eyes look at him very coolly now; I would be frightened if I were him. I drove her

57

down and have talked a lot to her about all sorts of things, theories of art, writing, people. I find her fascinating to talk to, extremely intelligent and stimulating. Bunny showed me a lecture he's written about Galsworthy and Morgan Forster. I read there a quotation from Forster – 'Kindness, more kindness, and even after that, more kindness; I assure you it's the only hope' – and was glad I'd not given way to my rancour against Julia. I nearly did, then I saw the folly and futility and dishonest reasoning, and merely sent a postcard asking her to lunch next week. If she comes, and I'm by no means certain she will, I shall bite back and swallow anything she could possibly take as critical. I think that remark of Forster's is profoundly true as a matter of fact, and I shall try hard to bear it in mind.

May 30th

'Kindness, more kindness, and even after that more kindness, I assure you it's the only hope,' and in spite of despair I walked out of the garden into the hall, heard a Siamese cat yowling, smelt lunch cooking, felt the warmth of the lawn underfoot and thought, 'I love the stuff life's made of.' Yet it is so beastly and cruel, like a hideous dress made of the finest velvet. In my despair I do, I must, hurl myself head first into the lives of others, attending only to the superficial sense-perceptions of my own. One suffers though for others. I notice poor Bunny's slightly bewildered loneliness because of Angelica's withdrawal, and his kindness and sweetness to his children touches me also. I feel Angelica hates this house or at least takes not the smallest interest in it. The meals have been fairly perfunctory, I was put to sleep in dirty sheets (a thing I don't relish); the bath towels are frayed rags. No love for poor old Hilton from her now.

June 3rd

I was right about Julia. She *has* put me in her 'doghouse', and so we reach a semicolon or some such thing in our long relationship. My postcard last week merely asked her to lunch on Thursday. As it happened, I invited Eardley to join us, so there would have been no private conversation. Her short reply arrived yesterday and I suppose the most significant thing about it is that it begins, 'My dear Frances', after a lifetime of writing 'Dearest'. I found myself wondering what trains of thought and feeling had led her to hatch this egg. 'Thank you so much for your nice card,' she began, and then excused herself from lunch by saying that she was 'just making a start at spending the day at the London Library' (not 'writing' there, just 'spending the day'). She goes on to say that I mustn't worry about her, she can only get along by not thinking or talking about her troubles, and has decided to 'have a hermit period for the time being, without meeting more people than necessary'. Finally she says she'll communicate again when she wants to see me.

What do I feel? Anger and sadness at the waste and the rejection of my concern and affection for her. A definite element of relief at not having to face the strain of our next meeting under pressure. What turn will she take next? Am I to be treated to a cut if we meet in someone else's house or just go back to the 'vicar's wife' style?[1] Will she have any regrets? asks a base murmur from the undergrowth.

This has filled my present sky with a great damp cloud, and lopped away yet one more stem of the few connecting me with some sort of reality. I had none to spare.

June 4th

Julia's rejection, snub, or whatever it can be called, was sufficiently bruising to make me very glad of any extra kindness from other friends. Janetta has been a great comfort, and we had a lovely evening going to *Ernani* at St Pancras. One of Rachel's fat, full letters landed on my hall floor, heralding her approach. I was touched by her ending, after a long amusing and gossipy letter, 'I think about you so much and Burgo comes into my mind so often. I feel his loss must come home to you more and more, though I expect you do have moments of consolation. I would only like you to know that I realize what you must feel, and that there must be awful times of loneliness and dreariness and poignancy. It must be hard not to feel that everyone forgets, when they just go on as if they weren't aware.'

June 6th: Lawford Hall

Came here yesterday afternoon, with Phyllis Nichols[2] and sweet Jo-jo;[3] later joined by Leslie Hartley. Walked out with Phyllis round the

---

[1] Henry Bath on seeing her at Stokke said to Mary 'Who have you got here? The vicar's wife?'

[2] Widowed owner of the house.

[3] Her daughter.

garden under a washed pale sky, rich smells coming on all sides from the damp plants and earth, ducklings in a small flotilla on the dark waters of the biggest pond. As ever, I was drawn to her by her honest friendliness. She began to talk suddenly after dinner about the next world, spook manifestations. I couldn't make out how far over this dread cliff she had already toppled, but she tried to resuscitate the case for Borley Rectory, spoke of 'the sense of evil', and ended by saying that when Vera Birch and she were talking in this very room, the drawing-room, Vera asked her 'Did you notice that the handle of the door was turning all the time?' Implying – for Vera was an old flame of Phil's and I suppose they were talking about him – that he was signifying his spiritual presence. How *can* she get comfort from such futile suppositions, quite apart from being able to believe them? Trying to conduct the conversation onto a more feasible plane I asked Leslie Hartley and Jo-jo whether they believed in and longed for an after-life and in what shape or form they envisaged it if so. I don't think it was resented exactly, but it surprised them. What surprised me more than I can say was that while they all believed in and desired it and I could get no support for my longing for total black oblivion, they were one and all unable to give any sort of picture of what they envisaged – perfection of some sort, eternity with all the joys of life but without end.

Leslie talked about 'morals in fiction', a subject he had discussed with David on the wireless. I brought up Morgan's runic 'kindness etc.' It left both Phyllis and Leslie totally cold. Their response was: 'Some people aren't worthy of it, they'll only take advantage of you.' Take advantage!

The house dog, a very beautiful, sleek pointer Phyllis calls Rocco, as usual produces the court jester element in Lawford life, pointing all over the place out and indoors, and submitting one to over-familiar snufflings and lickings and shufflings under skirts.

June 8th

Drove back late last night with Jo-jo, arriving after midnight rather exhausted. Julia's rejection is like a painful thorn; I can't forget it. It's the first thing I remember every morning. I dread its turning bad and festering. Why is it that it rankles so?

In the middle of my unhappy restlessness the telephone rang and it was her. Her call couldn't have come at a worse time, with my hurt feelings lying so close to the surface; and to hear her saying, 'I hope you weren't offended by my hermit letter', or words to this effect, was too much for me; then, as I hesitated, she added: 'You sound as if you were.' I said something about the feeling of being 'totally rejected' not being pleasant, and that I hoped she would let me know when her 'hermitage' was over. I should be delighted. She did just say, 'You're not totally rejected', before I rang off, and I felt indignant at being thus officially honoured with readmission. My feelings distressed me by being so out of hand; I was shaken by heartbeats for hours after. Oh *hell take it all*. A lot of things have combined to make me feel all on the wrong leg somehow.

June 9th

As I almost expected, a letter from Julia in the post. What it would say I hadn't really pondered, yet having read it I feel I might have guessed. It is still 'My dear'. 'For a long time now', she writes, 'underneath all your *intense kindness* I have felt, palpably and unmistakeably, a hostility there in you towards me. Whether you are aware of it yourself or not I don't know. But at any rate you were so tart and unfriendly, again, when we last met at Percy St that I just feel too crushed to face it all for the time . . . If you are not aware of the feeling yourself no amount of going over our words and conversation would avail for in my view it is not in the words so much as in your whole face and manner. For of course such feelings are catching, one reacts defensively and gets hostile also, so by this time I too have got prickly to say the least of it. I think the fact is our feelings for each other are ambivalent . . .'

June 10th

After all this I realize I now should simply dread a meeting, and that I believe she is suffering from persecution-mania or something very near it, and I remember how every *woman* we saw in Rome was described as 'looking at her oddly, having such an unfriendly manner' – Alvilde and Joan, for instance, but *not* Jim Lees-Milne nor Cochemé.

Last night Nicky[1] had a twenty-first birthday party, and I went for a while, and presented her with a silver necklace which she put on

---

[1] Loutit, Janetta's eldest daughter.

and it looked fine on her. The glamorous young (art student friends) thudded and pranced in the crowded room and I would have been happy to watch them for ever.

June 25th

Shocked by the terrible news of the death of Arthur Goodman in a shooting accident, while Celia was at Aldeburgh. What will this delicate and sensitive creature, with two children to support, do without the husband on whom she seemed to lean for everything? I can't forget it. A nightmare feeling hangs in the hot air. I have felt tense all day, hurrying from one thing to another.

June 26th

Vague and fruitless longings: for the energy and concentration to read something tough and stimulating. For such books to appear, crying out to be read. For a less literal mind. For the power of getting off the earth more frequently into the less stodgy atmosphere of imagery and analogy – I do so enjoy it when I rarely do. For calm, to be turned on like a hot-water tap.

I went to Wimbledon last week, with Nicko Henderson, Janetta and Georgie – the first time for over thirty years I reckon. Sat in the best position in the centre court and was ticked off for talking too much by a fanatical pipe-smoking addict in front. It was an absorbing, but not really exciting nor beautiful spectacle. Long ago I seem to remember agile, athletic white-clad figures leaping like gibbons against the smooth green background – but not a bit of it now. The modern male singles player is not a beautiful specimen. Often round-shouldered (occupational disease I'm told) even bandy-legged, awkward and ungainly, he plods rather slowly, head bent, back to the service line, goes through a ritual childish bouncing of the ball on the ground, has a painful epileptic fit and (if lucky) sends his first service so hard that his opponent doesn't even move towards it. If unlucky it's a double fault and the plodding starts again. There are of course rare moments of emotional tension, match point etc, and one does become strangely involved, but modern tennis reminds me of those rams one reads about, whose horns grew so long and curly that they pierced their own brains and killed them.

Into my mind flashes a picture of dining with Clive and Little Barbara at the Travellers' Club a few days ago. Clive, as always, courteous and gentlemanly to everyone including the negro waiters, turning their services into an act of special and friendly kindness on their part – yet he incongruously and distressingly arrived without his teeth, brought a white pasteboard box from his pocket at the dinner table, fished them out and put them in. I can't help blaming Barbara for contributing to this atmosphere of nursery physical intimacy. He had left off the 'collar' he has had to wear lately for his rheumatic neck, and was just beginning to forget about it when she must needs ask, 'Do you want your collar on, Clive?' It was obtrusively present in a plastic nanny's bag, and another contained some wild flowers brought from the downs for me. My hard heart ought to have been touched. I can't help wondering how poor Clive stands the intensive boredom of her conversation – perhaps he can't, and that's why he keeps suggesting 'going into a home'.

July 1st

Shall I begin with last night? I shunned the great Hill party for Lucy,[1] fearing to feel 'caught' far away at Hampton Court and ill-equipped for such an endurance test, yet half regretting it because of the number of friendly faces I would have seen and the interest of watching the orgiastic young. But when I rang Janetta about six and heard her exhausted voice, with a dinner party for ten or more (including Julia!) ahead of her, and her hair dressed for the occasion so that she couldn't even lay it on her pillow and rest, I was glad not to be going. I'd asked Bunny to dinner to cheer my last evening and prevent my going to the party, and also because I had felt sorry for him lately. Quite unnecessarily – he arrived in a self-confident, ebullient mood from his publishers' cocktail party where he got off with a young female writer. Just before leaving, his voice churning almost to a standstill, he told me this strange story: a fortnight ago he had fallen asleep after lunch in his boat on the embankment (whose Yonghy Bonghy Bo discomfort I'd quite needlessly grieved over). He woke and saw in front of him 'the extraordinarily beautiful colour and texture of naked human flesh'. A woman he had always loved and been attracted by – and been to bed with a long time ago – had come to see him, found the door of the boat open and him asleep, and

[1] Their second daughter.

63

got into bed beside him. A few months ago, he told me, he had felt there was no point in life. Now he was better.

Devoted to Bunny as I am, his mood of sensual self-satisfaction has always faintly embarrassed me, yet I wouldn't have missed that curious boat story. We talked a bit of the past – of how Molly MacCarthy had long ago (in the first war) refused to believe some sexual adventure he was describing – he was making a mistake, it didn't happen, she implied. I visualized suddenly and very clearly her knitted brows and pursed mouth, shaking her head, tampering relentlessly with reality. Of Vanessa and Clive as man and wife, he said that Clive's 'enormous vitality, noisiness and vulgarity' had been just what Vanessa needed to release her from the bondage of Sir Leslie Stephen. She had been very beautiful, very gay, with a streak of *enfant terrible*. When on a trip to Greece she got dangerously ill with typhoid, Clive wouldn't go near her – he had even then a morbid horror of illness, and she was nursed by Roger Fry; he fell in love with her and they had an affair. Clive's with Molly started about this time and (Bunny thought) was a major circumstance in the drifting apart of Clive and Vanessa. The sequence of these emotions and relations has become confused even in the memory of those closely involved. The Clive–Molly affair was long and serious. Desmond and Clive were close friends throughout. How was this managed? Had Desmond already begun to be unfaithful?

Marriage – infidelity – divorce. How can the equation be solved? Talked about this to Robert and Cynthia[1] the evening before. Robert, doing a telly programme on divorce, had some amazing stories: of the wife whose husband hadn't spoken to her for years but wouldn't 'give her cause' for divorce, nor did she dare leave him because she would lose her means of subsistence – the six pounds he handed her 'in a fan' every week. And of another woman who had lived as the wife of (and had children by) a married man. His wife wouldn't divorce him, but pestered him for maintenance money until he committed suicide. His insurance and pension goes to his legal wife. The mistress, Robert said, was obviously an awful character, but the tears flowed down her face as she talked, and she showed Robert the suicide notes to her and her children which were deeply moving. Her old father had had a seizure and died from the shock of the news.

Very good description by Robert of the state of being at one and the same time deeply moved and completely detached and cold while he

[1] Robert's second wife.

listened to the weeping woman. A different attitude to suffering was described by Bunny about Nerissa[1] who had been attending the murder trial at Leeds of a man who had strangled (or shot) his mistress. 'Could anything be more boring?' she asked, but luckily the visual aspect of a trial had fascinated her.

I spent last weekend at the house of Julian's parents: I'd not realized it had been his grandfather, Hilaire Belloc's house, bought sixty years ago, fitted up and left unaltered, not a thing done since, hardly a cobweb removed, no electricity or telephone, ceiling so black with lampsmoke that Tristram Powell said 'how nice to have black velvet ceilings!' Hundreds of books of sixty years past, pedigrees of family cats with details of their lives, crucifixes, holy virgins, presentation objects covered with inscriptions, rooms pitch-dark, and painted dark brown or red. It is a civilization of a sort as original and odd as Charleston but how different. I saw that Julian loved it and I found it lovable through his attachment to it. The country round is exceptionally rural without being wild: fine oaks; grassy lanes; fields of plumy grasses taller than Rose[2] with the evening light shining pink through them; a wild garden in which a comfortable vegetable plot had been cleared, and a small lawn enclosed by fruit trees, shrubs and purple lilies made an outdoor 'room' where we ate our meals and read. Julian was thoughtful, and neat in a sailorly way, an efficient housewife. I drove Georgie and Rose down on Friday night – Janetta having been kept in London by her brother Mark's having been desperately ill. She came for the day on Sunday. As always I enjoyed talking to Julian enormously, and gave no thought to the passage of time.

A bad mark to Cyril Connolly. Bunny asked him why he thought it was that his first marriage was the most important to him. 'Because it took place in church with candles, veils, and flowers.'

July 2nd: Skelwith Fold, Westmorland

Arrived in brilliant weather, hot and cloudless. Walked with Tom and Nadine[3] down through fields where hay was being picked up and filling the air with its smell, to a broad river edged with a little cliff. Yes, the beauty here is as great, greater than I'd remembered and it does inevitably seep healingly in at every pore. The solid little

---

[1] Twin daughter of Bunny and Angelica.
[2] Janetta's youngest daughter.
[3] My brother and his wife.

farmhouse too, the whitewashed walls, greenish slate, the intoxicating scent from three cabbagy red-pink roses in a vase by my bed coming to my nose through the darkness, Tom and Nadine's married happiness – all combine to give an unnightmarish view of the world.

July 6th

I am sitting alone on the terrace of the Old Farm enjoying my solitude and the matchless view down through the rough garden with its foxgloves, roses, ferns and a few lilies, to the valley and the knobbly fells bloomed over with bracken beyond. My co-guests are Mimi, Nadine's cousin, and her husband Sir Geoffrey Harrison, late ambassador at Tehran – pleasant people but who talk a language I don't understand or anyway can't speak. The conversation is for the most part lacking in toughness; when anyone brings it round to a generalization on politics or religion or education it is Tom. I am very fond of Tom and Nadine, they've shown me great kindness. Indeed there are many things giving me immense pleasure here – and Oh the beauty of it all! The weather has been for the Lake District superb, and we have done each day a splendid excursion, twice climbing sizeable mountains from which one has the miraculously exalting experience of being up among the other summits and looking down over the silver lakes gleaming between them. We ate one picnic lunch by a brown stream tearing down the hillside, and sheltering from the cold wind behind a rock as grey and portentous as a fossilized primeval animal. Yesterday afternoon we had the most taxing walk of all – drove to Patterdale and went over Place Fell and Knight's Crag to the verge of Ullswater, arriving there pretty weary only to find there was a four-mile walk along the lake shore home. I'm delighted to find I can do it, and beside the satisfaction of achievement there is the sudden silence and drop of wind and staggeringly beautiful view from the top.

July 15th

When I got back to London I found a short letter from Darsie Japp saying that Juanita[1] had had an acute cerebral haemorrhage and died

---

[1]   His younger daughter.

without regaining consciousness. I went with Kitty West next day to the Requiem Mass, feeling that it was the least one could do for the poor old pair. The beautifully sung music seemed at first impact the best and most effective form of catharsis for the mourners. Then the mumbo-jumbo began: a bell like a dentist's summons to his assistant tinkled urgently; little boys moved compulsively to and fro altering the position of books and chalices, raising the tail of the priest's gown, moaning and droning the while, and such words as I caught were grotesque and inappropriate, and begged us all to prepare for our own ends. (Yes, indeed we must, but how?) As we left the church we found the Japps and Olivia[1] and the poor old bridegroom-elect (who looked dreadfully stricken) waiting in an emotional foreign group to receive our condolences. The outlook is black-edged and I am obsessed with the thought of death. It is as if one had been on a long walk and suddenly turned and found death had been for a great while pacing alongside. How differently I now wake each morning, without any thought of planning, any hope, any expectation, yet in a sort of way I feel nothing could ever be shocking again. I marvel at the serenity of people who have not been bereft. How can they go about so calmly? In fact I felt David Cecil was the only sane one among us when he told me how he became frantic when Hugh didn't come home from a party and was out in the car, and rang up the police.

At the Cecils' I again met Iris Murdoch and John Bayley. I have not taken so much to a pair for a long time. He, with his dryness, great humour and effervescent vitality, provides the right seasoning to her charmingly unselfconscious solidity, good head and warm heart. They are deeply devoted to each other.

Yesterday to hear *Curlew River* in Southwark Cathedral – Britten's latest exploitation of cruelty to boys. It didn't stir me, musically or dramatically – I didn't know what he was after. Very different were two Handel operas last week, especially glorious *Semele*, put on with unspeakable visual vulgarity (Woolworth gold, a decor like the Follies in about 1900, a large gilt crescent moon beneath which Semele lay among shot silk pouffes, women's dresses of the same period with heavy head-dresses, prim and respectable).

Janetta's sweetness has been a specially great consolation to me lately. I think that in these last weeks I have been able to sit

[1] Juanita's daughter.

67

back a little and look at what remains of my life with a certain detachment.

July 26th: Crichel

I'm here in divinest summer weather, still and almost too hot, the flowers very gently turning themselves inside out and then falling on the short grass with a plop; windows open wide onto the dark breathless night let in the insistent remarks of wood pigeons. It has been so far a contented stay. Andrew Porter[1] is also here. I like him; dark, rather good-looking, intelligent, perhaps a little competitive. We have been visited by Kitty, Lettice Ashley-Cooper and an *antipatica* little musical lady who is writing a book on Finzi.

So here we are in this house, four singletons, each preoccupied with our own interests – Raymond with his health, Desmond and Andrew with music and myself with bare survival.

Yesterday passed serenely, reading, writing, talking, croquet, all against a background of blooming blowsy summer and 'I *can't* say cuck-oo' from the wood pigeons. Cecils, with Laura, Hugh and Hugh's girlfriend (a friendly orange and pink creature) came for a drink.

Raymond has thrown up his plan to go to Venice in three days' time. He certainly doesn't look well and with increasing feebleness, the feminine aspect of his appearance is emphasized. But he seems anxious to entertain me (and heaven knows there's no need for that), touchingly laying down at my feet books such as a history of English vicarages – what a dusty subject! – and unaware of how alien to my taste that is and that I like books that entertain, are works of art or make me think. Biographies and histories proper qualify only insofar as they do that.

July 29th: London

Last days before departure to Spain[2] overcast with thundery sense of doom and restlessness. Last night I spent at Jonny and Sabrina's with an all-young company – his brother Sammy, Harriet and Tim Behrens.[3] I drank rather a lot and hope I didn't talk too much in an

---

[1] Music critic, friend of Desmond's.
[2] To stay with the Hendersons, but above all to see if Henrietta and Sophie were 'all right'.
[3] Elder daughter of the Hills and her husband.

68

effort to remember that the young are bored by one stressing the difference of age (so I've often been told).

⧯

August 3rd: Alhaurin de la Torre[1]

The plunge into all this dreamy heat and scented beauty was more effortless than I had expected, but (hot as England has been lately) it has had the combined effect of a huge injection of some over-agitating drug.

On Saturday I handed in my trusty little Mini, friend and companion for nearly three years, in exchange for a new one I have ordered. Then, having said goodbye to Mrs Ringe I made my slow preparations to go over the top. Mary, Alexandra and Nicko picked me up at four a.m. Having gone to bed at ten I felt I'd had a night's sleep. Calmly and effortlessly we were off. It was already almost light, but the cabin lights were put out so that we could snooze and I slipped into a strange no man's land, until at seven a tray of breakfast sausages, coffee, toast and marmalade was set before me.

Now it was Sunday. Hazy, hot and fine at Gibraltar. We crammed somehow, luggage and all, into a small, new, blue car and sped off. Stopped and bathed on a nondescript beach, in a fairly warm sea. Soon after eleven we drove up to El Rascacio where Henrietta, Sophie and Nerissa were supposed to be. It is a charming white farmhouse set back from the road in a bower of trees and geraniums. I asked a maid for Henrietta. 'No está. Está a Malaga.' Was Sophie there I asked (explaining that I was her *abuela*), or the *hermana* perhaps? Yes, Sophie was here and awake, the *hermana* 'está durmiendo'. We walked out on the terrace where waiters were clearing the tables and there under the shade of a tree was a pen in which were a couchant, brown dog and Sophie, sitting erect and solemn and rather pale, almost unchanged from when I last saw her except for paler hair. I was too dazed to make much sense of anything, so that when the maid called me to say that Henrietta was on the telephone, and I ran up and found a sleepy Nerissa with her hair cascading round the receiver softly murmuring into it, my wits were loose and jangling as she handed it to me. A faint far-off

---

[1] The house had been previously taken by Janetta, and now by the Hendersons.

69

voice said: 'I'm in Malaga . . . Have you heard all the awful things that have been happening?' 'No, what?' (bracing, as now I always do, for the worst, and more than the worst). 'A friend of mine from Dartington was horribly beaten up by her boyfriend, a Puerto Rican, at the Rascacio; he hit her with a bottle and she had a miscarriage and had to come to hospital. It was awful. I couldn't leave her.' 'Is she going to be all right?' 'Yes, but I can't leave her.' 'Where could I get hold of you?' She only said in this faint, far-off voice: 'At the Hospital.' And then I returned to try and take in Sophie and ask Nerissa what had happened and if she was all right there, and see that the Hendersons weren't kept waiting too long. Impressions of Sophie: she was calm but a little less dynamic than she used to be – the heat? – a few insect bites on her delicate cheek – a lovely curly smile, much interest and affection from all the maids and men, the gardener included.

August 4th

My mood of angst could not survive this fabulous all-drugging heat. However one may scream at the horrifying new sky-scrapers sprouting along the Costa del Sol, there are still a few places that have kept all their vivid attractiveness unaltered. For instance our *pueblo* here – Alhaurin de la Torre. Less squalid perhaps than it once was, the main street is a succession of snow-white one-storey houses each with a flowerpot hanging and a figure, male or female, precariously tilted against the wall on a strong straight-backed chair. The inhabitants greeted us with relentless Spanish stares and warm Spanish humanity when we applied to them for help or information, and let us into their shops although it was Sunday and they were really shut. This house, pool and garden is far more delightful than I remembered, the two servants more ravishingly pretty and amiable. In Alhaurin two men on horseback were caracoling about the streets in happy, unbridled exhibitionism on pretty, excitable horses with small, pointed heads, red-tasselled saddle-cloths, no stirrups.

I took the Hendersons to visit the Brenans last night and this was a great success. The garden was bursting with huge yellow canes striped with green, rare plants and creepers. Gerald went swiftly away and picked a 'moonflower' for us – which had just that minute taken five minutes to open its snowy five-inch saucer on a long slender tube.

Back to our dark patio for a marvellous meal of gazpacho, chanquetes[1] and salmonetes.

August 5th

We all read and swim by turns; today we wrote letters and postcards. I scribble quietly in this. In the evening we went in to Torremolinos under a fainting lavender sky: all my horror of the place returned – it was full of stampeding, red-faced crowds, every shop a trap for tourists, phoney, noisy, without a drop of real blood in its veins, synthetic as those artificial morning-glories on balconies, *beastly*.

I'm enjoying reading the books I find in this house. Have finished Rose Macaulay's *Fabled Shore* and moved on to Baudelaire's *Journal Intime*.

August 7th

Henrietta is here. Two days ago she telephoned in the afternoon and we arranged that I should borrow the car and fetch her from the hospital for a day or even a night. Yesterday I went off alone into the sultry heat of Malaga (95° in the shade most of the day). The sweat was pouring off me when I arrived (after two boss shots) at the right hospital in the Limonàr district, walked upstairs and found myself in a large, light room with bed and sofa, terrace and washing room. Henrietta was with a fair, pretty girl whose face was contorted with pain as she sat on a chair while her bed was being made, and the Puerto Rican lover, a lizard-like, smooth young man in blue jeans and sandals was treating his victim with tender care. There was coffee, and brandy being poured into it. My urgent desire was rescue – to get Henrietta away as quickly as possible, and I did so. She filled in the details as we drove. She had invited the girl out to stay at the Rascacio and she had brought Andrés (who is disapproved of by Sarah's parents and had already beaten her up before). At the end of the evening session Henrietta was clearing away when she heard a terrible noise like a dog howling – it was the wretched Sarah, and she was covered all over in blood. He had cut her face and lip with a bottle, and beaten her about the head. The nightmare was that Henrietta had to go with her and her now distracted lover to search for Jaime Parladé and doctors in Marbella, who couldn't be found

[1] Tiny little fish, special to Malaga.

for some time. I can't really bear to think of any of it, and when I saw with what relief Henrietta slipped into the pool here and fell asleep on the grass, and responded to the kindness of the Hendersons, my own idea was to prevent her going back to the hospital at all, where she had led a ghastly few days, not going out, or hardly, devoured by mosquitoes, and with no bathing to refresh herself. Seeing her relief at the idea, I urged my attack more forcibly and now I'm afraid I may have overdone it. She must of course do what she wants. I think I can perhaps deal with the money aspect, as Andrès hasn't a penny; Sarah's mother is 'very rich but mean'. Another complication was that Sarah was pregnant and had a miscarriage after this battering. She then seemed much better, but when Henrietta rang up the hospital yesterday, she had had a high fever. I want more than anything else to extract Henrietta from this sordid imbroglio, but I see the danger of pressing her until she behaves below her standard of what a friend should do. For she has some, if not very strong, affection for Sarah who to me is nothing at all but a pathetic piece of flotsam, and though her drama makes me feel sick, it is sickness coupled with detachment.

I'm writing in bed before breakfast. The zz of a mosquito woke me very early and when I had my light on hunting for it Nicko called me out to look at a passing Sputnik. The garden was deliciously cool and the morning star shone brilliantly in the pale sky. The Sputnik moved along at a pedestrian pace and was an unromantic spectacle.

August 8th

The fierce heat continues. Yesterday it was nearly 100° in the shade. Mary and Nicko drove off to Ronda for the day leaving Henrietta, Alexandra and me – for my part only too thankful to relax – on the brink of boredom, sweating in the shade or on the bed. Alexandra is a sensitive, intelligent little girl, very responsive to any move towards her. After the long, hot afternoon the three of us walked down the road to the *pueblo* and braving the intensity of Spanish stares and an attack from a child with a water pistol, bought a little rocking chair for Sophie. Nicko and Mary returned after dinner fairly exhausted.

This morning Jaime has arrived, like a good fairy, bringing the £100 it is thought Sarah will need for the expenses of her lover's savagery. This is the payment for some pictures Henrietta is painting for a house he's doing. Meanwhile, Henrietta has gone off with him to Malaga to hand it over and get back her clothes, and the future

72

seems to be taking shape. But OH, the heat! It is too much. I've sat since breakfast listening to the fresh, cold water filling the swimming-pool, and I'm sweating into my clothes. There's a sort of voluptuousness in it, but it drains all one's energies.

August 9th: El Rascacio, Sophie's first birthday

102° in the shade yesterday. But though the wolf's bite was so ferocious, it was heat of a less crushing abnormal sort. Lunch at the Cónsula[1] under the trees. Henrietta was there looking ravishing with a blue band round her head, Jaime, Mrs Rupert Belleville, and two American members of Café Society – Ethel de Croisset who has considerable elegance, and a white-faced creature who has none.

Henrietta went off to the Malaga bullfight with Jaime and then to the Rascacio, where I too am, having been driven over before lunch by Nicko and Alexandra. Will I be able to stick it here? I'm by no means certain. A nice young man called Martin (friend of Henrietta's) is here, still pale-skinned from England (he is supposed to be playing his guitar at nights); Nerissa too, fierce and purposeful. We all got lunch, with great difficulty, for the vagueness and incompetence of the organization is great; Sophie sat gurgling her little Spanish gurgles, on various people's knees and when asked to 'baile' she will curl her wrists in a very authentic way over her head. She is much more 'all right' than I thought at first, but the girl who is engaged to look after her is a rat-faced little creature, horrible and untrustworthy, and Nerissa is determined she should get the sack, saying she stole, wore Henrietta's clothes and dropped Sophie in the pool while she was away. Now I have retired to my room for a so-called siesta. It is one of a row of old cow-sheds converted into rooms by curtains and when the door is shut there is practically no ventil-ation. What to do therefore, when I leave it?

I am virtually living in a night-club. It comes to life about nine p.m., when the red-sashed waiters hurry round laying the table, the grill is lit and lamps set burning under the trees. Last night Nerissa took me in hand; she's a splendid girl – intelligent, realistic, burning with purposeful desire to find out about life. Talking to her was like talking to a contemporary; she was the making of my evening. My trouble is that I'm used to spending my evenings in talk

[1] Where Bill and Annie Davis lived in Churriana. Both Americans, Annie was Cyril's sister-in-law.

or reading or music, and if those fail I go to bed. Whereas almost everyone who frequents this place expects to drink and bray steadily from about nine until three.

This morning my breakfast came like lightning. A new and unpleasant thing is a raging wind, tossing the eucalyptus trees and making my door and the yellow striped curtain that hangs over it flap frenziedly. I hear strident voices from the children by the swimming-pool. No other sign of life at twenty to eleven.

Last night Henrietta was rather seriously gliding about among the guests, taking orders for dinner. Enid, the English lesbian proprietress, stood hump-backed and soft-voiced in front of the grill in the garden.

Janetta, Jaime and Julian arrived last night, all in the last stages of fatigue. Julian seemed near tears and said he was sorry but he was half mad with exhaustion and must really go to bed. The golden-brown image at the other end of the table looked at him but made no sign. The poor fellow sat down again and I remembered what it was to be involved with Janetta's strong will, and resolved always, somehow, to keep my liberty of action. I felt too sorry for Julian to stay, and it being about twenty to two I said goodnight and went to bed.

What is wrong with the life of the expatriates out here is that they are entirely cut off from the stream of civilized life, threats of war, new books, or ideas, but lie drowned in heat and coaxing themselves into oblivion with drink, sunbathing and swimming, and living mainly in the dark when sensibilities are anyway lulled.

8 p.m. Dusk is creeping over the Rascacio, and the loud chattering of birds in the eucalyptus tree has begun as they settle down for the night. From the cowsheds comes very faintly the persistent thrumming of Martin practising his guitar. He plays well and seriously — more about him I'm unable to discover. I've been out all day with the three Js who descended unexpectedly in the middle of the morning. We picnicked and swam from a deserted beach beyond Estepona. Then Julian went off to meet his friend Ed Gilbert at Gibraltar, Jaime on some business errand, and Janetta and I established ourselves on the airy terrace of a hotel.

Back at the Rascacio I have just been talking to Enid Riddell (the proprietress) by the pool. It's clear that, as I suspected and feared, she feels that Henrietta, Martin and Nerissa aren't helping her enough to pay for their keep.

August 14th

Isobel Strachey's arrival and mode of 'taking' Spain has been marvellous. Fresh as a flower she stepped from a taxi just before lunch-time, wearing a charming striped cotton dress, and was at once (and has remained) delighted with everything. She complains of nothing, even if the light in her bathroom won't work, and appreciates everything, doesn't fuss. What a difference from Julia! Everyone likes her and she speaks slow but fluent Spanish in exactly the same languid drawl as she speaks English. Her pleasure has increased mine no end.

Martin the guitarist has been disgruntled and unhappy and then rather ill. He is now better and happier-looking, and has started to play the guitar in the evenings. He does this beautifully and with great sensitivity. To hear him thrumming gently in the half-darkened garden, even though it is to an audience of chattering French tourists with potbellies or dyed yellow beehives and silk pyjama suits in peach or turquoise, is something I've greatly enjoyed, and so do they. Last night a large party got him to sit at the end of their table and looked really appreciative of his delightful playing. I like also to watch his pale, dedicated face, turned sideways into the darkness. I have now realized that he was the young admirer of Henrietta's I heard about in pre-Burgo days. He is gentle and intelligent and sweet to Sophie. I like him, though he might be weak and too dependent to give Henrietta the support she needs.

We dined with Jaime in his delightful new Marbella house two nights ago. Isobel and Nerissa came, and Ed and Julian were there. Jaime told us it was his first dinner party and we sat at a white table in the darkened patio.

August 17th

Jaime has managed to pull a new nurse for Sophie out of his hat and the change in her has been amazing: she has come to life, developed adventurousness and energy – this I think the rat-nurse had contrived in one way or another to quash, principally by putting her to sleep half the day.

Nerissa appears unable to understand why she shouldn't continue to stay here free, nor does she show any desire to do anything in the way of work. I spent a lot of time writing to Bunny, and then tearing up my letter and starting all over again. In the final form I told him they were leaving here but made the least possible of the reason for it. I said nothing about the beating-up.

Last night Henrietta, Isobel and I sat under the trees playing Scrabble while ants crawled along the branches and dropped into our hair.

August 21st

On my last evening at Marbella Henrietta arranged to rent an ugly but well-equipped, little house, bought a new cot and a push-chair and ordered a mattress. I told her I'd contribute towards all these expenses. I left them all gaily packing up and even sweeping up the unspeakable filth and mess of their quarters to go to the new house. I hope they will be all right, poor impractical dears.

Tomorrow I leave here, driving with Jaime and Julian to Portugal, where we are all due to stay in a house rented by Janetta for herself and her children.

August 23rd: Portugal, the Algarve

Here we are blessed with a much purer air and sea, great beauty, a beach of fine, soft sand, kept somehow or other scrupulously clean and enhanced by the very pretty striped tents and awnings under which sit monumental middle-aged women looking out to sea. Janetta's house is modern, airy and spacious, furnished with local things – rugs, stuffs and plain furniture. It is all much much nicer than I expected, and waking each morning (this was the second) to peaceful cluckings of fowls, and voices of maids, one looks out through the long-skirted fig-trees to a bluer, calmer sea. The sun seems more burning, the air more translucent, a greater sanity and serenity prevails.

August 24th

Last night as we dined by the light of candles and a great harvest moon, Julian launched an attack on Bohemianism. 'At the other pole you get conventionality' I suggested, but he wouldn't have that and

76

substituted 'a dashing upper-class life'. Jaime said that Henrietta and Nerissa were the only true Bohemians he had ever met and he found them 'absolutely glorious', pleasing me with his appreciation of the two dear girls in spite of the muddle that went with their vitality and spontaneity.

August 26th

An expedition to Cape St Vincent was a wild success. When we reached it the strong wind magically abated and we gazed down over the stupendous cliffs into the deep, dark green, gently sucking, gurgling tide. We walked on each headland in turn and picnicked on a sandy beach between Sagres and St Vincent, so beaten upon by sun and the glare of the sea and stung by occasional eddies of wind and sand, that I for one was overwhelmed by the vastness of the horizon and the all-encircling ocean, and my wretchedly inadequate identity was for the moment completely swallowed up in it all.

September 16th: West Halkin Street

Back two nights ago, and though London has drenched us with rain and blasted us with wind, I returned to find it loveable and even welcoming this time. Indeed if only I had a piece of interesting work I believe I could settle down and face what comes next. I would like to dig in here for a good six months, and an excited letter from Eardley about a project to take a house on the lake of Orta together next spring leaves me rather apathetic.

The bad news that one always expects to hit one in the face like a slap is here all right – poor old Clive is dying according to Barbara. Angelica had prepared me for this; on my return I found letters from Barbara and when I rang her she dissolved into tears and said he had pneumonia and cancer of throat and lungs, so the doctors believe, had no voice and couldn't swallow. How can one do anything but wish him to die quickly, dear and affectionate old friend. Half an hour later she rang up to say he was 'much better' and wanted to see me very much. Round I went, with an immense hitch at my moral courage I must admit. I suppose one gets a little more able to take these harrowing scenes – the shock at least is less, and I was fully prepared. He's terribly thin and has no voice beyond a croak or whisper. I kept up a monologue for about half an hour, dreading chiefly that I should miss one of his attempts at saying or asking something. Then I read to him out of *The Times*. Barbara says the doctor has faithfully promised he shan't suffer at all, so it's to be hoped he'll let him die as quickly as possible. How much he knows he's dying I can't tell. Barbara thinks not, as he wondered why the masseur hadn't been to treat his neck, and the reason was it was quite hopeless. He told her he had dreamed he was dead, 'and then I woke – and I wasn't'. I found myself wondering if it would be possible to talk rationally to a dying person with his death as an accepted fact – say in effect, 'Well, it's a loathsome world and you'll be well out of it.'

September 17th

Clive died last night, thank heaven. I went round to Barbara's earlier, with wine, grapes and a pie. She flung herself into my arms saying, 'Clive is dying.' I didn't know whether to believe it or not, gave her whisky, got her to tell me how the day had passed. She had noticed a decline when she went round that afternoon: his colour was very bad, his breathing difficult and he couldn't swallow at all. She wasn't very coherent, poor thing, and I gathered that she was alarmed by his difficulty in breathing and that matron had come up and told her she had better go home, she'd had enough. The doctor had been telephoned to and said that Quentin must be sent for. She heard matron tell the nurse she didn't think he'd last long. Yet he was thinking clearly and making his pathetic croaked remarks till she left and when she told him she must go as she was having supper with me, he said 'Give my love to Fanny'.[1]

September 19th: Thorington Hall, Essex

I was trying to brace myself to face a rather empty weekend in London when Margaret Penrose suddenly suggested my coming down here with her yesterday afternoon and I very thankfully accepted after a short hesitation. It's lovely being with someone who is always thinking, as she is.

---

[1] His nickname for me.

Yesterday we were joined by a bird-like woman doctor about fifty, a typical Penrose friend, bright-witted, no flies on her, quite funny in her cockney–Welsh way. She told us about an elderly patient of hers who was mentally normal except for the delusion that he was kept awake at nights by the loud banging of two blacksmiths, deaf and dumb identical twins, who lived next door. She described the case to her pupils adding, 'of course he suffered from high blood pressure and this delusion was his way of accounting for the beating of his pulse in his ears when his head was on the pillow.' Next day she sent her social worker round to check on her patient's living conditions. 'They're very good,' she reported, 'except for one thing: next door live a couple of deaf and dumb identical twin blacksmiths and they hammer away and make a fearful noise all night.'

Lionel arrived in the evening from Dundee where he'd been reading a paper. More stimulating talk.

September 21st

Driven back to London last night by Gwyn Johns, the woman doctor. I questioned her a good deal about her practice – mainly health patients, uneducated inhabitants of Fulham. Her humanity, dedication and common sense applied without rule of thumb to the problems they offered, all impressed me. We discussed such things as whether you should tell patients or their nearest relations they are going to die; she tells me there are new drugs dealing with schizophrenia and other forms of madness, which enable patients to return home and go to work and become the concern of the GP not the asylum – but still no more is known about the mental and physical causes of insanity. I didn't know, either, what an immense number of diseases were covered by the word 'cancer'.

September 22nd

Lunch today at the French Club with Philip Toynbee, Terry Kilmartin, and a pretty but slightly spotty Jewess, all of the *Observer*. I was touched by Philip's inviting me (the result of the letter I wrote him praising his book, which he'd sent me a copy of). He was very charming, wonderfully articulate, and surprised me by sudden human and outgoing remarks showing awareness of others. Why surprise? Because there's enough of the rebellious clown about him to rouse an expectation of his being somehow not always quite human. In fact, I like him very much, and do greatly admire his originality and vitality as a writer. Almost at once we got on to the subject of God – and *goodness* how I wish Ralph could have heard his extraordinarily accurate prescience justified! He always declared with absolute conviction that Philip would end up a mystic and probably a believer in God, and he admitted both these today. It was enjoyable to argue with such an intelligent and voluble supporter of religion. Oddly enough, his chief justification is the necessity for a first cause. When I brought up the problem of evil, he drew a picture of a well-meaning but *bungling* God, who simply hadn't succeeded in making the universe as good as he would have liked! 'And when I've finally proved he does exist, I promise you shall have the scoop for the *Observer*, Terry! "*GOD EXISTS*". You'll be able to splash it across the headlines.' (He failed to see that making God the first cause only gave a name to the enigma and pushed it one stage further back. What caused God?) There was a hint too of pragmatism – that if belief in God made you happier it must be true – and comic references to Sally being an alcoholic and having had recourse to the local clergyman, a Mr Sinker, who is trying to explain to her about the Immaculate Conception. She has joined Alcoholics Anonymous though it doesn't seem to have done her much good. Philip has been to gatherings 'on parents' day' and said he was impressed by their good sense and desire to help each other and lack of nonsense. It's ironical that after so many drunken episodes in his own life 'the dog it was that died'.

September 30th

A letter from Julia yesterday as friendly and affectionate as if no cloud had ever passed between us, and oh with what relief I shall shovel earth over that grave! But glad as I am, I can't help thinking that her behaviour taken in sequence has been rather mad.

A curious shifting within the foundations of my life has been making itself felt lately. My roots have loosened a little in the soil as if preparing to leave it, as if realizing anyway how slight is my hold and function on this earth. To adapt has become more and more my aim, though I dare say my friends would be surprised to hear it in view of the way I sometimes blurt out my views. None the less, from my vantage point within my ego I know this is true. I know I am 'an outsider' in everyone's 'life story' and that my own is virtually over. I begin to see too that some of the things I thought I valued – London, friends, work in particular – are just techniques for getting through the rest of my life.

A marvellously beautiful weekend with the Cecils, golden and blue September weather, perfectly ripe and still, made me feel that bolting from London to end my days in country peace would not be an impossibility. Walking in the fields one afternoon with Rachel and looking at the gentle curve of the grassland sweeping up to a row of just-turning beeches, a heady, sad waft of the magic of the Ham Spray country and my walks on the downs with Ralph came back to me. I visited Kitty West in her newly converted cottage nearby and saw her satisfied and completed by the beauty of what she saw out of every window, the lack of restlessness, the power to do something quietly and undistracted. It seems to me that even during my absence abroad this summer London has got more frantic and that the struggle to keep up is almost too much for me. Why this desperate urgency to get or do something at top speed? Advertisements promise to teach one's children to read much faster, understanding everything. How can their *minds* work faster? It only means they learn some horrid knack to whirl through a book without hearing the music of the words should it exist, presumably to find out what happens. And it's this same impatience – to get where they're going – that makes people drive so viciously and has turned the traffic into a dangerous nightmare.

In spite of my defeatist attitude quite a lot of things have stimulated me lately. Talking to the articulate young at the Cecils always fascinates me. Hugh and a friend were discussing the adamant hierarchy at Eton: how the worst sin is 'bumptiousness': for a boy to address an older or grander one, or even show high spirits or extreme cheerfulness in his presence. An absurd preparation for life, and why should the social system of school bear no relation to life?

The night before last there was a performance of *The Magic Flute* in Belgrave Square Gardens. Anne and Heywood had tickets and came for a drink on the way. Later on I walked out into the square and stood close to the wings. Above me the enormous trees stood silent in the lights from the stage which was enclosed in a vast baggy French letter of some plastic whitish material, with the audience hoisted high among the branches on a rickety construction of poles. Anne told me afterwards that it felt both unsafe and draughty with very uncomfortable wooden seats and that the noise of the traffic often drowned the music entirely. They left at the end of the first act, without their champagne supper. I too left then, chiefly because the performance was worse than mediocre.

October 3rd

Saturday afternoon in Belgrave Square Gardens. Two old ladies, deaf presumably, are bellowing at each other in deep, gentlemanly voices about the child of today – 'the nannies we used to have . . . the old fashioned type have gawn' etc. The sun is gently warm; big brown plane leaves rustle round my feet. Autumn suddenly.

Last night I went round to Angelica's studio and saw Sophie and Henrietta just back from Spain. Sophie is adorable; her hair shone fine and golden in the electric light. She studied me thoughtfully for quite a few minutes and then became extremely friendly and high-spirited. She walks quite well, a few steps at a time, lifting her feet like real walking – not toddling. I watched her bath and melted with love for her.

Dinner with Julia went off very well because of extreme care on both sides – but she hadn't really a good word for anyone. Bunny Romilly's food was very highly praised – she thought him 'a better housekeeper by the end of the weekend, but not such a nice man.' Poor Isobel, having kindly asked her to dinner, was hastily dismissed, 'a little square tragic skull-face, talking distractedly', and she had forgotten all about her cancer. She'd never heard that Clive was dead – odd that Lawrence never mentioned it at the weekend any more than the Cecils did to me. I suppose poor Clive had reached that anteroom to the grave where you are assumed to be already dead.

October 4th

As I left the Square Gardens today I found an elderly woman struggling with the wire that temporarily fastens the gate (until the relics of *The Magic Flute* are cleared away) while a Pekingese wound its lead round her leg. 'The whole thing's *damned* stupid!' she said to me. 'And of course look what happens, the *hoi polloi* come in and lie all over the grass. There they are now. They're not *our sort*. I don't mean it snobbily mind you', ('Oh indeed', I felt like saying, 'then what on earth *do* you mean?') 'but they just aren't.' I confess I was astounded.

Robert thinks the Conservatives will get in at the next election – maybe he's right.

October 5th

I spent most of yesterday with Henrietta and Sophie, taking them to Kew for lunch and to spend the afternoon with the Kees. Alexander[1] and his little friends were charming with Sophie, who staggered happily among them in a pair of green corduroy dungarees I'd given her, eating ice-cream cornets and playing with Alexander's mass of toys. She even went on a child's roundabout tenderly protected by two boys. Then we took her out for a walk in Kew Gardens in the Kees' pram. The gardens were deep in a dreamy, still haze, and crowded with Sunday visitors. On the whole the figures, whether romping children, old folk humped with age, or enlaced lovers, improved the landscape. As in a dream we mooned into the various glass houses, all lit with a pale glimmer from the autumn sun, and wandered in tropical dampness round pools with blue and pink water-lilies floating on them.

Last night as I lay in bed listening to the Brahms piano quintet on my transistor I thought its beauty seemed to be that of the savagery of life. I ran into Kitty Godley[2] in the meat department of Harrods and she almost at once opened the same subject, her eyes widening in horror at the thought of it.

October 8th: Cooleville House, Co. Tipperary

I'm here, in Irish peace, though I spent a far from peaceful, distracted morning preparing to come.

Arriving not much before seven, I was soon drinking whisky with Julian and Eddy and conversation went on all evening, ending in quite a lively argument about 'second-rateness'. It started by Julian's defending and my attacking Torremolinos, and the manner of his defence was to bring up Tim Willoughby[3] as an example of someone

[1] Their son.
[2] Epstein's daughter, wife of Wynne Godley, economist.
[3] An aristocratic young hippy, who later drowned when sailing in the Mediterranean.

83

who 'liked the second-rate'. What is one to make of such a line? Of course I rose to the bait and Eddy also entered in on my side, but listening to my supporter I realized he was using the word 'second-rate' solely in a class sense, and thought that Tim, as an aristocrat, was letting down the side. So there was I being priggish as usual about 'standards', Eddy defending class distinctions and Julian – ? well, I'm not sure. Nor did our discussion illumine my search for the germ that causes the prevailing diseases of modern life.

October 9th

Very dark morning: I lie in bed and intend to stay here for some time. The cold, out of doors, is bitter, and when we set off for an afternoon walk yesterday we were lashed by sudden rain. Much as I love this country of streams, ferns and ruins, I feel more disposed to sit reading by the fire than struggle out in such conditions. Eddy has surprised and charmed me by a new expansiveness, liberality and gaiety, and seems to have become less gothic and narrow in his sympathies. I delight in his company and conversation, and realize how original, well read and intelligent he is. Last night's chief conversation, after some brilliant imitations by Julian, which set Eddy rolling on the sofa, was about writing novels. Julian said he liked to write against interruption, so that if at any moment a dreadful blank came and he didn't know what his characters were to do next, or was searching for 'a bridge from one thing to the next', he could switch off and listen perhaps to a wireless announcer from the Bournemouth Pavilion and be amused by his voice and reflect about the old-fashionedness of what he said. Eddy was quite shocked by this. If after thinking it out, he didn't know (pen in hand) what his characters were going to do next, he said, he would take himself somewhere else until inspiration returned.

October 10th

As so often on a visit, even in the happy old days when it was less vital to be able to swim in alien waters, I sometimes feel my engine stalling and resenting being driven, a heavy effortful sensation which I shall hardly be here long enough to outgrow. Both my companions have been charming, and more than that I have felt warm affection and respect for them both. Is Julian unhappy? I don't think so, but he probably knows he will return to that state on Monday; he may, however, have achieved detachment from Ed. I suppose his chief trouble to be that he longs for mutual love, rather than more sex.

Last night a grizzled spinster with a red-lined nose like a rocking-horse came to play Scrabble and have dinner. I didn't like her.

October 12th

Total loss of voice was an embarrassment yesterday and the afternoon before. As liquid draws out more liquid by abhorring a vacuum, the hole left in one's brain by expressing thoughts in words produces new thoughts. Talking, particularly beginning to talk, suddenly became a great effort. I felt like someone trying to play on a piano with some notes that didn't sound unless struck in a very special way.

Eddy drove us up the Vee road, and away to the sea and a charming little port called Ballycotton, near which we lunched with a friendly, big, grey-haired Mrs Pearce. I liked her, and her slightly arty but tasteful room with its huge Irish Georgian windows framing the pure blue and green of the estuary, picked out with red hawthorn berries; she had a magnificent collection of records and some attractive books. After lunch we drove to the harbour and walked briskly along the cliff.

I've been much preoccupied by a life of Wilfred Owen by his brother, who is far from detached about Wilfred, and whose main concern with him is his need violently to express his own jealousy and vindictiveness. So that he depicts him as a monster of insensitiveness and priggish egotism. He was not this – the poems are evidence which *cannot lie*. I'm amazed that the critics didn't see what was happening, but took Harold Owen at his face value, as a 'sweet forgiving character', not realizing what a grizzly portrait he is painting of the distinguished brother he says he adored.

October 26th: The Noel Carringtons' cottage

Woken by a dream of bungling. At a nameless station in East Anglia I left my purse in the wrong train and saw it steam out. Here I was, without ticket, money or spectacles – helpless. Then, I suddenly came across Ralph who marvellously reassured me and told me what I should do; he was both in the same world as me and outside it. The dream was obviously a cry to Ralph: 'See how badly I'm doing without you!'

The birds under the eaves are twittering and making a sort of stitching noise. In the field sheep are baa-ing. I've been very peaceful here and felt better as a result, and am grateful to Catharine and Noel. Oh yes, I feel the rough gravel of the bottom on which I crawl very distinctly – but it has not yet quite destroyed my senseless love of life.

Noel has given me the typescript of Mark Gertler's letters to Carrington to read. A few days ago I was reading Gerald's to her. Gerald wants me to sell these to the Americans for him, and I feel copies should be made first of these very remarkable documents into which for some years he poured the major part of his writer's response to life. Gertler's letters are not really good, but from both rises the image of the fateful character to whom they were written.

October 30th: West Halkin Street

Henrietta and Sophie here to lunch yesterday; I had Sophie alone with me all afternoon, leading an intense unflagging mental and physical, exploratory life. I never tire of watching the expressions on her mobile face. How utterly impossible to look at its satin smooth, delicate curves and imagine old age, even maturity. She struggled to solve every problem the physical world presented her with, and when one – a zip fastener – defeated her she laid down her head and broke into a silent wail of frustration.

November 1st

Yesterday I came to Salisbury by train and am spending two nights in Kitty West's cottage, lying now in one of the beds in her small, snow-white bedroom, my breakfast tray beside me. The quiet of this beautiful year has gone on into autumn; not a breath stirs the trees I see out of my window, turning brown like toast in front of a fire. I try to compare Kitty's solution of the problems we all share with mine. I think hers is very good. She has made her house pretty and comfortable; her pampered, selfish cat occupies the central role, like a difficult husband. We talked very coolly last night of suicide (it's obvious she's considered it as definitely as I have) and listened to *Wozzeck*. She feels that both her children are unhappy at the moment. One of the things I've noticed so much lately is parents' transition from high hopes for their children to total, almost apathetic disillusionment. This passage must have been particularly hard for Kitty who is by nature an optimist. Anthony[1] complains of being hard-up and is getting Kitty to pay Edmund's[2] American University fees – this has set Rebecca West off in a frenzy of active interference: Edmund must be 'made to come home to England' and finish his medical training here. She says that 'the only thing Anthony was ever any good at was hating.' If so he got it from her.

November 2nd

It's as if I'd been washed into the silent backwater of an overgrown river, and enjoying such things is all I'm good for at the moment. All round Kitty's garden are tangled woods with a few dark yews among the brown oaks, and tufts of skeleton plumed grasses. Opposite, a small platoon of white geese cackle and get into heraldic postures, while in the evening innumerable moths beat softly against the windowpanes and last night there was a queen wasp in my room. I really love all this animal and vegetable gentleness and peace, though I doubt if, like Kitty, I could stand it all alone by myself. Indeed I know I couldn't, but I'm glad for her; it seems to satisfy her.

I suggested our going to Russia next autumn over our supper last night. She leapt at it, and I was pleased by her eagerness. I feel a little ashamed that while I felt rested and soothed, she lay tossing in bed last night, brooding over her problems.

November 12th: London

I've just walked briskly right across the Park with Little Barbara, seeing her home after lunch. Such beauty. This particular, wide avenue stretches straight and noble from Hyde Park Corner to Marble Arch. The air, no more than cool, caressed my cheek and brought down more of the leaves that still hang on the boughs, shrivelled though they are, because of the phenomenal stillness. Drifts lay at the edges of the paths and were being carried away in big, transparent, wire netting cages on lorries, looking like enormous packets of cornflakes. A pink-cheeked baby entirely dressed in white

[1] Kitty's ex-husband, son of H. G. Wells and Rebecca West.
[2] Son of Anthony and Kitty.

wool bounced rather touchingly up and down in its smart pram out of sheer pleasure in the beauty of the day, and with no encouragement from a sour-faced au pair girl in charge of it, who had obviously been disappointed in love. Small tailored poodles and children in coloured tights bounced too among the fallen cornflakes. Impossible not to feel a sort of exhilaration – an utterly irrational sense that the stuff life is made of is good. Even Little Barbara didn't irritate me as much as usual. She said as we parted that I was the only person who gave her a sense of security. God help me. I'm sure her life minus Clive to look after is very drab. A lot of the time she is talking to me of her sorrows I think of other things. Yet there is this agonizing, impotent, useless pain I feel on behalf of Janetta, of Henrietta and Sophie. How can one compromise between these two hopeless attitudes?

Last night I had a successful dinner party – I really think it was, and two lots of guests have rung up to say so. Eardley, Angelica, the Kees and Campbells came and we had a bottle of Colin Mackenzie's Moselle, two bottles of Derek Jackson's superb claret, smoked salmon and leg of lamb. I enjoyed it and did not feel exhausted, though owing to a bungle on my part it was preceded by playing quartets with Angelica and Margaret from tea-time onwards so that I had to baste the joint between movements. I am pleased that I felt equal to it all, and it signifies a little elevation from the recent trough.

November 18th

Janetta gave a cocktail party for Sonia[1] last night. I only spent a short while there, but long enough to pick up a number of impressions. Sonia looked buxom and handsome, with eyelids painted bright forget-me-not blue. But almost her first remark to me was one of fantastic pretentiousness and condescension, to the effect that she liked funny old London more than she'd expected to – everyone here was so slow-witted compared to the quick, intelligent French. 'Oh you mean all of *us*, do you?' I asked. The third person in this conversation was the poetess Kathleen Raine who stood before me like an unsmiling schoolmistress, and at one moment stared at me so hard I felt her gaze scrape my cheek. I realize now that my reluctance to go to the party came from knowledge that Sonia and I are incompatible. I dislike her pretentiousness and am pretty sure she dislikes me. So let's give it all up.

[1] Orwell.

Eardley had got into Julia's doghouse I realized the other night, because 'he never asks me to dinner,' nor offered to drive her down to the country. Which of us are going to measure up to her standard, I wonder? Not me I fear. When she dined with me the other night Mary and Charlie McCabe were 'socially impossible', Eddie Gathorne-Hardy 'too selfish and lazy to be borne', Jonny had 'lost all his looks', and Sabrina and Georgia never had any; she had 'never liked Raymond'. Only Heywood and Anne had an entirely blameless record.

November 20th

I wake every morning to total awareness of the grey world all round me – then, unable to come to terms with it, I instinctively snatch up a book and stuff it into my mind, as one stuffs a 'comforter' into a baby's mouth to keep it quiet. Or breakfast, or newspapers, or letters, whatever is appropriate. My reading became more serious and connected in the interim period when I was without work (and perhaps better none than the pointless book I'm now translating). Then I read Gombrich's *Art and Illusion* and started out on the complete edition of the *Goncourt Journals*, which has been something of a disappointment so far, too scrappy and superficial. I do like the continuity of the best memoirs or books of letters. Now I am reading Robin Fedden and find his poetical description of the mountains really moving and am dazzled by his originality. Little Barbara rings me up practically every day. A clumsy sense of boredom attaches to these endless self-pitying conversations. I am prepared to sympathize *ad lib* with her for her loss of Clive, but not greatly because the Jew who wants to take her flat tried to beat her down on the telephone. 'He rang up at eight-thirty last night and spoke for quarter of an hour. I told him I wasn't well. I was just eating bread and milk and going to bed. He upset me so much that I couldn't sleep all night.' I think self-pity is the nearest to sexual pleasure that she has ever known.

November 22nd: Charleston

Yesterday I drove Henrietta and Sophie to stay with Duncan and here we all are. As we approached the smooth couchant, enormously high shapes of the downs a pervasive calm and contentment enveloped us – Henrietta and me at any rate, for Sophie was by now asleep. It has been with me ever since. Plunged in this Old Bloomsbury civilization (for all we may have laughed at its 'croquet hoops', and the paint peeling here and there) I am overpowered with pleasure and emotion at the sense that all round me *real* values have been aimed at and achieved, and that the house, garden and all it contains is a unique work of art, something lovingly created and kept alive. Even now when nearly all of them are dead, it is the same, and I have been struck by the fact that the feeling I have for it is partly gratitude, such as a very good performance on an instrument produces. One thing I am absolutely convinced of is that the lasting value of what Old Bloomsbury stood for and did will go on being recognized – indeed it *is* being recognized. Duncan says that it is people between thirty-five and fifty who find his pictures too old-fashioned, and the young are beginning to like them again. A troop of young people came yesterday afternoon and sat in the studio and looked at them. Sonia (who is at the Connollys) said of course she didn't like them – they aren't nearly avant-garde enough for her. Her mind works in such a boring, intensely conventional way. You must always like the latest thing, support the latest writers. She's added several toads during a visit here and a visit by Henrietta and me to the Connollys, such as when we were talking about Arthur Waley, and Duncan said, 'I believe he's living with a very intelligent lady in north London.' 'Oh yes', said Sonia noisily, 'I did hear all about her and it's fascinating, and she does something very remarkable but I'm afraid I've quite forgotten what it is' – wanting to show that she was in the know but quite unable to make the smallest contribution. After she'd left here on Saturday evening Henrietta said, 'I think she's a huge *fraud*. I liked her voice and her looks rather, and her laugh and her strong neck, but she never says anything.' I tried, probably overdoing it, to be amiable to her, but another toad dropped out when we were talking about Charlie McCabe and I was giving a fairly unflattering picture. Was there nothing to be said for him? 'Yes, that he had quite a good head and used it to think for himself,' I said. Sonia (impatiently): 'Oh that's so silly – why not let other people do it for you?' (As she does, with fraudulent results.) Another time, after she'd admitted that she didn't like Duncan's painting and the Connollys said they liked it enormously, I asked her who would be her first choice to buy a painting by if money was no object? 'Well I think I'd buy a Francis Bacon,' (absolutely safe, well-established,

Left: Robert Kee thoroughly awake at breakfast-time, Ham Spray.

Below: Julia Strachey drinks a sherry on our verandah.

Left: Janetta.

Below: Angelica Garnett has tea on the terrace at Hilton.

Right: Raymond Mortimer exploring the strange streets of Alberobello.

Below: Joan and Jacques Cochemé picnicking near Monte Olioeto.

Above: Julian Jebb entertains Georgie and Rose, Janetta's daughters, at the Sussex house of his grandfather Hilaire Belloc.

Right: Isobel Strachey relaxing after arrival at El Rascacio on the Costa del Sol.

avant-garde choice), 'but of course I'd be much happier buying books.' 'What books would you buy?' 'Oh standard library editions of all the great writers.' She's perfectly dull and conventional, and a first-rate man like Duncan shows her up for what she is. But I for one have never never caught a tinsel gleam of what takes people in.

But why spend so much time uncharitably analysing Sonia's defects when I have been so emotionally stirred all the time I was here by the first-rateness of this Bloomsbury world, the charm of Duncan, the calm and peace which gently lapped us round from the beautiful downs which have been all weekend swathed in tepid mist, with a total result of great reassurance – it's like the repeated reassertion of something one believes to be true and is glad is true. Last night, very gay, delightful talk, and some television-watching in the studio for the three of us, Duncan, Henrietta and me. Sophie has all day padded happily about crooning in a sweet, high voice, with bright eyes and blazing red cheeks, interested in everything and occasionally pointing at the pictures with a little cry. She, Henrietta and I called on Lydia Keynes and the Connollys on Sunday morning. I had never been inside Tilton. Lydia's face is weathered like a nut so as hardly to be recognizable; she wore a handkerchief on her head and a small string cap on top of that, and was muffled in a fluffy dressing gown. She skipped agilely round us, greeting us with cries of welcome and ceaseless talk. She had to begin her 'pyottering' quite soon, that was why she had asked us to come early. 'I always do my pyottering – then I can talk to no one.' Her voice-production is marvellous, her choice of words very original – no Sonia she. She told Henrietta she was looking beautiful, snatched up Sophie and held her clasped on her lap for a while, and to me she said as I left, touching me greatly: 'It is such a long time since we met but I heard of you often, my dyear, and have thought of you with great tyenderness!'

Cyril and Deirdre were at their nicest. Cyril so adored showing off his bibliophile treasures that it was a great pleasure to flatter him about them. They both, and their little girl,[1] were exceptionally friendly and contributed quite a lot to the great cockle-warming-ness of this weekend. I am full to brimming with it, but now the time has come to face London and grey solitude. I felt it was essential first to try and shred apart the texture of my surroundings here and discover what is so valuable in it.

[1] Cressida.

I took Celia Goodman and Julian to *Il Trovatore* the other night. Celia liked Julian, who was, of course, all the time angelically attentive and kind. I myself was bowled over by the opera itself, and loved watching the elegant and dedicated movements of Giulini, as he conducted without a score, with difficulty glimpsed through the forest of heads. Before Julian came I talked to Celia for a little about her problem of where to live. She is more fixed on central Cambridge than ever, but no nearer finding a house. What on earth can one do to help her?

November 29th

I've been at Crichel since Thursday, all four present. Desmond arrived breathlessly for lunch on Friday looking like a black-beetle in a leather coat and turtle-neck sweater. This produced an audible groan from Raymond and a very strict po-faced speech of disapproval later on from Eardley. Why do they mind so much something that is purely superficial and unimportant, and to my eyes rather endearing? I suppose it's the unavoidable grating together of essentially different individualities. As with old married couples, this stridulation increases with the passage of time, but is often less painful to the participants than the observer might assume; the converse pleasure in each other's quirks remains constant. Eddy and Raymond were rather fiercely critical of the fuss Eardley and Desmond made over social occasions, after a quite easy, pleasant lunch party (Reine and Jemima Pitman, Mary Potter).[1] 'Desmond isn't much good at making conversation,' Eddy said accusingly. They neither of them seem to think it rational to find it a boring way of spending the time. As referee on the sidelines, I tend to be recipient of these criticisms of each other.

Another bit of inter-Crichel criticism: 'Raymond is extraordinary,' Eardley said to me, 'he's just like a little boy. He came into the drawing-room yesterday and said: "I've had a sleep and done an hour's work and now I'm going to have a bath." Or else he says: "I've been reading for two hours and now I'm going to bed".' I do notice, now he mentions it, this slightly eccentric habit of Raymond's. Old age? Eddy shows this in snoozing off for quite long periods, a look of sad boredom on his tilted face, and perhaps an occasional tiny snore.

[1] The painter.

One can't help, in this headquarters of homosexuality, being slightly aware of one's sex, though I believe I think of it less than most females even of my age. Eddy and Raymond have an old-fashioned view of the female character, including sillyness and illogicality – the opinion of a 'cracker-motto' in fact. If he feels likewise Desmond is too good-tempered to let it show. With Eardley I really feel most at ease with my unfortunate disqualification, for I believe he thinks it a good and civilizing influence to have a female about. On a walk yesterday Eddy, Eardley and I passed close to a bull which was in the act of hoisting itself onto the back of a young ruffled-looking heifer, with its long sad-looking penis preparing for action. 'No sight for a lady,' said Eardley.

Meanwhile I'm happy here, as I used not always to be in the past. I have my book to translate, I'm reading David on Max with mild pleasure, we have music (a complete recording of *Fidelio* on Friday, but last night some songs by John Ireland and Frank Bridge sung by Peter Pears which I found antipathetic). Conversation of course is endless; Eddy rather more grand and conventional than he was with Julian and me in Ireland, can't understand 'people having difficulty in finding *servants*' – the word is always said on a low stressed note – 'it always means they don't know how to treat them properly.' Any mention of someone suffering discomfort and austerity arouses disapproval rather than sympathy. The pained side of him is in fact more in evidence, the gay and funny less so. No arguments on ideas unless my taking up Raymond for repeating the old cliché that 'blackmail is worse than murder' can be so called. Perhaps I was too aggressive, but I said I couldn't help questioning his premise, and that violence of all sorts seemed to me far worse. Desmond backed me up. He had experienced both blackmail and violence, and violence was far worse and more frightening, he said. I maintained that it was only the victim's feebleness that made him a victim of blackmail, that if he went to the police his privacy would be guarded and he wouldn't be charged with his offence. Raymond said categorically *no*, that he had read of an appalling case, but was quite unable to remember anything about it. Kidnapping is different – there is a real risk of the kidnappee being murdered, but what most blackmailers want is money, not to hand you over to the police or the anger of your deceived wife.

Eardley took me into his studio and showed me what he is now at – representing the last Beethoven quartet in patterns of what he calls 'royal' colours. I was very much interested in what he had to say, but the visual effect left me cold. It was nice all the same to be surrounded by such an aroma of busy happiness mixed with the smell of oil-paint and the warmth of a stove.

December 1st

When I cross logical or intellectual swords with Raymond, as I did after lunch yesterday afternoon, I feel we are two chamois butting at each other with pretty nearly equally powerful horns. The subject was an old one – whether there existed any evidence for extra-sensory perception. I said if there had been it would have made money at roulette. The banks would be quickly broken by only a few such 'sensitives'. Raymond said, dogmatically and fierily I thought but without chapter and verse, that there was such evidence, but that the mysterious faculty only operated intermittently. We've had other, more light-hearted conversations. Another about bohemianism. Eddy 'can't BEAR it' and doesn't distinguish it from squalor – only Eardley agreed with me that it also involved freedom, dislike of living by rules, spontaneity, flexibility, originality. I was amused, remembering our conversations in Portugal, that Julian's name was the first to come up as a Bohemian. 'He doesn't turn out lights and so on, you know,' said Eddy. Well, here I am in a hot train steaming back to London and its complexities full of gratitude to these four dear and kind friends for taking me so very kindly into their home. Each time I go I feel more 'at home' there. Yesterday morning the garden and fields were white with frost; it salted over the roof of the pretty little church too. Then out came a mild sun covering everything in rosy bloom. Eddy, Eardley and I stepped out for a brisk walk with dog Moses in the afternoon, as we did every day but one. By then the sun was fading and the trees were pale dove-grey shadows swimming in artichoke soup. I enjoyed my stay unreservedly, yet there were moments when I looked at my poor old face in my bedroom looking-glass and thought 'how have I the courage to go down among them all?'

December 9th

Last weekend with Robin and Susan Campbell in their coastguard cottage on Southampton Water. What met the eye was marvellously beautiful, disposing itself in horizontal streaks of silver water edged with bistre rushes, the low grey hills of the Isle of Wight and the streaky grey sky above. It was a pleasure, too, to be aware of Robin's adoration of it all, his feeling of possessiveness (as it is the country he lived in as a child), the intense satisfaction with which he identified birds and pointed out such and such a sluice, bridge or dyke, with much the same topographical love that the other Robin (Fedden) writes about the mountains or the Seine in his books. I don't think I quite realized what a true love the lie of the land can inspire.

The coastguard cottages stand alone on the wild shore looking out to the island. Within doors family life reigned – the two charming little boys were dominant until bedtime, a plump cooing French girl in charge. Susan working like a fiend to reconstruct the small garden, hauling huge stones about, her eyes gleaming through her spectacles, Robin busy bringing wood and coke and filling lamps, tired but happy, patient and loving to his little boys, the 'family' collected round a large table with oil lamp for meals.

December 10th

Just back from dining with Frances Phipps and Puffin Asquith. Frances looked lovely and romantic in a rich blue velvet dressing gown and a red scarf. The combination of characters, however, didn't work. For an intelligent sweet-natured man, Puffin Asquith is curiously enough something of a bore. His idea of human contact stemming from kindness was firstly to send Frances a huge bunch of red roses for her red room (and even bring me a little one when he heard I was coming) and then 'entertain' us without stopping, with a continuous stream of anecdotes, each story reminding him of another and (when they failed) a detailed account of the plots of all his films. Neither of us could get a word in edgeways, nor was there any attempt at generalities. I was fairly flummoxed, because the boredom was painful at times, yet looking at his kindly face, his gesturing hands, and blunt-nosed, black schoolboy boots, my heart went out to him. The intervals between stories were filled by a strangely equine indrawn breath, a sort of neigh. It must be that he is carrying out the Asquith idea of conversation – goodness how they all talk! But sheer quantity of talk is no good at all. As in music, the rests are all-important.

Before I left to go to Onslow Square I sat at the piano and played a Handel fugue. What magnificent sanity. In a few bars he convinced me against all reason of life being worth living, conveyed its curiously indelible excitement. No literature can sum up a philosophy of life so surely as music can, and I believe it would be theoretically possible to state all the composers' messages in philosophical terms.

The effect of Puffin on Frances was to make her laugh in a girlish, flirtatious way, and become very feminine.

December 12th

I was not disappointed in thinking I should get some backwash from Frances about our evening with Puffin Asquith. It was not his boringness that upset her, but his musical snobbishness. I noticed it too, but Frances is so sensitive a plant that she stayed awake all night thinking of it. He had remarked that when the Governor in *Fidelio* calls Leonora '*Die echte Frau*' there is an implication that she is '*hochgeboren*'; also that one feels (in spite of his infidelities) that the Count's love for the Countess, or reunion – I forget which – is something deeper and more important than Figaro's with Susanna. I noticed the little smile with which he made these remarks, a little smile of 'we, the elect, the privileged' so often seen on the faces of the upper classes. I do loathe it, as much as Frances does, who wailed that 'it came from deep Edwardian "U" feelings, snobbish to the very root.' She was too loyal to criticize Puffin apart from this, except to say that she believed that at the deepest level he was 'cut off and alone and in despair'.

Cambridge. At E.Q.'s[1] little house, in pouring, lashing rain. I came here yesterday with Wynne and Kitty. Last night Horace[2] and Rachel came to dinner; Horace seemed a kindly well-informed man, practically a stranger, Rachel a handsome old lady, trying too hard to be 'with it'. Intelligent too. I don't know what it is about blood relations that clogs and at the same time splits one. We were fashioned in the same mould, yet the process of growing up has entirely consisted in developing independently, along what seem chosen lines even if they were determined by the same conditions. It has not, has never, seemed to me pleasant to be reminded of the past in this pungent, tangible way.

December 16th

I finished a very difficult translation sample yesterday but was left too wound up by it to stop jigging about like a monkey on a string.

---

[1] Nicholson, daughter of my friend Leo Myers, and widow of Kit Nicholson.
[2] My eldest brother and his wife.

Last night I dined with Adrian Daintrey in his new studio beside the Regent's canal, which glittered between the trees and festoons of freezing mist. Other guests were Edward Le Bas and a sophisticated grey haired lady, thin as a lath and with a beak like a bird, the living spit of Osbert Lancaster's Maudie Littlehampton and this was almost her name – she had plenty of sense, a deep voice and quantities of jangling bangles. We sat on a backless bench and there was no hard liquor – only thin white wine. I drove them all home and then slept like anything, to wake this morning in a curious state of euphoria.

Julia rang up this morning to say she had been badly let down by Sonia who for ages has been suggesting they join forces in a house. When Sonia was in England a house was found and bought for her by Michael Pitt-Rivers.[1] She told Julia there would be a ground floor for her, Janetta took Julia to look at it, and both she and I tried to infuse Julia with enthusiasm for this new project. Now Sonia writes from Paris to say that Michael has been 'so sweet' about the house that she can't ask him to pay the extra to convert the ground floor to Julia's use. 'Never mind Julia, we'll find you a nice flat quite close.' Poor Julia – it is food for her persecution mania. I had been so moved by this helping hand Sonia was offering Julia that I nearly wrote to say how all Julia's friends felt grateful to her. The only thing I was prepared to credit her with – good-heartedness to her female friends – now seems to have to be discounted.

December 23rd

I dined with Julia last night – she showed me Sonia's letter: a discreditable maundering of egotism laced with protestations of friendship and 'I mean's'. Was distressed by the sharp note of fear in Julia's voice – she can 'only just get along with the help of her Purple Hearts', 'fears she's heading for a mental home somtimes', 'feels quite suicidal especially since this blow of Sonia's', 'simply HATES and is TERRIFIED by living alone'. We drank a good deal together, and got on very well, thank heavens. With pencil and paper we tried to work out what her finances are, they're not bad at present, but she feels, and very likely rightly, that she is going to be gradually cut down.

Before this I called on Henrietta and Sophie and gave Sophie my

[1] To whom she was briefly married.

97

Christmas present, a woolly push-along dog, large and I hoped comforting. She seemed to like it, pushed it about a lot and screamed passionately when an exceptionally sweet young man who was there took it away to oil the wheels for her. Their gallant life touched me to the quick. Henrietta has made the flat look much more human, even gay, and is altering the Ham Spray library curtains which I gave her, which should humanize her sitting-room.

December 24th: Christmas Eve

I'm here at Sandwich Bay in the huge Edwardian monstrosity of a house lent to Magouche and Janetta by Michael Astor. Just been down (10 a.m.) for breakfast. Franca[1] gave me a warm croissant, and some coffee, not a cat stirring. Met Janetta in the passage and she said, 'Oh yes, they're all lie-abeds.' I'm grateful for a Christmas refuge. But it's like living in a golf club. Perhaps that's what makes me uneasy. Magouche's mother, Essie, is here too and is just the sort of lady you'd expect to find in a golf club. Erect, grey-haired, brisk and friendly but basically conventional. I see now that I'm designed as her opposite number. The children make up slightly uneasy pairs and have not quite shaken in with their mates yet.

A thick sea mist encloses us, the sun – briefly visible – has now vanished. It's absolutely still and absolutely silent. This is no more stifling in effect than our totally tasteless millionaire surroundings. Out of the window, so far as I can see, *three* perfectly flat golf-courses lap up to our very walls and reach away in every direction until the hulk of another millionaire's house rises out of the mist, a dim shape. My bed is soft and warm, there is mock Tudor furniture and a dressing table with skirts, prints of ships on the wall. The house belonged to Lady Astor I find, and it is her personality I suppose which stamps it. What a neutral one! Oh POUF! Give me air! I have been deeply disconcerted to find myself so put out by a house's atmosphere. The natural antidotes would be work, if I can do some, or going out walking, but the thick white mist is not inviting.

Strange that the civilization hanging in a house like smoke remains so potent, even when the owner is away, even when she's

[1] Magouche's Italian servant.

dead, that one can hardly breathe at all and certainly not sleep in it if one finds it uncongenial.

Christmas Day

The sight of stockings stuffed with really valuable things as well as all the immense riches under the tree, but chiefly the background of what this house represents makes one willy-nilly feel that a redistribution of wealth would be a very good thing, and I hope that Mr Callaghan will succeed in extracting some of it from the pockets of such as Lady Astor. For just as Mary finds 'the smell of money' attractive, I always find it repulsive.

December 26th

All day yesterday the cold northeaster blew, covering the distant hills with snow, my walk along the shore was a *supplice*, and the Christmas bubble burst slowly with the opening of the presents round the tree during the morning. An enormous quantity of mainly pretty, unexpected, imaginatively chosen things. What is there about this Christmas? What strings of family affection does it twang and why? I've dreamt of Ralph and Burgo continuously, as if they were still alive, but since my drive down with Janetta I've had no real conversation with anyone.

December 27th

Things going from bad to worse, and I feel sunk by my own inability to compete with my surroundings. Like an unco-operative sulky adolescent I have withdrawn a good deal into the privacy of my room. I find no driving force – what should it be? social sense – to impel me to go out and make an effort with Mr and Mrs Edward Rice at lunch, nor yet to face an intrusion of young Rices and Byngs here. A cruel plan, the latter seems to me, for it will plunge all the young here into embarrassment. Making conversation, as against talking – what a miserable thing it is. We had a big dose of it last night: first the arrival at seven – much too early for the late dinners of this house – of Edward Rice, an attractive, extremely rich sixty-year-old and his younger, smart, knicker-bockered, self-confident French wife. Leonard Byng, Isobel's friend (and I suspect ex-lover), also had a

French wife, a governessy, pretty, little smug thing. The ethos all these people brought with them was 'Money is Power.' 'Democracy is dead,' they cried, but also 'George Brown is one of my best friends,' and 'Wilson is too much of a conservative for me.' A veneer of culture thinly disguising jungle behaviour in the department of sex and fascist beliefs. The whole lot made my hackles rise, very likely without due reason. Achilles is not the best judge as he sits sulking in his tent.

Magouche came into my room this morning to say we were invited to lunch with the Rices. Would I like to come? Prepared by Janetta, I begged to be let off. Then she said that that would be quite all right as Maro[1] was longing to go. And I could keep an eye on the young here. It turns out that the twenty-year-old French nephew of the Rices and three of the young Byngs had been asked back to lunch here. This would seem to be head-losing at its worst. The four youngest never spoke to the visiting adolescents when they came last night but withdrew onto the stairs by themselves. Natasha[2] is in bed and refuses to come down; this leaves poor Georgie to be responsible for the visitors. She caught Janetta in the passage just now and almost screamed for mercy.

Everything is made more tense by the fact that an easterly gale is tearing at our windows, a liverish sea tossing itself on the shingle and terrifying Janetta who is due to cross it with Rose on a visit to Derek[3] the day after tomorrow.

2 p.m.   I am feeling appalling guilty. Having been down to the kitchen to scrounge a bit of cold turkey for myself, I found the poor children collected there in an agony of social dismay. What was to be done? How *could* they get through lunch? The visitors wouldn't do anything but talk. Why not force them to play games – cocky-olly or racing demon? I suggested, everybody would be happier. But they seemed to feel it was hopeless.

Yesterday was a wonderfully beautiful day I forgot to say – iced blue from morning till night, very little wind. I walked alone for about an hour and a half along the wide, wet, glistening beach towards Ramsgate. A few happy elderly couples and their dogs were pacing too. Men were digging up cockles from the damp sand just

1   Gorky, Magouche's eldest daughter.
2   Gorky, Magouche's second daughter.
3   Jackson, Janetta's ex-husband and Rose's father.

left by the sea, which retreated with extreme suddenness over the flat waste, almost out of sight and noiseless, and then as suddenly began to tear back again. This walk on a shining plate of wet sand between the vast sky and the vast sea was a great pleasure. But I shall be glad to leave here, and go back to my own cubbyhole tomorrow. One of the troubles is the physical and nervous tension this east coast atmosphere produces in some people – I am one and Janetta I think another.

December 28th

London again, and it gave Janetta and me a beautiful, pale, frosty welcome as we drove over Westminster Bridge. Since getting in at lunch-time I've not seen anyone except shop assistants, yet I've been in a way less lonely than I was at Sandwich. My God, in what a dismal dejection I went to bed last night, in spite of the great kindness of Magouche and Janetta, the charm, grace and sweetness of the six girls. As one visitor, French Mrs Edward Rice, said, the house was like a Turgenev novel, with the children playing cards on the floor, Natasha and Maro bending over their embroidery frames and at the same time chattering and laughing – the cap fitted and I fitted only too well into the role of ancient great-aunt or governess, sitting in the corner with the samovar, to whom everyone is kind but who serves no function. It's this I've felt – useless, desperately lacking the fertilizing warmth of being loved and having someone with whom I can laugh and who is interested in anything at all that I've done or thought, and vice versa. So a draining away of confidence, a shrivelling dislike of my own character – all this dreadfully overloaded my boat yesterday until the great grey-green waters of despondency nearly came over the gunwale.

How much are other people aware of such inner struggles I don't know. Probably hardly at all – they have their own problems and preoccupations. So I hope that my anti-socialness didn't get through.

Actually the evening passed gaily and with relaxation, playing racing demon and watching the girls twist to the gramophone. Susu is a marvellous little dancer and it was a joy to watch her, but she stops at once if she sees your eye on her. She's a very attractive little being. I tried to express some of my gratitude as Janetta and I set off up the lightly powdered road to London.

101

1965

January 2nd

The New Year has made an aquamarine-coloured, chill, transparent, scentless entry. It is like a 'new page' covered with austere pale blue squares in an arithmetic book, and its aseptic flavour, perfectly tolerable by day, gives way at nights to a rather dreadful bleakness, while I fetch about – look everywhere, think of anything – rather than accept its presence. I've had some bad moments, sounding the depths and scraping the edges of the bucket of my loneliness, being assailed at odd moments by vivid memories of Ralph and Burgo and finding myself defenceless and unprepared.

I drove down to Lord's Wood to see Alix and James yesterday morning – no change in the way of life here, with all its eccentricities and endearing inconsistencies. A walk with Alix, dressed in Canadian-looking long fur coat and top boots, through the winding paths she has cut through the bracken and brambles on the common.

'From here, you see', she says, 'one can either take this wide path where we can walk two abreast or go single file under this natural arch covered in ivy, but I don't like going too far in that direction because that's where the dog-fanciers live.'

Much talk about the Labour party, which they both staunchly support, and prison reform, education and so on – but never stodgy or dull. They both remain intensely interested in the way the house is run; there is a revolving electric grill and spit in the kitchen. Otherwise the same stuffy heat, windows draped with crackling plastic curtains to keep out the draughts, the same getting up and washing the plate you've just used in the middle of the meal. They live mentally speaking entirely in the psychoanalytical, Strachey and political world. Michael Holroyd has produced the first volume of his life of Lytton for James to read and James was appalled and said it 'simply wouldn't do'. Lytton had been made a 'disagreeable, weak, silly and laughable character' – none of the force of his personality has come out, nor his wit. Holroyd mocks at G. E. Moore and 'the Society'[1], which James still holds in religious respect (when I asked if he could tell me if it still went on he replied, 'No, I can't: I daresay you can guess the answer from that'), but is totally unaware that he has presented an unflattering picture. The question is whether any picture could have satisfied James. To what lengths does his hero-worship obscure his judgement? Also, what will happen? James thinks he has the power to suppress the book entirely *at a pinch*, but obviously doesn't intend to. He has insisted on Holroyd making a lot of changes, and also that the first volume shouldn't be published until the second (which takes over at the moment of Lytton's literary success) is finished. Alix's view was that there was something 'frog-like and unfeeling' about the book and that Michael Holroyd had no real interest in Lytton or Bloomsbury.

I'm delighted by Alix's occasional sallies into fantasy. Last night we had a fine leg of mutton cooked on the electric spit. After we'd cleared away our plates she said thoughtfully: 'There's something *disgusting* about mutton, which I don't feel about beef – a sort of heavy, cloying breathiness. You notice the same thing if you meet a shepherd in a lane. It's the sheep, I suppose.'

January 3rd

Every strange environment takes a little getting into, but this – and it's certainly strange enough – takes less than most. I've walked out into the woods several times with Alix, enjoyed the pure piercing smell of the earth, moss, frost and rotting bracken, the delicate compositions made by trunks of trees that are too slender because of competition from other trunks. Indoors – physical stuffiness and a smell of old clothes and covers that need cleaning; *anything* but mental stuffiness; idealism about the United Nations and the need to improve the lot of the poor, inconsistently blended with *folie de grandeur* about all Stracheys and anyone connected with them ('My cousin – what's her name? – Peggy Ashcroft'), and Eton and various other nuclei round which snobbishness may gather. Admirably well informed about international affairs, they reel off the names of the presidents of small black or brown States in a way which makes me ashamed of my ignorance. Naive interest in television's most humdrum and soppy

[1] The 'in-term' for the Cambridge Apostles.

programmes about the Wild West, policemen or lawyers. These I enjoy, but I couldn't if they weren't a rarity.

January 6th: London

The tempo has slowed to a gentler andante, and piano. I have seen people every day, and most of them rather sad. Mary came yesterday for a while and told me with tears trembling at the back of her voice about her latest difficulties with Charlie. They can be summed up by saying he's intensely selfish. When I said to Mary, 'He's a strange man, your husband,' she said, 'Of course he's mad.' Like many others – Julia, for instance – his difficulties in getting going with work are internal but he can't face the fact, so he blames Mary who really does as usual her 'level best' to encourage him. Magouche begs her 'to ditch Charlie as soon as possible'. But I don't quite know what she wants herself. She told me, and I believe it, that she thinks he would be 'broken up' if she abandoned him.

Magouche looked splendid and behaved with her typical gaiety and dash when I lunched yesterday with her, with Mary, Johnny Craxton and Paddy Leigh Fermor. Delicious food and lively conversation.

A story I liked in the *Goncourt Journal*: young gentleman to actress who has raised her skirt and is warming her behind at the fire: '*Si c'est pour moi – pas trop cuit.*'

January 12th

Janetta sweetly gave a dinner party in honour of Dicky Chopping's[1] first novel, *The Fly*. Julian, Julia, Nicky, me, and Dicky and Denis who arose from the basement, booming: 'We're absolutely *sloshed*.' Dicky had given lunch to his publishers and then had a television interview, Denis had been telephoning and visiting booksellers all day. Emotionally exhausted, they had then taken to the bottle and Denis somehow picked up a young German on the way home. Dicky was smiling and weeping uncontrollably by turns or even at once, and kissing everyone. I ordered him an elaborate buttonhole from my flower shop which reduced him at once to more tears and kisses. The effect on Denis was more peculiar. We have all been anxious at the way he has been for weeks inflating Dicky's literary debut –

[1] Painter of flowers, who had been my collaborator in a botany book (never finished).

implying that his name would be a household word, duchesses falling over themselves to invite him and so forth. Luckily his publishers seem to like the book and have puffed it; luckily, too, he got a very good review in the *Sunday Times* as well as a personal piece and a photo in *Atticus*. But the *Observer* was crushing and other papers may be likewise. Last night however Denis's full ambivalence came out in striking black and white – or rather in black alone. He was running Dicky down right and left: to me he said that he didn't like the book at all himself – it was 'a horrible book' and Dicky 'was the laziest person in the world'. (*That* I couldn't let pass. 'No, really he's not, Denis – I think you're a great deal lazier yourself.') And when he came out to see me into my car he again said: 'Of course it's not a good book, it's a horrible book, but at least it's better than his other work.'

January 14th

Janetta came to lunch and told me that she had been reading *The Waste Land* obsessionally and with an almost total incomprehension that had reduced her to tears. I spent yesterday morning doing the same and I can understand her attitude. Is it a great take-in studded with flashes of true poetry from the author of the *Four Quartets*? Incomprehensibility, and especially obscure and erudite allusions that take the reader by the lapel and draw him into the same college common room, are as much of a bait as shockingness. People so love to think they are among a few initiates. I don't think, and never have, that it's a *great* poem. The relief when one strikes a line of Marvell, Webster or Spenser shows it up. Exactly why it had such an enormous success I'm not sure – but believe it was partly chance.

Rain fell out of the sky in pailfuls after Janetta and I had pleasantly eaten our boiled eggs and grapefruit together, when Cyril [Connolly] arrived to pick up some shirts she had bought him from the sales. He was genial, even benign, brought out a bag of lychees and sat eating them, leaning back with a napkin spread over his broad front, peeling them voluptuously with stubby fingers. Janetta had said: 'Don't ask Cyril about *The Waste Land*.' 'I think I *will*,' I said, and did. What's more, it was a good thing because he loves instructing and did it extremely well.

Janetta is off to Spain, Magouche with her. She won't tell me when, yet I've asked her several times. Does she know with her acute sensitivity how dreadfully I miss her?

Julia? – alas, alack. A bad evening. Was I off my guard because the last went so well? One can never afford to be that. But today she savaged everyone and got under my skin in the end: Dicky and Denis, of course, had been 'too babyish for words' with their 'birthday boy' attitude to the publication of *The Fly* and Denis's childish jealousy. Of Julian – 'Well, since you ask, I *can't respect him*, but let's not say any more about him.' Then there is her attitude that everyone else has all they want in life and no right to complain. The Campbells, for instance, had 'no right to complain' of the interference their children were in their lives, yet she would hardly accept my view that they both adored their little boys. In fact, I don't believe she sympathizes with other people's troubles or joys *at all*.

January 18th

Last night I dined with Bunny, just back from America, and Angelica in her bohemian studio. It was freezing cold – the studio stove just warmed the side of the body toasting in front of it. Angelica was wild-haired, beautiful and grubby, and had an outsize baking 'potato' in her stocking. Bunny was magnificent – brave as a lion, full of interesting news of America and Mexico and his lectures. At seventy – or more? – he's planning a trip to Mexico again next Spring, and meanwhile to drive with Angelica all the way to Greece, Jugoslavia, Macedonia, Bulgaria perhaps this year. I think this is the most sensible thing to do – wear out one's remaining years with exciting and exhausting travel rather than carefully preserve them for the sake of tame and prolonged existence.

Isobel and I went to 'that RUS-sian film they say is so good. It's called HAMlet'. She was in her scattiest mood, regretting her wasted youth in the Argentine playing tennis and golf, not being properly educated nor active enough in the pursuit of young men. (Ralph and I always thought Isobel *too* active, and that she frightened them off by her determined pursuit, so incongruous with her flower-like femininity.)

Bunny and Angelica seem to have re-entered an area of mutual warmth and affection most delightful to witness.

January 19th

A dinner party here last night, the company – Johnny Craxton, Godleys, Georgia [Tennant]. Conversation streaked along without flagging till they left.

Winston Churchill has been dying for the last three days. My theory that the crowds waiting for this event are re-enacting the scenes at Tyburn was not accepted by anyone, yet it seems to me self-evident. They are trying to get a 'kick' – in this case from the drama of the grand old man's slow demise. If they were to go away for a cup of tea just at the moment that the notice of his death was posted on the door or given to the press they would feel cheated, like someone who left a football match just when a crucial goal was scored. Wynne accused me, burning-eyed, of being averse to all irrational behaviour. In the course of the evening we talked also of T. S. Eliot and incomprehensibility in poetry, of Hedonism, and finally of drug-taking, à propos of *The Naked Lunch*. Georgia spent a long time trying to tell us, with obvious sincerity but uncharacteristic inarticulacy, how the attraction of 'junkies' made other people take to drugs out of admiration and emulation. This was partly their being against the police and the Establishment – the bad boys of the school; their recklessness gave them an extraordinary glamour in her youthful eyes. I asked if it became legal, would people still want to take drugs. 'Oh, NO!', yet when I said the problem seemed simple, then: make it legal and it would stop, that wasn't acceptable to her.

Then we got to the mainsprings of art and Bunny's theory that its purpose was to enlarge one's experience; because one can, for instance, only be either male *or* female, and has in other respects limited opportunities for knowing about the world and people and life. Wynne and Kitty, orientated psychoanalytically, wanted to define it (art) in terms of 'resolution'. 'Fortinbras', said Wynne, 'resolved the tragedy of Hamlet and made everything all right, so that one wasn't left in despair.' Kitty said books she greatly admired – Henry James for instance – left her in deep sadness, and quite 'unresolved'. To my hedonistic eyes, Fortinbras is totally unimportant, and I believe it to be mainly the aesthetic qualities – the poetry, the satisfaction one gets from the formal relationships, shape and development – that make *Hamlet* so magnificent a play. I suggested that literature is always impure, and depends on being connected with reality at as many points as possible, not abstracted from it. Abstract art has pushed the emphasis on formality to its logical conclusion and that has proved absurd. It is as if a couturier were to lay such emphasis on the style of a dress that he ignored the female inside it.

January 22nd: Crichel

In my comfortable refuge bedroom, from which I look out on a bright pale wintry scene. I have been here for two nights alone with Eddy and Eardley. Snow was falling lightly when I arrived. Most of the time I am content and relaxed here. This hour after Mrs Spicer has brought my breakfast is my most private time.

Eardley took me into his studio yesterday to look at his 'Big Picture' representing a Beethoven quartet. He showed me sketches for it last time and has been working on it hard and obsessionally for two months ever since. The huge canvas covered most of the end wall of the studio. It is purely abstract. A central panel of interlocking rectangles of flat colour floats on a pale background and above and below it are strips which look like castle walls against an evening sky, with scarlet flames licking up from below.

January 23rd

Eddy said yesterday: 'I've never come across anyone who wouldn't rather have an inherited title than one bestowed by the Queen.' Faint murmurs arose from Eardley and me – supposing the inherited title was recent and undeserved by the ancestors? Wasn't it better to have your own achievements recognized? But we couldn't even get through to Eddy, past the blinkers of his prejudice. Eardley said afterwards that he'd 'felt his blood beginning to boil'.

Happiest moments here have been perhaps those when I've been alone in the garden fumbling with short-stalked snowdrops and aconites, or taking particoloured ivy leaves from the wall. At lunchtime came Desmond, and in the afternoon he and Eddy and I (and of course yellow dog Moses) went a long walk, ending up by slowly ascending a beautiful, winding, shallow valley with fields of large, strong-looking, long-legged sheep who were frightened by Moses and turned their multitude of black faces in his direction as one sheep. They reminded me of the crosses on the German graves in the battlefields of France.

Talk of music, and gossip about musicians. Nothing has been heard of the Harewood divorce, though he has (or is going to have) a child by his mistress. Eddy thought the Queen and Princess Royal must have brought pressure to bear to keep appearances going. Benjamin Britten has taken explicit and violent sides ('but he always loves doing that,' Eddy says). He isn't on speaking terms, therefore, with Harewood at present.

Basil and Frances Creighton[1] are here now. Desmond complains of the formality of the conversation and the way we all break up into pairs. I agree with him. Eddy likes it. It isn't quite the same happy and relaxed ease we had before, extremely nice as they both are. But they're not at home here entirely. Frances Creighton is very pretty, beautiful one might say even, intelligent and sweet-natured. In some ways she reminds me of that other sweet Frances [Phipps], but lacks her sudden ferocity and fun.

Records in the evening, chiefly Liszt, a composer I've never much liked. 'Soupy', Eardley called him. Eddy is exactly suited by Liszt's odd combination of banging and trilling (rather as if you came across an occasional bone in a mousse or soufflé, or a piece of armour were trimmed with lace), and kept exclaiming, 'What a marvellous composer!' The faces of people listening to music: Desmond pinker than usual, with set, almost cross features and sudden involuntary gestures. Not altogether an appearance of pleasure. Eddy like a cat that has swallowed a saucer of cream, his face bristling with a barely controlled sensual relish according amusingly with its neat oval; foot and head waving, and his unexpectedly square, strong hands from time to time accompanying the pianist with a rapid trill on the arm of his chair. His excitement over this to him entirely congenial music caused him to make characteristic quick, darting rushes about the room like a water beetle to look at the score, or – once – play a few bars on the neglected piano. Basil Creighton sat still and looked gloomily preoccupied. Frances leaning forward, erect, very slightly swaying and glowing, dedicated.

My days here have gone very fast and here begins the last of them with – as usual – quite a definite pleasure at the thought of returning to my nest.

The news that Winston was at last dead dropped soundlessly yesterday into our quiet pool.

January 28th

The last day at Crichel was marred by a fit of sadness (perhaps?) on Eddy's part. He slept more heavily even than usual after lunch in his

---

[1]   A cultured elderly couple. Basil had been a translator from the German, Frances a good amateur pianist.

armchair, complained constantly of the cold, and shut windows opened by anyone else. He and I drove to tea with Kitty, and his good manners smoothed the surface of whatever dismal or ailing sensations he was enduring until dinner-time when his poor little spotty, oval face drooped rather and he became inordinately silent. We were to listen to a wireless concert after dinner and he retired to the red room to do this whilst Eardley, Desmond and I remained in the drawing-room. This really seemed rather *marqué*, and I was worried about what was the matter, but Desmond said Eddy was just feeling 'East-windy'. The other two became somewhat uproarious in his absence and mocking about him, and Desmond insinuated that he drank much too much whisky. Poor lonely fellow, for I think he's shut away in an iron reserve from everyone except his God. Next day I drove to London with Eardley.

Today has begun Janetta's long absence, and I have to screw myself up to face it. Magouche has gone too, so that there is a definite sense of absence. Janetta came bringing me a huge bunch of flowers yesterday.

January 30th

Listening to Winston Churchill's funeral, now in progress, I wonder exactly what causes other people to feel so much while I remain totally blank. The paraphernalia of mourning, honour, exaltation and grief have been heaped so high and into such a cumbrous pyramid that it was bound to topple and collapse into the near-grotesque. Yet people have shuffled for four hours in biting cold to look at the catafalque. The symbolism and the universal and endlessly moving drama of death itself must, of course, have something to do with it. But I think millions of people really do believe what is constantly being said, that he was 'the greatest Englishman' – Shakespeare even included! The whole of London therefore seems to be awash in this deep black soup of emotion, though any individual (like Mrs Ringe)[1] I talk to is 'sick and tired of it all'. And I don't doubt those who have stood all night to see the procession go by will experience some devastating but satisfying catharsis. Even I find it hard to turn off my transistor which is blaring out funeral music, the occasional ludicrously fierce bark of sentries and the agonized voice of a female announcer 'carrying on' bravely

[1] My 'daily'.

110

in spite of her voice being almost annihilated by tonsillitis (as it sounds). The Archbishop's voice, rather groggy, offers up 'a hearty vote of thanks to God' for delivering this our brother out of the miseries of this sinful world and begs that we may all be speedily so delivered! The choir bursts into a sing-song used by soldiers in the war: 'John Brown's body lies a-mouldering in the grave.'

January 31st: 5.30 p.m. Sunday

And I've been alone all day though I've heard a few voices on the telephone and walked out once to post a letter and look at the state of Belgrave Square Garden. I have been grovelling in the past making dubious extracts from letters and diaries for Michael Holroyd and his biography of Lytton. It is a pretty lowering business and has left me trembling.

February 2nd

My 'grovellings' went on yesterday and have raked up a substratum of confused feelings. Do I want this young man to have access to any of it? Should people in no way concerned with feelings that were private, tender or painful have access to them? I'm aware of such conflicting motives in myself that I don't trust my own judgement and am seized at moments with a desire to burn all the papers I have. Yet the obstinacy of Noel Olivier in refusing to show Rupert Brooke's letters to his biographer has always seemed to me irrational and selfish. Last night Leonard Woolf talked on the wireless with dignity and perfect taste about Virginia. What would Ralph have said I should do? I feel desperately the lack of his judgement to consult. The whole surface of my mind feels tender so that the notes of a Beethoven 'cello sonata seems to bruise it as they fall from my transistor. Shall I ring up James and ask his advice? But I know that it is on my own assessment that I must ultimately rely.

I'm collecting reactions to the Churchillian frenzy. Julian, whose response appeared to me 'sound', said that some of his friends had been in a state of tense emotion and glorification of Churchill. Dicky took it for granted that the past week had been one of agitation and excitability (and therefore of drunken outbursts at Wivenhoe) and when I asked him why? – 'because it stirred up feelings about the war'. If this is true, if Churchill's death and the panoply decorating it, has glorified, idealized and romanticized war and disguised its sordid

111

beastliness then it has been disastrous indeed. And I rather fear it is so. What surely is certain is that the mass emotion we have just witnessed is not really, as some describe it, a 'sense of loss', for the old man has been dead and gone these last ten years.

February 3rd

Yesterday I made a great effort, pulled myself together, and decided off my own bat and without recourse to James, what to give Holroyd this evening. Possibly my interview with him will raise further echoes, but at the moment my feeling is all for the truth and nothing but the truth.

February 4th

I was right – my evening with Holroyd did raise echoes – and they kept me awake until about three last night. But I liked him. I was pleasantly surprised by his friendliness, quickness in the uptake, accessibility and (so it seemed to me) good judgement. At one moment he started to talk compulsively about himself, and I feel a little compunction at not having led him on further. Anyway, we passed three hours talking without *gêne* about the past and looking at photographs and I had no difficulty in deciding which, or what to say, nor do I think I ever saw reason to suppress the truth.

February 6th

The best has been said for the Funeral by V. S. Pritchett in a remarkable article in the *New Statesman*, which I prophesy will be quoted in all history books for the period. Even he doesn't answer the question he himself asks: What were the feelings that touched personally every man, woman or child who saw it? His real answer seems to be a response to the perfection, imagination, and admirable timing and taste with which the performance was carried out, though he seems to *think* he's saying it was the nation's recognition of greatness. Tristram Powell, who had been a moved spectator of everything, contributed to this same effect and also thought that it was as a symbol of mortality that it was particularly moving. He added descriptive touches that made it vivid – like that of a little man in a Russian fur hat suddenly seen walking in the middle of the processional route, bowed forward with his eyes on the ground, who then suddenly indicated a patch of the road that wasn't adequately sanded, and minions hurried forward and did it. He was the Chief Gritter!

I took Henrietta, Tristram, and Julian to see *Ballo in Maschera*, an indifferent performance of one of my favourite Verdi operas. What a *Maschera* I'm wearing, I thought, pretending to be enjoying the *Ballo*, and trying to forget the despair in my heart. The decisions I make to do this or that are purely arbitrary, like arranging a school timetable. It might just as well be Algebra instead of Biology. And when I look at my torn sofa-cover and muse about possible new stuffs for it, my thoughts die for lack of water. What's the good of making a nest when there's no one to make it for?

February 9th

I'm very glad indeed I got Julia to come to dinner last night. She is, after all, the person with whom I am most at ease, the oldest of my friends. I'm glad too that I decided to behave as if our last meeting had been perfectly normal and easy. It's possible she even thought it was – she says now she was feeling very strange under the influence of some new drug now abandoned. Last night there wasn't a breath of difficulty between us.

February 21st: Crichel

I was intrigued enough by what Raymond told me last night about Mycenae, Pylos and Knossos to spend the whole bitter cold afternoon reading the book he is reviewing. I've for so long pushed the phrase 'Linear B' to the back of my mind. Now it turns out to be perfectly simple, something one can grasp in five minutes.

The arrival of Desmond brought a rush of friendly warmth and tail-wagging about tea-time. There's always a certain amount of friction between him and Raymond who becomes a trifle governessy and disapproving with him. When Raymond had left the room Desmond said to me that he was getting rather fussy, there was surely no need to be 'cross all yesterday' just because of missing his train.

February 22nd

Raymond's Mycenae–Crete obsession became almost comic in the end – he could talk of nothing else at all, and as he had been mugging up his facts from several solid tomes Desmond and I were at a disadvantage. As we drove yesterday to lunch with Lady Juliet Duff I knew that Desmond was longing for the lecture to stop, as I was, especially as there was so much to look at in the way of pale beautiful sweeps of hillside, all the colour drained away by a sudden onset of cold, except for the faint brown of twigs and their buds. At lunch we had Beverley Nichols, Lilian Braithwaite's daughter, Joyce Carey, and, of course, Simon Fleet – with whom I think I got on quite well. The tall handsome rooms were full of lovely things including a table covered with pots of flowers – large pitcher orchids, jasmine, aconites and snowdrops – and looked out on the beautiful frozen garden. Roaring fires, voluptuous cats; talk about cats, 'the young' and Alcoholics Anonymous. But oh, poor Raymond – he looks awfully thin and worried, and takes life so hard. His seventieth birthday is approaching and two parties in his honour are being held – one by the *Sunday Times*, one by Hamish Hamilton – to both of which I've been asked. I don't think he's happy and I feel sad when I think how little human contact we made this weekend. He took no interest in my life, but heaven help us, what is there to be interested in?

February 26th

I must really put an end to my inward-looking temperature-taking; forget myself utterly for a while and sink into the concerns of other people. This I have in fact been doing the last few days, caught up without effort or by design in the affairs of Mary in particular. We were to go to a matinée on Wednesday afternoon, lunching here first, so when she rang up on Tuesday and asked if I had a few moments during the day I sensed an emergency under her calm tones and was not at all surprised to hear her say as she sat down on my sofa, 'I'm wondering whether to get a divorce.'

March 3rd

I have two books to translate if I want. I am doing a French life of Conan Doyle first. I feel breathless. Calm, calm is my objective but I doubt if I shall achieve it. I'm lying in bed looking at thin snowfall on the already covered roofs. Total silence. A feeling of boundless strangeness. Who am I, and what am I doing on my island mattress?

Yesterday I went to lunch with Faith[1] to meet Boris Anrep who looks a really beautiful object now in his reduced but dignified old age. He turned to me at lunch and said, 'You know Helen[2] died two days ago?' It so happened that I had been looking nostalgically at old photos of her at her most charming, pacing the Ham Spray verandah with Bunny, only yesterday, and reading bits of my earliest diaries, which give a cynical but affectionate picture. It was a shock, though I have for the last years thought of her with guilt, because I didn't go and see her and knew I ought to, but couldn't face the uneasiness of her welcome. It wasn't possible to think my last visit gave any pleasure to speak of to Helen. Ralph and I both expressed our affection for her in the old days – he particularly: it's lately that I've been remiss. I think perhaps she was a little, too. What a very strange character, compounded of vanity and charm. The vanity may well have been based on a sense of inferiority to Boris, as one is tired of being told, but what struck me most was that she underestimated her *real* qualities – talent for life, gaiety, good taste – and overestimated those that didn't exist, such as being a pundit about the arts and the mentor of the young, infallible. She was erratic, wayward, graceful, amusing and charming; and a lot of that charm was bound up in her appearance – her marvellously fresh complexion, untidy silky white hair, elegant movements, and eccentric, dilapidated style of dress.

Julian came to dinner a few days ago, Tristram to a drink. They had returned from making a film in Segovia and were full to overflowing with impressions and conclusions not all of which could they convey though I eagerly held out a bailing-tin to catch them.

March 9th

Georgia Tennant and I drove to visit Georgie Kee at school, speeding out of London through an iced fog like milk of magnesia, lunching in a very grand restaurant lodged inside a wayside inn near Compton.

I am enormously impressed by Georgia. What a really glorious girl! Intelligent, articulate, warm and funny. We talked hard all the way to Farnham, mainly about the ethics of the love affair, ethics in general and how they were related to Christianity. She was not so antagonistic to this as I am – she thought the Christian ethics were still valid and didn't mind faith being taken as a basis for accepting

[1] Henderson, mother of Sir Nicholas, and a great friend of Boris.
[2] His estranged wife, who had left him to live with Roger Fry.

them. She was very good about the promiscuity of the present young, agreeing that the check on it should be fear of debasing the gold standard of love and sex. Another thing we agreed about was the monstrousness of Reader's Digestism – cutting down long books just because they are long, not just because they are dull. If interesting, the more of them the better. Certainly some of the *Goncourt Journals* are dull, but when I got out a single volume of *Pages From* recommended by Cyril from the London Library, I was appalled. It's like having a few toe-nails from a beauty chorus – fragments of mince from a saddle of mutton; and the condensation is so great as to *have* to be haphazard. Just as Julian was going the other night we started talking about this and he was rather severe about it, as if it was priggish and wrong to mind cutting books. Georgia was enthusiastically on my side.

Julia came after I got back from visiting Georgie. I was so dead beat I'd fallen asleep, but I couldn't say no to her. She hates London weekends so. It was, alas, a story of desperation. 'I've begun throwing knives now,' she said, and described how she let off her feelings by pitching books about the room and banging doors – rather alarming.

I believe few people – Ralph was of course one – feel love and criticism towards the same person at the same time, as I do. I had a conversation on the telephone with Julia this morning about the 'horror of not being able to communicate'; she said, 'If one is an artist and writer, communication is important to one.' I said even though I was no artist and no writer I understood this very well and had found it agonizing to accept when Ralph died. 'How did you manage?' 'Simply by trying to spread my communications into whatever channels kind friends offered.' 'Well, you see, I don't find there are many people who understand, who speak the same language, have crossed the same bridges.' She went on with amazing unconscious vanity to expatiate on how few worthy recipients existed for her thoughts. It wasn't exactly 'I am holier than thou' but 'I am more of a special person, an artist, original, than thou.' I gave her a big – and truthful – sop to her vanity I hope, by telling her how many people greatly enjoyed her company.

March 11th

Margaret Penrose on the telephone spoke about existence very much as if it were a makeshift, a coat bought off the peg, not made to fit.

What *IS* it like? I never stop thinking about it and in the course of my long life my views undoubtedly change. Although one loses the youthful sense of its malleability and its splendid possibilities, its loveableness goes on, and this seems to me strange considering the fearful battering it gives one. 'It' is an always felt, even dominating presence, a bicycle to be ridden, a horse to be mastered, an adversary to be wrestled with, sometimes a purring cat lying on one's lap or a draught of heady wine gulped quickly down. Now – at sixty-five – I do think of it as a makeshift but still with a certain glow about it; a threadbare carpet with a worn but glorious pattern. Margaret seemed to feel that most normal people could have taken unto themselves a large number of different mates, and this I suppose must be true – because it would be purely superstitious to believe in the gravitating together of kindred souls – yet I find it impossible to accept in my own case.

March 21st: Sutton Woodlands

Kitty West's cottage. Not fine and mellow like last time, but gentle, soothing and sweet, with grey skies, fleeting patches of blue, and a soft wind. I've just been in the endless quiet woods, looking for and finding wild daffodils, sheets and sheets of them, coming up through dead bracken under short hazel trees with dangling catkins. Picked as many as my hands could carry, in tight buds. The blue tits swing boldly about outside our window on a lump of fat, that looks like a Francis Bacon portrait. Kitty and I saw a beautiful new-hatched Brimstone butterfly rolling intoxicatedly over her damp field. I stayed out longer than she did, hating coming in, yet it is she who loathes London and I who love it. Part of loving it is the great pleasure of the plunge into this cool freshness – there's no time for it to rise up and choke one before one's out and away. The quiet and stillness is dense like thick felt, long trails of marbled ivy hang motionless from the trees into my path like lianas. Through the marshy fields lots of little channels of water chuckle along, and beside them I saw a few primroses and celandines.

March 23rd

One of Gerald Brenan's 'spiky' letters, chiefly to tell me that Henrietta was not happy and Sophie running wild, ending, 'I thought you'd like this budget of news.' After his well-known 'desire to cause

117

pain' what a relief to lunch today with Anne [Hill] who loves passing on good news and had a good and cheerful letter from Henrietta to Harriet to report on.

April 3rd

Yesterday began a 'great' weekend at Stokke, lovingly planned by Mary for some weeks – me, Julia, Jonny and Sabrina, Ben Nicolson.[1] Ben is evidently moved to find himself here after ten years; shades of the past envelop him, his long Spanish face falls into deep melancholy and then lights up into hectic mirth. Julia is the one we are all anxious should enjoy herself and I wasn't sure she was doing so at dinner last night, seated between Charlie McCabe and Ben. She has backcombed her hair into an enormous frenzied haystack, otherwise she seems on the spot and her original and amusing best. I say 'otherwise' because it is, I think, a form of concealment or fending off the world. Jonny and Sabrina delightfully loving to one another. Sabrina is pregnant and I was touched by Jonny's look of real consternation when I said I thought the farmers were watering the milk. 'Good heavens! What shall I do? I must get cream or something for Sabrina.' I like her thoughtful search for the words she wants to express her ideas, often very successfully. Talking at dinner of religion or mystical experience, she described very well how once after being 'terribly afraid' she got an almost mystical experience from the sense that she was *accurately* able to orientate herself again – as if that accuracy came from outside. An uneasy moment when Charlie, feeling perhaps that he wasn't registering, began to shout a story down the whole table to me, and Mary thoughtlessly tried to 'take it away' as a footballer does the ball.

I do feel glad I don't any longer have to be responsible for large house parties – what a sweat and anxiety!

April 4th

The weekend is now going along merrily, and I take off my hat to Mary for her excellent compounding and arranging of it – seeming effortless, though of course it is not. Balmy, heavenly day yesterday. At lunch I told Sabrina about Jonny's remark about the cream – her face softened into a smile; then after a brief pause she said: 'Did he

[1] Art historian, son of Harold and Vita.

118

really say that?' 'Yes.' 'Tell me again.' Work and croquet in the morning; after lunch a walk in the forest with Julia. She was appreciative of Mary (who has been in and out of her famous 'doghouse' more than once) and even of Charlie to some extent.

April 9th

I have been making a crazy pavement of my various activities and every moment full. I'm almost too horrified by what is happening in Vietnam even to read about it – but no country now ever makes a move of friendliness or understanding to any other. They merely threaten each other with financial weapons, and bombs. At home the same fizz and crackle of hatred fills the air. Hooligan children derailed a train a short while ago killing two people and injuring fifteen, but that is far from an isolated instance.

Last night I dined with Boris and Maude Russell.[1] I was shocked at dinner to see her lose her temper brutally with her aged Austrian servant, shove her away and mutter, 'Get *along*!' She saw my horrified look I think, for she expatiated on the stupidity of Austrian peasants. I was ashamed suddenly to feel a *serf* was waiting on us, older than nearly all of us, but hobbling patiently around. It was a glimpse of medieval attitudes to the lower classes.

April 11th

At the Cecils' at Cranborne. It's Sunday morning and I'm lying in bed, having woken fairly early and started reading Lady Cynthia Asquith's diary, one volume of which is here in TS. David, Rachel and Julian Fane[2] (who is my fellow guest) rave about it and her. I think one can detect a lively character full of charm but the diary is not really good. Why, I ask myself? I think she's fallen for the fatal temptation of feeling she must write something every day, and recording movements and facts rather than responses to them: 'Beb[3] and I took the motor to lunch at Downing Street, Winston, A. J. B., etc., etc. Sat between X and Y, interesting conversation.' Disconcerting references to 'lack of whimsicality' as if it were a defect; pure gush like 'she was so darling'. Here was this poor woman with her

1 Hostess, beloved of Boris.
2 Writer, charming aristocrat, at that time a bachelor.
3 Herbert Asquith, her husband.

husband at the front, many of her friends being killed, her eldest little son turning out to be mad, and she writes lists of social engagements or 'shopping at Harrods'. One almost feels she is cold-hearted, certainly vain, and I note the absence of anything visual. The best things are remembered remarks – like Margot's of Katharine Asquith, who lacked vitality: 'Death could take nothing from Katharine.' I'm anxious lest too much of my critical feelings should come out to these hero-worshippers, who obviously loved her and treat her like a rare blown egg in cotton wool.

As usual it is a very comforting house to stay in. Many enthralling conversations, about *Hamlet* one night, violence the next, a walk yesterday afternoon through a sparkling wood carpeted densely with fresh green garlic leaves, anemones and tufted primroses. Hugh and Laura[1] are here – Hugh the more inarticulate, yet one is aware he has plenty of thoughts. I admire David's fatherly patience while he struggles to express them. I like Julian Fane: he is like a blond pale Leo Myers,[2] but without Leo's formidable cynicism and intelligence. I have the feeling Julian Fane finds me too unfeminine, but can't be bothered to try and seem less so. At lunch I did of course make certain criticisms of Cynthia Asquith's diary. Did toads leap out? Or did I successfully gulp them down again? I'm not sure.

Laura is now reading the diaries and takes a position closer to mine than any – she sees the funny side at least of the way Cynthia is always 'going shopping': 'to Harrods to buy a white suit' immediately after seeing her husband off to the front or hearing the ghastly news of a wounded friend. Julian Fane with rather anxious blue eyes tries to get me to admit they are 'brilliant'. I hedge – hoping to confuse the fox-trail of my fairly strong dislike of them, and not only of them but the whole civilization they stand for. Or at least feeling that it lacks something of the more integrated realistic ironical civilization I most admire. But what, exactly? After Julian Fane had gone, David brought down from an attic two thick tomes, privately printed – one to the memory of the Grenfells, another to the Charterises killed in the First World War. Such books are always horribly painful with their mixture of the steel of genuine agony with the golden haze of idolatrous love. I pored over the Grenfells, from curly-headed angelic boys to a really terrifyingly tough-looking Julian, who wrote *Into Battle*, that paean to destruction. All the time

[1] Younger Cecil children.
[2] Writer and my cousin.

David paced the room, making no bones about being emotionally stirred by the unwrapping of these coffins. Of course he was: this was his world and these were his values; he has the same conviction as they did of belonging to 'the chosen few'. Yet with the best will in the world, I could smell nothing but dust.

April 12th

I've been working, working all day, not unhappily though utterly alone. I've been elevated, intoxicated by hearing masterly perform-ances of all Beethoven's 'cello sonatas by Rostropovich and Richter. How extraordinary that their splendour can produce such a radiance of exhilaration that the whole world is illuminated by it, Vietnam, cancer and all.

After four and a half years of solitude I am only just learning that the task of the solitary is to make something of her lonely life as such, not try by distractions to deceive herself that it is anything else. The result has been a surprising reluctance to have that solitude broken.

Good Friday, and cold dead religious silence. I'd forgotten what it was like to wake (after a long sleep) to no post, no newspapers, an all-prevailing hush. But I soon pulled my new-found solipsism together and abandoned myself to it, turning the big wireless on full strength to break the godly quiet and pour Mozart and Schubert as far as the bathroom, where I lazily splashed, feeling like a pasha or a cart-horse rolling in a field, tufted feet in the air.

Last night I had dinner with the Campbells in all the happy domesticity of their little house, prettified with new wallpapers. Very nice. Real love pervades the house, and after dinner little Arthur came downstairs from bawling in his cot and trotted to and fro or reclined in his mother's arms with the abandon of a Roman Emperor. At dinner quite a long and – to me – bewildering conversation about Religion. How were they to answer William's questions about what happened on Good Friday? I couldn't see the difficulty. But Robin had a lot of fuzzy things to say about Myth (like Father Christmas), religion being 'a work of art', and the necessity of 'thanking God' for the goodness of the world. What about its badness, then? Ah, this a child couldn't yet understand. Susan cried, 'Well, he's been christENed!' therefore the clergyman now 'expects' him to go to Sunday school.

April 15th: Thorington Hall

With Lionel and Margaret [Penrose]: 'Are you SURE you don't mind sleeping in the panelled room?' This is because it's supposed to be haunted and many people would die rather than sleep there. 'Not in the very least,' I say, forgetting that perhaps because unloved it has its disadvantages. Rather large and square, it has only one picture on its panelled oak walls, an eighteenth-century portrait of a man 'who is always looking at you'. A small bone-hard child's bed crouches against one wall, and there is virtually no other furniture. Having no heating or fire of any description the chill of all the past winter hangs in it, but going to bed in vest, cardigan and dressing gown and clutching my hot-water bottle, I managed to sleep.

Staying here is a nice mild American medical scientist, working on a book with Lionel, whom he clearly adores. His face is oval, dusky and unformed like the pictures of Nabokov but less tinged with emotion. Last night Jonathan,[1] with his quite pretty wife Maggie, arrived too. I'm very grateful for the chance of getting out of London, shall enjoy Lionel and Margaret's company greatly and hope to get on with my work.

Last night a story of Lionel's delighted me – it was about W. H. Rivers, expert on shell-shock (indeed, the man who discovered there was such a thing). He was lecturing on the subject and had an intermittent stammer; suddenly he got absolutely stuck and after wrestling with the word for ten minutes he seized a piece of chalk and angrily scrawled on the blackboard the word: TERROR.

April 16th: Easter Day

I've been given the 'telly' room to work in: here I spent all yesterday morning, and propose to spend this, with my work spread out on an oceanic dining-room table – happiness. I have pulled up an electric heater and am doing my best to warm up after the rigours of the night in my quite exceptionally cold, dark room. The weather has turned bitter cold and an intermittent gale battered my windows; now and again a yew tree just outside struck them with a loud bang and at 5 a.m. the door of the priest's hole creaked and then crashed open – this lies behind the idea of the haunting, I dare say. Yesterday an art master from Lawrence's school – Francis Hoyland – came to lunch to see about renting Lionel's barn as a studio. Talked to him about

[1] British chess champion for ten years, and youngest son of the house.

his methods of teaching art. He suddenly became enthusiastic and said that as works of art all started from the body of the perceiver – here he seized a bottle of HP sauce, a tomato and a loaf and arranged them roughly – he taught his students to go back to their own bodily sensations. When I suggested that perception was not purely bodily but also mental and that the knowledge of what HP sauce was, for good or ill, played a part in the act of perception, he got almost angry.

After lunch Margaret, Jonathan and Maggie, George Smith (the nice American) and I got onto five bicycles and went spinning round the lanes. Uncertain at first, I was delighted to find I could still do it, after at *least* a twenty-year gap.

Our evenings are spent in the telly room. Last night I looked round during a Sherlock Holmes film and saw that Margaret, Bessie and Freddie (the staff) were all fast asleep sitting bolt upright.

April 20th

The intense cold tightened its pincers and three nights in the glacial dankness of the haunted room were quite enough. All the same, I loved being with Lionel and Margaret, and liked the gentle American also. As for Jonathan, he was almost completely silent, though he doesn't seem unhappy. I pleased the Penroses by saying their house had the atmosphere of a 'reading party' and though I've never been to one I regard this as high praise. Lionel and George worked at their book on imbeciles; I at my translation; Maggie at something to do with maths papers and Jonathan at chess. I think Margaret, in spite of having to cater for us all, felt a little short of somewhere to discharge her warm and boundless energy, her considerable intelligence.

A conversation with Lionel about scientists comes back to my mind – he said how maddening the French ones were, insisting on being so logical, as if no one else was: how peevishly they quarrelled over some minute piece of knowledge, and who was to have the honour of first discovering it. 'One scientist I shall always remember because he said, "Knowledge is extremely important, but who discovered it is of no importance *at all*." I thought he deserved a great deal of honour for saying such a thing but the worst of it is, I can't remember what his name was.'

April 24th: London

I met a new and very likeable character last night – David Sylvester, the art critic. A large, plump man with big, sad, dark eyes and a jet-black beard crawling all over his cheeks and surrounding very red lips. Clearly extremely intelligent, not very happy, emotional, both gentle and violent (the two at war with each other) and anxious about himself. The conversation was interesting and moderately excitable – centring round religion (we're both anti-Christian), teaching children to read (we didn't agree there) and violence. I said that it could be statistically proved from criminal records that men were more violent than women. He took this up rather hotly, as if I'd said they were *wickeder* (which of course I hadn't) and declared that if men were violent it was because women so wickedly refused to breast-feed them – this was *always* possible if they really wanted to, he said – and also wickedly 'castrated' their sons and husbands. I looked at him rather sharply and said, 'Have you been psycho-analysed?' whereupon everyone laughed and it seems he's still at it. More than once he charged me with being 'sophisticated' – 'a person as sophisticated as you are'. That's not a word I've ever applied to myself.

April 26th

I've already noted Eardley's suggestion that I join him in renting a house in Orta, north Italy, but without enthusiasm. However, the 'yes-person' in me has taken over, and we are setting off in a few days' time. I shall stay a month, Eardley longer. The house belongs to Nigel Dennis, author of *Cards of Identity*.

April 29th: Paris

The first night of my journey to Italy with Eardley. Here after all I am, lying on my comfortable rough-sheeted platform bed waiting for *petit déjeuner*. The walls and curtains are covered all over with *coquet* bunches of flowers on an egg-yellow background. I look out onto the quiet courtyard.

The days before departure saw the overcoming of various obstacles. I gave a dinner party to Heywood, Julian, Henrietta, Mark Palmer and Georgia – the young stayed late. I felt Heywood to be an elderly ally and he amused everyone with stories about Harriet's six-year-old twin stepdaughters. He had just taken one to the Zoo. 'How can you tell a man-bear from a woman-bear?' 'Well, you look underneath.' 'And what do you see there?' 'You see some balls and in front of them a penis.' Slight pause. 'Now you've embarrassed me, Heywood – you see, I call them something different.'

On my penultimate day, I went to the lunch in honour of Raymond's seventieth birthday at the *Sunday Times* – I suppose about thirty of us in a long boardroom with printed menus with our names on them. I sat between Morgan Forster and Leonard Russell (one of the *Sunday Times* staff and husband of Dilys Powell). She, Lady Clark, Lady Churchill and Janet Adam-Smith were the only other females. Leonard, Duncan, Dadie,[1] V.S.P.,[2] and Roger Senhouse[3] were there, and the room was full of affection and good feeling. Lunch disgusting, and not much to drink; afterwards, Raymond rose to his feet and spoke uneasily from a fluttering piece of paper. I gave him a little Georgian silver pillbox, which I think he really liked. Though a purely formal occasion there was a sort of glow left behind by it and I travelled home on a bus with Duncan.

Now D-day – yesterday. Eardley had to go back for his spectacles, didn't allow enough time to get to Southend, and left most of the maps behind. We got on fine, though, yesterday and I only hope it may continue. It's always a surprise what rough, wrinkled, noisy, bumpy aeroplanes car travellers are expected to go by – but pleasant being one of a half a dozen, and soon with no effort we were spinning off over the pale spring-green plains of northern France, under fierce showers and long periods of sun.

April 30th: Nancy

Divinely beautiful town. We have spent the night in the large sumptuous hotel that overlooks the Place Stanislas. A festival of university actors (amateurs) from all over the world is going on in the

[1] George Rylands, doctor of English literature at Cambridge.
[2] Pritchett.
[3] Publisher and love of Lytton Strachey.

theatre here, a magnificent building lined with cherry-coloured velvet and the twin to our hotel. One of the very nice things about Eardley as a travelling companion is his eagerness to go to anything of this sort, and go we did, coming out afterwards into the splendid square, discreetly floodlit so that the stone ornaments along the roofs stood out almost meltingly against the night sky, and the fountains and gilt gates at the corners blazed brilliantly against the equally brilliant green of the trees behind them.

The performance consisted of three troupes: Americans from Indiana, Turks, and French. The Americans were deplorable in their complete lack of talent, and clumsiness; the house booed loudly. The Turks, though – what an experience! They were really first-rate, and the audience applauded them wildly. (These were mostly charming young people from the university here, or the visiting teams.) Stylized rocking, springing from foot to foot was the basis of all their gesture and movement – as if to show themselves alive, or as a child will pick up and thump on the table the doll or creature that he is making perform in his play. At one side sat a man beating out a rhythm with his hand on some sort of drum, or occasionally picking up a trumpet and blowing it. Within this extreme formalization the characters were brilliantly differentiated by the exact way they bounced to and fro. It was like ballet, so that the fact that one understood nothing hardly mattered, even when the comic character recited a very serious poem in a funny way.

May 1st: Luzern

We are supposed to arrive at Orta today – what angsts, surprises or disappointments may that bring? From beautiful Nancy we drove yesterday morning to Colmar and spent some time looking at the Grünewald *Altarpiece*. Both agreed, as we got back into the car, that we felt shattered and disturbed. I think I 'liked' it less than Eardley did – the great thing about it is the extraordinary intensity of emotion it contains; I can't think of any other picture that arouses it so violently, unless perhaps the Piero *Resurrection* at Borgo San Sepolcro or the *Lamb* at Ghent – but both are much better pictures than this. What is more, though there are these disturbing, violently emotional passages in the Grünewald, there are others of real falseness and sentimentality. Nor am I greatly impressed by what many modern painters have apparently been struck by – the grim reality of the crucifixion. But should a great work of art leave one disturbed, agitated and confused? Surely not – however deep it goes, the Piero, *The Burial of Count Orgaz*, *Othello* ought to leave the problems resolved and smoothed out. Why the Grünewald doesn't do this, for all its mastery is a problem to which I see several solutions. First: the very intensity of the emotion like an overpowering smell pours from the picture and prevents one reacting to its beauty, colour, design as much as one otherwise would. Second: it taps the unconscious, as Bosch does, by means of horrifying creatures, and suggestions of unspeakable desires and deformation – and leaves these substrata in unresolved chaos. And third: the passages of sickly, vulgar unreality and sentimentality – vulgarity of a specially German sort – make a clanging and unpleasant discord with the sombre grim realism of the rest. So, though I came away feeling I'd had a sensational experience, I do most definitely not bow down to Grünewald in deepest awe and respect; in fact I resent not having been left with that golden sunset glow a really great picture leaves in one's mind.

The Swiss – that's the other subject I've thought about. To cross from depopulated beautiful unspoiled France (though Nancy it is true, is hardly to be taken as typical of any country) into this small over-populated, stodgy, methodical, prosaic land, is a portentous experience. At once the houses began closely edging the roads in interrupted villages, the cars crawled in an endless queue. What can have made people propagate so much faster one side of the boundary than the other? Then every material thing is ugly, or rather made without consideration for beauty or taste. The rich damp green fields with their kingcups and cuckoo flowers, the tearing streams were some relief as we drove up into the hills, but everywhere, everywhere man was vile – or rather, *deadly dull*. A glorious natural vision before we plunged down into Luzern was provided by the pale, huge, pinkly-lit transparent-looking Alps hanging high and ethereal far above us in the sky, and seeming grand and pure compared to the crawling grubby cars, people and concrete or wooden houses below. Our hotel is all that's most Swiss. Everyone speaks excellent English, but treats us in a slightly governessy inhuman way, without the real humanity of Italians or Spaniards, or the intelligent crossness of the French.

May 2nd: Orta

Well, here I am in my bleak un-windowed bedroom at 7.30 a.m., with the rain falling heavily outside. We arrived yesterday, mid-afternoon, May Day and a weekend, to find the pretty little town jam-packed with humanity, and cars forcing their way slowly along the narrow streets. We broke our way into the garden of 'our' house – a strip of rough grass, very narrow like a London back garden. It goes down to the lake's edge where a pretty willow tree droops over it and makes a tiny region where one might eat out. The house itself is very narrow and tall. When we had collected the keys and made our way in, the dankness of having been shut up all winter hung everywhere. At the moment it doesn't seem extraordinarily feasible, but yesterday our immense desire to make a go of it was augmented by the astonishing arrival of Bunny and Angelica almost before we had looked round. All the floors are made of rather dusty brick-coloured tiles. Nothing works, including an electric fire in the top room (where Bunny and Angelica are sleeping in their sleeping-bags). The room I'm now in has no window or heating, and I had to lug upstairs a mattress from Eardley's room so as to have something to tuck in; but we drank whisky, made up the beds, went out to eat in a restaurant and were very jolly.

This morning my mind is full of problems. How long will the Garnetts stay? I feel responsible for their being here, though not perhaps for their forgetting our dates and coming so early. After they've gone Eardley and I will each take one floor and arrange accordingly – I don't think I mind which. Hope of a glimpse of the *douceur de vivre* has temporarily gone with the sound of rain, through which for some hours I've heard the Italian birds chirping stridently, on a very different note from the twittering French ones. Then I feel responsible – why? – for keeping Eardley's spirits up. I was tremendously aware as we arrived yesterday of *his* feeling responsibility for the place, and desire for me to like it, so with the ludicrous inversion human beings go in for I strained every nerve to reassure him. Both of us are worrying hard.

How I long for some physical satisfaction to hang on to! – warmth of a fire, sun, coffee. We have none of these.

May 3rd

Now all is well – very well, I think I can say. The Garnetts with their bravura and appreciation saw us through our teething problems. The rain stopped soon after Bunny and I had stepped out together along the narrow streets (whose roofs almost meet overhead and so keep off the rain) to buy bread, milk, coffee and butter. There's an extraordinary satisfaction about acquiring these prime necessities, and by the time the table was spread and hot coffee being poured into cups, the sun had almost come out and we felt much warmer. A splendid honest *donna* of seventy-seven called Herminia came and cleaned the bath (left strikingly dirty by the Garnetts, who have evidently been roughing it); we found deck chairs and dragged them out into the garden, bought eggs and salad and fruit and cheese and bunches of herbs. Halfway through the afternoon we walked along the shore of the lake by the narrow marge left between the softly lapping water and sloping luscious fields full of fruit trees, small, intoxicatingly sweet narcissi, and large white violets. Everything was pretty.

May 4th

Today has been a full and important one. The morning was radiant and balmy. While the Garnetts went off to telephone, Eardley and I set about like two ants, rearranging our quarters. He is to have the Garnetts' bedroom: the black hole behind it where I slept the last two nights is to be a dressing room with clothes-hanging space for both. I have the *sala* to work in, and sleep in the bedroom behind it. This is dark, but not so bad as my recent hide-out and I have moved the bed to give a magnificent reading-light. I dragged beds, pushed and shoved, unpacked everything down to the last pill bottle and spread out my dictionaries. I have even done a good day's stint at my translation, and changed £10 of traveller's cheques. We are in fact afloat. We have even called on the next-door neighbours, the Cappellis and taken a drink with them. Middle-aged both, with rather quizzical faces, they hint at many mysteries connected with our house and the Nigel Dennis family.

I feel *peace* descending and that I shall be quite content here with Eardley and that we have made the Casa Forbes into *our* house. We now *live* here.

May 5th

First breakfast *à deux* cooked and eaten. Herminia is crashing about in the kitchen. The top lavatory is not working, nor are the electric fire and sitting-room main light. The Dennises either have strikingly little love for their house, no taste or sensuality, or no money. There's not a single carpet or picture in the whole house. In the afternoon we drove up the hill behind the village to its summit, finding a place where great quantities of big blue gentians were growing, and on and up, to small elegant pure white crocuses and dogtooth-violets. Though there are not many flowers, what exquisite ones! We ate indoors by the heat of our god-given butagaz fire, for though it is warmer already, it's pretty freezing in bedroom or kitchen. Yet how marvellous to look out and see a clear dark sky, stars and a crescent moon.

Herminia treats us as though we belonged to a superior order of beings, both delighting and embarrassing us. When we got back from the mountains we found her hurrying excitedly along the street with a bundle wrapped in newspaper. She had brought us some lettuce thinnings, radishes, and a huge bunch of buttercups, daisies and dandelions!

May 7th

A pearl-grey day. Sounds come clearly across the silver lake. The peace is incomparable, and one cannot believe in the invasion of weekend tourists which will begin presumably tomorrow. Yesterday the sun came out. Sitting out in it and reading the newspaper was so delicious that translating my verbose French professor[1] (who has just compared the Sherlock Holmes stories to *Paradise Lost*!) was set aside; this was too good to miss. A visit from the Cappellis, bearing a huge and splendid gift of azaleas. Fearing that Herminia might feel her buttercups outclassed, I was solicitous to give them fresh water in their jam jar, but the vase shortage is so great that I had to rush upstairs and fetch the lavatory brush container for the azaleas.

Full days, scented evenings, really hot sun all afternoon. Each morning Herminia brings more and more bunches of flowers; when she has something worthy of her – lilac or may – she really arranges them very prettily. We try and keep her fed with short snatches of such conversation as we can manage. Yesterday, admiring my sheets, she said how extraordinary the Forbes were to have such a fine house and no nice things at all. 'What about the Signora?' I asked. 'Does she do anything in the house?' An owl's hoot went up. '*Hoo! Dolce far niente, tutt'il giorno!*' She illustrated this by resting her cheek on her hand. Then she told us how the *Arandora Star* (the ship that was sunk full of Italian waiters) included her son-in-law and two other relatives. And a pacifist chorus followed from us both.

[1] Pierre Nordon, author of the *Life of Conan Doyle* I was translating.

An expedition by car up an endless series of *lacets* to a mountain village where the old people still wear the clothes you see in Victorian prints – gold earrings, headscarves, small shawls and very full skirts.

The regular life in sweet surroundings with a companion who likes much the same things as I do should be and is very soothing. Indeed, I've felt relaxed and contented. Up on the hillside yesterday I got a waft of mountain magic: every sound carried, crickets and cuckoos and a dog barking in each farm, and the extraordinary clarity and distinctness of female Italian voices. One farm had some baby rabbits lolloping round it, loose. The path wound into pretty woods and out again. I longed for Ralph to admire it with. I think of him and Burgo a great deal here, and dream of them a lot.

The nights are the least pleasant part. Facing my cold dark room is a slight ordeal, lying under the thin blankets patched with Nigel Dennis's underpants, waiting to get warm.

May 14th

As the weather grows more summery, our petals gradually unfurl. People have begun to bathe in the lake. The nights are perfectly clear unless for a slight haze, and the beauty of the twinkling lights across the water seen between the tall shapes of the cypress trees is almost too obvious to react to. Eardley and I have talked of all sorts of subjects, general ones like art and war, and personal like our pasts or homosexuality; and last night he talked a lot about life at Winchester and his feeling for his brother – these I believe to lie deep in a guarded region of his ego, and I am flattered that they came out spontaneously.

The day before yesterday there was a major event – the kind Cappellis from next door arranged to get us seats for *Simon Boccanegra* at the Scala. I felt an intense thrill at finding myself here in this famous opera house about to see the opera that was almost first on my list of desiderata. When the lights dimmed, they for a while left all the boxes faintly lit – the prettiest sight in the world, like a honeycomb of cherry-coloured silk hung with occasional clusters of moon-like lamps, and we heard beautifully from our seats in the galleria.

We flew home swiftly through the night.

May 18th

The other day Eardley took me to call on two aristocratic elderly Italian ladies, Bianca Negra and her sister, who live at the village above us in a magnificent house (a 'national monument') painted all over the outside in dull purple, ochre and blue, but mostly shut up now as they can get no servants. They were a delightful pair, intelligent, civilized and amusing, speaking excellent English. A little puzzled – as the Cappellis were – as to what terms Eardley and I were on, they quickly thawed and showed us one small charmingly painted room. I mentioned wild flowers. Their eyes lit up. The younger sister said, 'Some people have a normal love for flowers, some an abnormal one. Mine is *ab*normal.' They began to tell us where to go, and above all to the Val Formazza above Domodossola. The very next day, though it was Sunday and looked unsettled, we were off like a shot.

We drove up the long deep valley from Domodossola towards the Swiss border, winding gradually between its steep granite sides and clambering by *lacets* among enormous grey blocks fallen chaotically from the mountains. We ate our picnic leaning against the noble slope of one of these, which had cherry-coloured primulas growing from its cracks. Then on again up and up, past a vertical waterfall and *then* we entered a new world which I hope I shall never forget the look of in all my life. A high valley, a basin of short turf, with the snow mountains all round and melted snow from them running in a stream down the middle. The smooth slopes were thickly sprinkled with marvellously clear-coloured alpine flowers, a beautiful mixture of purple and white crocuses, very blue forget-me-nots, yellow pansies, gentians big and small, primula farinosa, orchids yellow and red, a glorious pale yellow pasque-flower and two other anemones. My reaction was certainly 'abnormal', worshipping and intoxicated. We shan't find any other flowers here to equal them. We drove on till the road was blocked with snow and then turned home. After this really immense thrill, it was almost a relief to find it raining when we surfaced yesterday and it kept quietly on all morning.

May 21st

Joan Cochemé's arrival has only slightly ruffled the even surface of our pool. She is very appreciative, seems to like the place, the house and the arrangements we had made for her comfort, and has settled in here very snugly and sweetly in fact, like a cat making the best of a not-too-soft cushion.

May 25th

After a day of much rain with the dank chill of a wet face flannel, it suddenly stopped yesterday, the sun came through and we went out and hired a boat to row across the lake to Pella and back by the island, for Joan to see the church. It was a perfect evening to glide over the lake, whose faint smell of mud and rotting vegetation rose to one's nostrils; the surface glassy, turning later to milk, a thin mist wreathing Pella and the hills above; towering thunderheads faintly bloomed with pink from the setting sun; reality and reflection forming a dreamy, blurred, quiescent unity, the air full of the screeching of swifts and the musical dinging of church bells near or far.

May 27th

Joan has left. Eardley got slightly drunk the night before she left and at dinner at our local trattoria we talked of love. Joan and I both stuck up for love but not for loyalty. Eardley was inclined to put loyalty above love. Then homosexuality, and how it led to promiscuity; and how the passion for youth came into it.

May 28th

Yesterday was Ascension day, and according to Herminia it always rains then, because of the impact of Jesus Christ – or was it the Virgin? – with the clouds. '*Capisce?*' Eardley talks a lot about Mattei.[1] The conversation nearly always ends, 'I *do* hope we get some fine weather when Mattei's here.'

Thunder and lightning and a migraine broke over my head together, and I hope may have explained my extra feeling of stupidity. But I am also oppressed by the thought of return to London and the unknown problems I may find there. It is no longer possible to live in the *now* and *here*, try as I will.

May 29th

Eardley has gone off to Milano to meet Mattei.
  Some time afterwards: the bell rang shrilly and when I called to

[1] Radev, his Bulgarian friend, due to arrive next day.

ask what it was Herminia shrieked, '*L' albero*!!' In the centre of our narrow lawn a tall seedy-looking cypress has been all this time spoiling our view. Eardley wrote to Nigel Dennis lightly suggesting it would be better to cut it down: since when a whole series of enterprises have been set in motion. Signor Cappelli has been written to, a woodman engaged, and on this day of all days when I was alone in the house he arrived to do the job. He was a magnificent dour-faced seventy-year-old with thinning grey hair and very strong, but rounded shoulders; his equipment was an axe and a billhook (lovingly slung over his bottom), a ricketty home-made ladder and a remarkably small piece of string. My heart was in my mouth when he climbed the ladder to the very top, with no one standing on the bottom rung. But he descended looking worried; the tree was rotten, he said, and couldn't be cut in two bits. It must be felled in one piece. Now Signor Cappelli arrived, and told me the old man had 'infinite science and skill' and would drop it just where he wanted. The woodman encircled the tree with a rope, took his axe and began to take measured and scientific chips from the base of the tree and at the moment that Eardley and Mattei entered the garden the tree began to waver. Eardley, Mattei and Signor Cappelli went out into the lane and pulled the string – it couldn't be called a rope – it broke and Mattei went flying. A few minutes later the tree fell exactly where it had been intended to. I have never seen such convincing knowledge and skill matched with such pitiful equipment.

The fall of a tree is a sort of execution and I was aware of desperate longings for a reprieve. 'Tell him not to cut it down – before it's too late,' I think I said. Did the crowds at an execution feel the same *détente* and triumph and pride in the executioner's skill when the head rolled on the ground? After all was over the woodman's wife arrived, thick as a tree herself and much like one, with legs as straight as logs of wood, a stocky body and tightly drawn back grey hair. Speechlessly she helped him drag bits of the fallen victim away.

May 30th

As I lay in bed last night listening to the crash and roll of thunder and hearing the rain lashing down, I felt differently towards this peaceful little enclave. I think too that we have more or less exhausted its possibilities and I don't envy Eardley his extra month here.

June 3rd: West Halkin Street

I have re-entered my life at full gallop with rather unearthly energy and am already almost 'straight'. To my orchestra the night I got back and also to see Janetta. Yesterday Mary came to lunch and Julia to dinner. I have spoken on the telephone to nearly all my friends. Mary sounded cheerful about Charlie's new job – which makes them far better off and improves his morale, 'But he's jolly disagreeable, all the same, much of the time.' She'd just had a flaming row with him about Magouche – he had practically said she must choose between him and Magouche, that she was 'bad news', a 'nasty piece of work' and other equally revolting phrases.

Julia and I discussed the Colmar Grünewald. She praised it for giving a lifelike and convincing picture of Christ's sufferings on the cross 'instead of just a young man with flu'. What perhaps worries me about Julia is that she avows that she wants to find a new life-companion – this, at sixty-three, and regardless of her extreme fastidiousness.

June 5th: Lawford Hall, Essex

I thought as I got into my soft bed last night how uneasy I had for many long years felt in this house and that now I don't – not in the least, here or anywhere else. I've been broken in, exactly like a horse, made to go round and round under whip and bearing rein until I simply can do it without minding. Will this state of things last? Or will it crumble? It is a comfort, that's the best that can be said about it and what I've learned I've learned in the school of utter loneliness.

Talking to Janetta two nights ago, I mentioned Julia's desperate craving to find a new mate at the eleventh hour, which I can barely even understand. 'Oh, but almost everyone I *know* is trying and longing to do that,' said Janetta with a furrowed face. 'They may be miserable in their marriages and want to get away, but it's the one thing they think of – to find someone else to share their lives.'

Thank heavens then for this one small mercy that I've never, never for a second envisaged or hoped for a second best.

June 7th

Back from a walk in the marsh with Phyllis Nichols. She has been talking to me just now about mediums and the next world and communications with the dead – it's like a foreign language. To begin with wish fulfilment makes nonsense to me of the idea of a future life – it is such a dreaded and dreadful thought. Yet Phyllis longs to believe in it, and I suppose many people do. This life, they say, is meaningless otherwise. And meaning is given it apparently by absurd messages from a dead son saying, 'I hope Daddy is wearing my old dressing gown.' I've been deeply touched by Martin[1] and by similarities with Burgo, particularly the combination of over-confidence and the reverse, of the life and the death principle, and the sense that he is vulnerable and terribly needs luck. I like Francis[2] even more than before – there's a good, responsible, kind person. He has a good head and likes to use it.

I have felt unexpectedly aware of the gap left in this family by Phil's death, and thought of him a great deal and felt his absence like a hole in a carpet. I even walked to the churchyard and looked with a pang of horror at the green grass between the sober headstone and foot, so like the ends of a bed and thought how terrible it was to preserve the mouldering remains of a dead person thus in an exact spot and put a little bunch of white carnations on it.

June 14th: Crichel

Where I've been for two and a half days, alone with Raymond. Desmond arrived last night, newly honoured with a CBE, excited by Glyndebourne, and anxious to turn on Donizetti's *Anna Bolena* on the wireless. He welcomes life in the modern world; Raymond tries to flap it away rather plaintively as if it were a mosquito, sighs for the past, and quite often just sighs. He didn't like the Donizetti at all, was crushed by a visit from Kitty West that he insisted on arranging (murmuring after she'd gone, 'The years like great black oxen tread me down'), and was very disapproving because Edmund West has married in America at twenty-two while a medical student (because he 'ought first to have enough to support a wife on' and 'perhaps it's a good thing I've no children, I should be very grumpy').

June 15th

It's borne in upon me that the *most* that lies ahead of me is ten years of dwindling sensibility. Or worse. I wish in a way I knew, and could

---

[1] Younger son of the house.
[2] Elder son.

make appropriate arrangements. I have come upstairs to bed after a real spell of pleasure – listening with Desmond to Tippett's *Variations on a Theme of Corelli*, a rich profusion of beautiful sounds.

June 18th

I notice somewhat ruefully but without surprise, that I often spend long hours with people without their asking me a single question about myself. Kitty, for instance; not a word asked about my five weeks in Italy. Bunny came to dinner last night and was a delightful companion; we talked of all his daughters and their problems in turn, about his work, about William,[1] the question of where to live, and finally – in a voice that trembled a little – about his relations with Angelica. So happy they had seemed at Orta, but (as Henrietta suggested) they have floated apart since their return. Angelica has talked of 'coming back to live at Hilton'. But now she has found a 'little rather slummy house near the Angel' and is all agog for that. As I heard his sad and quavering voice saying how he hated the idea of living in London, that it tired him dashing up and down and he got melancholy and lonely at Hilton with no one but William, my heart contracted with sympathy and affection. But not one word about *my* life. I have none, and everyone knows it. Perhaps that's the answer.

Yesterday I lunched with Magouche who, not being trained in Bloomsbury's school, did ask politely about myself.

June 20th: Stokke

I sit in blazing sun on the lawn; the 'others' have gone over to Stowell to bathe. What lovely peace. I've come down from my bedroom for a dose of it before returning to the grind through the last trees of my translation.

There was a jolly party of young people for dinner (and some to spend the night) on Saturday: young men who had been playing cricket against Stowell village, their wives or girlfriends. The Jellicoes and their guests – Mark Bonham Carter and his wife – made us up to fourteen. I sat between the nicest of the strangers, Julian

---

[1] His younger son by my sister Ray, his first wife.

Ayer and Bonham Carter. Julian Ayer, officially the son of one philosopher but really of another (Stuart Hampshire) is a charming good-looking, intelligent, alert, interested boy, who loves exchanging ideas. I took to him greatly and was afterwards blamed by Mary for not keeping up the traditional dinner-party rhythm. Mark Bonham Carter was anyway happily flirting with pretty Mrs Peter Baring. The hostship was chaotic, and I expect nothing from Charlie. But the meal didn't appear till nearly nine-thirty, meanwhile no one offered the Jellicoe party drinks. Charlie, well supported with a stiff whisky, mumbled that 'people should help themselves.'

June 24th: West Halkin Street

Listening to Callas in *Tosca* as I stirred a mayonnaise. Last night and tonight were devoted to Handel operas at Sadler's Wells.

Magouche seemed horrified when we got there ten minutes before the curtain went up, and suggested our fighting our way through the milling crowds to get whisky. As we'd each swallowed two quite stiff ones in my flat, I counter-suggested that we shouldn't. 'But what shall we *do* for ten minutes?' she said very spontaneously. I didn't say 'talk', or look about us – in point of fact we hardly had time to read the plot of the first act. But I was interested at this idea that if they weren't drinking there's nothing two people have to say or do after a certain hour. Another phrase in common currency: 'I need a drink' or 'I don't need a drink but I'd like one.' How many whiskys a night are *needed* by whom? I certainly need one. What would happen if we were wrecked on a desert island?

After the opera last night, Magouche and I went to the Campbells where Susan had provided a really magnificent spread of curries for us and we fell on them greedily. Little Arthur as usual woke twice and came down and sat on Susan's lap, surveying us out of his enormous blue, wide-set eyes.

Janetta came with me to Handel's *Rinaldo*. She described the party at Chatsworth for the coming-of-age of the heir last week. The special train with people in evening dress (including Princess Margaret) was watched by spectators as they trooped sheepishly up the platform. Then the great house, where everything was perfect – beauty everywhere, banks of flowers, delicious food, baths full of champagne, but Janetta was dealt a blow at the start by hearing from the conversation of two strangers that Andrew Devonshire was ill in bed with a high fever. He appeared for a very short while looking hectic and strange, and was then sent back to bed and visited by a doctor with a hypodermic. The great barrier of the house and all it stood for, the conventions and the Establishment, prevented Janetta going in the most natural and friendly way to visit him in his room. This is one of the things I loathe about conventions – that there are places where they sharply cut into warm, good, human feelings at their tenderest points. The party had been fixed for June in hopes of the pleasures of a summer night, but the rain lashed the great windows mercilessly. As all the Rembrandts, etc., are of priceless value every corridor had a 'watcher' in it. There was nowhere for the young to go and spoon, away from the eyes of the hordes of elderly female relations, great- aunts and grandmothers who were ranged round the walls, watching more keenly than the official watchers. The younger generation were kept in awe by the elders of their own kin.

June 29th: Timor mortis conturbat me

It has arisen from the depths of my unconscious like a bubble, and broken the surface with a hollow sound. I dreamed of some unexpected social occasion in which I was mixed up with Princess Margaret and the Duchess of Northumberland. Awoke and opened my *Times*, and my eye fell on a notice of the Duchess of Northumberland's funeral, adding that 'Princess Margaret was unable to be present.' What would Professor Dunne have thought? I merely thought that I must have previously read somewhere of the Duchess's death, and either wished to be dead too, or not to be.

July 3rd

Conan Doyle is really and finally *done*, and the last package sent off to Murray.

Living alone resembles living with someone else, in that one can have strange and different reactions to one's partner – one's Self. It can get on one's nerves; of course one can criticize it sharply. At the moment I'm doing all of these things. A loving mate sympathizes and encourages and tells one it's not too bad (and one is not too bad) really. Alone, I castigate myself unmercifully – for an impatient, arrogant, inconsiderate, bungling brute. And what good resolutions can be pulled out of the bog? Never to speak one's mind sharply,

139

always to be patient, think before one speaks, put up with things. How dull . . .

I want today to be a parenthesis – a long leisurely ————. I wonder if I shall achieve it. Literally having posted off the last dollops of Conan Doyle yesterday, I realize that it requires an enormous effort to be still, to relax; so at eleven-thirty here I am still in bed with the Sunday papers spread over the alps of my knees. Last night I was at Glyndebourne with Isobel, Anthony Blond[1] and his very pretty and quite intelligent friend Andrew. Anthony is an extraordinary mixture of tough crudity and good sense. You never know which side will be uppermost. Last night the good sense was. He really admires and appreciates Isobel (and how she blossomed under both their appreciation) yet I know he has sometimes been unkind to her over work. Black and white, a chequered man, whose saving grace is that he wants to be liked. Not to want which makes one appallingly uncivilized, but it's a rare thing, luckily.

The wound-up, never-say-die part of me is trying to read an article on President Johnson's attitude to the spread of nuclear arms and read it critically. Something else, the hedonist perhaps, wants to slip away and not attend. But on the whole I enjoy the thought of a quiet recouping day, with a human contact in the afternoon to stave off possible loneliness.

The satisfaction in trying to face some small bit of reality comes I suppose from the need to armour oneself against the horrors of life (knowledge is safety – the only real weapon of defence). Indeed the desire for knowledge may have its biological source in this same instinct for self-preservation, but seems to have become a craving on its own, with its own special gratification. And there is the converse anguish about the corners of dark reality that have not been faced. These I feel link up with childhood fears, peopling the corners of 28 Bedford Square with imagined monsters, which must surely have been the horrors one knew were waiting to spring out from the very stuff of life, as much a part of it as the thorns on a bramble. I'm sure that this facing and acceptance of reality and exploration of it in detail is an intense pleasure. Other people's feelings are a large part of reality, so that it leads to making contact and trying to sympathize and understand. It is, I suppose, Freud's 'reality principle' I'm groping after. I keep being reminded of my school-days. I see myself at the blackboard trying to construe a piece of Virgil or something,

[1] Publisher and friend of Burgo's.

140

and Mr Badley tapping his impatient sand-shoed foot and saying in a soft irritable voice, 'Get it right, Man! Get it right, Man!' I've been *trying* to 'get it right' ever since, but with long gaps of inertia and idleness.

I wonder what's happening to Julia. Would like to 'get her right'.

July 6th

Two mornings ago Julian rang up to tell me he had heard a rumour that Eddy Sackville had suddenly died. There had been a crackling on the line, and, unable to hear anything but the voice of bad news, my heart stood still for Janetta who had been flying to Gibraltar. So that when the truth got through and was confirmed, it was almost a relief. I have ever since felt increasing sadness – waste – loss – a hole in the world. This grizzly snatching by the hand of death of someone who (though always delicate) everybody believed would live till ninety like his father, someone of my generation, does bring it home how our ranks are thinning. Very grimly, one does ask who will be the next – it might well have been Boris, Leonard, Craig Macfarlane, even Raymond. Life suddenly seems a mere antechamber to the tomb, and I really feel at the moment I should live as if it were, though I know that isn't sensible. And the inescapable fact that the ranks will go on thinning steadily, hole after hole, till I leave them myself stares me bleakly in the face.

When Julian told me the news I could only clutch at the consolation that there would be no one total wreck of a person left behind. A great many people do mind dreadfully, though. I spoke to Desmond on the telephone – 'I shall miss him *terribly*,' he said in a broken voice. So will Raymond. Last night a woman who said she had met me in Ireland and whom I couldn't remember at all rang up and talked to me about him for ages; after first asking 'could I tell her anything about it?' she kept saying: 'He was *so* fond of *you*,' and I felt I should say the same to her but was deterred by not knowing the face I was speaking to. People have a curious desire to get together round the memory of a person who has died, and to insert themselves as far forward as possible in the ranks of the bereaved. How do people who believe in foreknowledge make it work out? Would they have translated their last meeting with Eddy in some peculiar way? I'm trying to remember when mine was and I think it was when he dined here and we went to a play about three months ago and we talked particularly happily and easily for hours after. And as

141

Desmond said, 'What will happen to Crichel?' – that delightful anachronism.

Gerald has written one of his tart missives about his letters to Carrington. He harps on his poverty, and says his plans for foreign travel depend on his being able to sell them. (He forgets they are legally my property and that he rejected my offer of them.) He and Gamel are coming to England on September 1st and he will then, he says, ship them to America, typed or not. Well, I must fuss round and get someone else beside Georgia to type them.

I rang up Frances Phipps just now. She's going to Eddy's funeral, most gallantly because otherwise she'd feel 'that she hadn't said goodbye to him'. 'Eddy's form of Catholicism made him believe in heaven – so I hope he's in it!' she said with her delightful laugh.

July 8th

I was afraid my outlook was becoming threadbare and suddenly yesterday evening events crowded in on me. A visit from Eardley, looking lean, brown and handsome, just back from France and on his way to Eddy's funeral. I saw no great signs of grief or regret in him. He seemed indeed alight with some inner jubilation, probably because Mattei has been ill, and when he found a message of 'Grande Urgence' awaiting him in Paris, for two hours he 'thought it was Mattei'. Relief, perhaps. While he was here Georgia rang up – in a tragic voice: 'I'm so worried about Julian.'[1] I tried to reassure her, indeed felt there was no need to be anxious but it seems I was wrong; the poor dear little chap has collapsed somewhat, is seeing his doctor, lying in bed with drugs and giving up his ticket for *Tosca* tonight to me. Georgia has been with me also most of this morning, hinting at grave 'anxieties' of her own, but not quite wanting to tell me what they were; we also have the matter of Gerald's letters to Carrington to discuss. It's clear she won't ever get them done and Gerald is beginning to tap his foot with impatience . . . I've just been reading some, and goodness, how good they are – just as good as I thought, I'm pleased to find. Another call: Julia. I think what struck me most was her phenomenal egotism. She spoke as if where and how she'd been all these weeks was the sole subject anyone (certainly I) could be interested in. Vietnam, Eddy's death, didn't exist for her. When I mentioned the latter she said perfunctorily, 'Oh yes, too terrible. Who shall I write to, I wonder?'

[1] Eddy had been a great friend of his.

142

The evening ended on a rather disagreeable note. I had been quite looking forward to dinner with Maude Russell and Boris. There was only one other guest, a rather smooth man called John Malet. Suddenly – or gradually – I became aware of the self-satisfied line-up of the rich, however civilized, against all that I think of value. The unsympathetic generalizations came thumping out of them one by one. How awful it was that we were trying to be nice to the Germans. They were bad through and through, never had been anything else. ('Mozart, Beethoven, Brahms, Einstein?' I murmured.) The Treaty of Versailles had been far too lenient. (F: 'Then you think one shouldn't try and forget or forgive?' 'No, no, *never*.') I said my piece about it being easy enough to put up with and understand those one liked and sympathized with, the important thing was – if one didn't want wars – to try and understand and put up with those one didn't. 'Oh, we none of us want *wars*!' they cried. (But they are going the way to produce one without fail.) I even extracted from Mr Malet a comment that I was 'of course right'. But he was 'afraid I had illusions about anyone seeing reason of that sort'. 'No, I have no illusions. I'm deeply pessimistic,' I said, 'and believe we'll all go up in smoke within the next few decades.' But international affairs weren't the whole of it – the Labour Party were of course 'farcical figures of fun'. The young were all 'dirty' because their hair was long, their music and dancing 'quite hideous'. Everyone should have had 'their bums whacked' – this was Boris – when young, and perhaps then they would have learned something useful. Old age and ill health have had a cruel effect on Boris; he looked really angry and ferocious when he was uttering these menacing views – a fierce old Slav with burning eyes and a curiously white upper lip. We stayed quite late and I said – insincerely – how much I'd enjoyed myself.

July 15th

Julia to dinner, looking young and pretty in black spectacles. She put some distance between herself and Lawrence and Jenny, and admitted that she half wanted to stop thinking of them altogether. A good and healthy symptom. Also she is going out into the world more, and accepting and enjoying invitations.

Some pleasant things have happened – an invitation from the Lennox Berkeleys; a visit from Jonathan Cecil[1] to ask advice about

---

[1] Actor, elder son of David and Rachel.

going to Spain for a holiday. He took me out to lunch, and his friendly sweetness and spontaneous kiss on parting touched me greatly. In the London Library yesterday (how I love the particular smell of the dusty books) I ran into Mary Clive[1] and Robert Kee at one and the same time, and it was a delightful and characteristic collision of two unique heavenly bodies. It looks as though I would actually go to Russia in six weeks' time, amazing thought! A very nice fat intellectual American woman on the bus engaged me in conversation of a reassuring sort. Murrays have asked me to read a book on Madame du Barry by an old lady of ninety – to prepare myself I did some homework on her yesterday and found the subject absorbing. The personal side of history is easier reading than fiction – but when I got to the French Revolution my nightmare feelings about it got the better of me. They date from my childhood and I picture the scenes with all too much vividness. The above scrap-bag paragraph represents pretty accurately my scrap-bag existence. I would welcome a long trail of thought, research, connected occupations.

July 16th

Frances Phipps to lunch. We had rather a mortuary conversation about Eddy's funeral, to which she had been. For some time I have had a sneaking feeling that she was trying to make me see the religious light. She is a born proselytizer, and I suppose that it was foolish of me to think I could sometimes question her about her faith because we are such great friends and because she seems to hold it in such unorthodox form. I have made no bones whatever about my own disbelief, nor have I been in the least tempted to be aggressive about it. She is lavish in her protestations of friendship and often says that I'm 'the only person who understands' her feelings about peace and war, left-wing politics, etc. But then – in the way thought and feeling are translated into physical signs – I've learned to recognize the occasional proselytizing mood in her lowering her head, fixing me with melancholy and mesmeric blue eyes; her voice subdued to a chanting drone. She described the suitableness of Eddy's last resting place, the green village churchyard, the reactions of various people, Paul Hyslop's[2] unbridled tears and other friends' disapproval of him,

[1] née Pakenham.
[2] Architect, old friend of Raymond.

144

the earth thudding on the coffin, the genuine sorrow of some of the people who worked for Eddy. Well and good, and I was moved and interested. Then she told me details of the actual seizure that killed him, how he had come gasping into the bedroom of a priest who was staying with him, then shut himself in the lavatory, locked the door and was found there dead. There followed a gossipy anecdote about the friends in Ireland deciding it 'was better to say he died listening to music'.

All this interest in the manner of death and the disposal of the remains I find utterly antipathetic, and I became inarticulate in my attempts to express to her that I felt the moment of death final, and that any attempt to extend one's love to the corpse and its trappings was worse than a mockery. That should be reserved for memories of the person – the only things that endure. At the end of our conversation the real kernel of her discourse was laid on the table – Raymond, she felt, '*should* have come to the funeral', he should have turned back and 'seen the last of Eddy'. I at once realized I too was being condemned. I defended Raymond of course (including myself mentally in the defence); but she is I think incapable of understanding the rationalist's attitude. No one expects her to share it, but I hoped she accepted my irreligion just as I accept her religion. When I tried to close the subject of immortality by saying that I had no desire for it whatever and the thought was quite appalling to me, she attempted to convince me that it could be both desirable and thinkable. She again said how frustrated she was by the fact that she couldn't get on more intimate terms with Raymond – but alas, I know he finds her irrationality upsetting.

The injustice of her attitude to Raymond and Eddy's funeral was underlined by a call from him, now back in England, sounding terribly broken-hearted. He said my letter had 'reduced him to tears' and he comes to dinner on Monday. I was much moved by the desolation in his voice and his wanting to come and see me. Whatever I wrote him was from a better motive (sympathy) than my letter to Frances – self-justification inspired that, and I already regret it.

July 18th: Doddington Hall, Lincolnshire, Sunday morning, 8.15 a.m.

Rather glad to have woken a little early and be able to compose myself to my surroundings. We arrived on the evening train on

Friday – Ralph Jarvis,[1] Caroline[2] and I and the chief guest, Steven Runciman, whom everyone is anxious to please and propitiate. I took to him very much, and enjoyed his anecdotes and his way of pulling down his upper lip like a stage Irishman and staring fixedly at one with a 'What do you think of *that*?' expression after making a *bon mot*. Other guests – who should they be but 'delightful Peter Hesketh' whom Julia marked down years and years ago as a possible husband, now matched with an elderly-looking wife. I wonder what Julia would think of 'delightful Peter' now. He's an architectural expert and for many long hours yesterday – six about – we all racketed around looking at houses all over the flat plate of the Lincolnshire countryside. I enjoyed visiting Grimsthorpe, built by Vanbrugh and inhabited by the Ancasters, parents of Jane Willoughby. Lady Ancaster showed us round – there was something raffish and feline about her which appealed to me; slight form, darting movements; precious emeralds and pearls round her neck and an emerald brooch clasped on the top of her straight, brown hair. The only son and heir disappeared off the Costa del Sol about a year ago, was presumed drowned, and obviously was. He seems to have been a charming bad lot, drug-taker and heavy drinker. His parents and Jane are still heart-broken, and I was touched by Lady Ancaster's method of distracting her mind – 'occupational therapy' as she called it – painting in the sow thistle and other weeds in her Bentham and Hooker. Then 'delightful Peter' insisted on taking us to look at one of his old homes now an open prison, gloomy, derelict and charmless, and kept up a running commentary of 'There used to be a wood here. My father planted this avenue. There used to be five gates on this road.' Steven Runciman looked round and muttered to me, 'I'm not impressed.' The general conversation in the car was all about properties, inheritances and ancestry. The extraordinary smugness of tone – 'Who was *she*?' 'Oh yes, that belonged to old Lord Liverpool.' 'Oh, was *he* the one with the wooden leg?' 'Yes, did you know him?' 'Why, very WELL INDEED!' 'Oh, really?' The snobbishness, the slow self-confident drawl in which all these exchanges were made – and they were pursued to incredible lengths – gradually sickened me.

I like all three Jarvises and Steven Runciman, and they have

---

[1] Owner of the house, a music-loving banker.
[2] His daughter, afterwards Lady Cranbrook.

interesting things to talk about. They were not responsible for such politely civilized competition in which everyone tries to show that he has the entrée to more different worlds, calls more noblemen by their christian names, and has more expert information than anyone else. Boasting, not communication, is the petrol firing these engines of talk. Ideas, where are they?

Altogether, though I spent a peaceful morning among the roses in the sun, reading my old lady about the du Barry, there was too much of the afternoon's excursion. What is one at? I think of machines in fairs – there was one called the Allwyn de Luxe, into which you popped your penny and a silver ball appeared at the top, hurtled from obstacle to obstacle, not stopping for a moment and then sank at last into oblivion at the bottom. I'm that ball.

At the moment I long for a quiet stretch – an Orta episode. But like thunderclouds in the sky, quite a lot of 'things to do' between now and Christmas are collecting.

The sky out of my mullioned window is an ashy greyish white. I can hear Ralph playing one of his three pianos. My room is handsome if a bit gloomy, high and ill-lit with a huge four-poster, its curtains heavily embroidered with russet-coloured wool flowers. Ah, it has begun to rain.

July 19th

In the end we drove home, five strong, in 'delightful Peter's' car, arriving 1 a.m. Not one whit deterred by the long drive, he made a detour at this hour to show us the modern block of flats *replacing* the house 'where we used to live'! Christ! the boredom of it, it's a monomania, a *folie de grandeur* entirely unrecognized by the possessor. This morning I feel white and drained with exhaustion, hardly able to face the week that lies ahead.

July 20th

I'm horrified by the way the loss of a loved and lovable human being is quickly translated and degraded into material terms, and I can't help connecting this with this preoccupation with tombs, services, and all the rest. Wills inevitably come next. I cling to the recollection of Eddy as a unique and lovable person, and hate to see his figure distintegrating, as a tower crumbles when blown-up by dynamite on the cinema, and turning into *things*, properties, material obligations.

Yesterday Eardley came to see me and we walked round and round Belgrave Square. Afterwards Raymond came to dinner. Eardley gave a very different account from Frances's of the funeral – not an unfeeling one, though I don't think he greatly loved nor misses Eddy. The rigmarole and mumbo-jumbo had appalled him, and seemed a dreadful mockery. He described vividly the one moment that had been 'touching and beautiful' – when two strong men with long shining spades had started shovelling earth on the coffin with heavy thuds. But both he and Raymond were preoccupied with bequests and lawyers. Eddy left all his pictures (worth thousands of pounds) to Eardley, all his books to Raymond, and his records to Desmond (neither of whom want any more), his house in Ireland to his heir's eldest daughter. Raymond is obviously 'cut up' as the saying goes, and mentioned Eddy's death almost with tears, describing himself as 'numbed', as feeling as if 'half his brain had been shot away'; 'Eddy had a much better memory than I have,' he said, 'and he knew far more about my past than I do myself.' Eddy had been much his oldest friend. He looked shrunken, pitiful, crushed. 'I was so sure he would outlive me. I don't feel I shall live much longer.'

Eardley had told me he didn't want to go on with Crichel and couldn't possibly afford it. I thought probably Raymond might hope that it could be prolonged in some new form. But no. No question of their being able to afford it. Yet he hates the thought of the sorting, moving, selling, and doesn't relish the idea of living in Canonbury altogether. And then – in plaintive tones – he said that Eddy had promised 'to look after him in his old age if he got too tired and ill to work', but he has made no provision for this. Poor Raymond, he feels bereft and just when he most needs security, insecure. And yet, and yet – the material considerations did seem to me to oust the human and psychological and emotional ones a shade too quickly, and I feel the closing of the happy, brilliant, charming Crichel episode sorely.

July 22nd

Dinner at the Lennox Berkeleys'. I went off in an apprehensive mood, passionately wishing I had someone to go with. Pushing my way through dense hedges of dripping hollyhocks I was in a moment in the drawing-room being introduced to two men – I nearly laughed aloud when each in turn said, 'We've met before – at Maude Russell's,' and they were *two* 'smooth men' I'd had as fellow guests on *two* separate occasions and felt alien to. We were eight in all. I attended violently to my companions. Freda Berkeley is handsome, good-natured and friendly. The person I found it was least easy to talk to was Lennox Berkeley himself. I've met him only a few times and always greatly liked him, and felt a sweet and sensitive character to be looking out of his small, intelligent squirrel's face.

The best part of the evening was provided by several couples in turn sitting at the piano and playing Schubert duets with immense brio, their heads nodding and their whole bodies responding to the music.

July 25th: Litton Cheney (chez Reynolds and Janet Stone)

A bad night in my small bedroom slung high among the beautiful trees: my sleeplessness had nothing to do with my surroundings, which are peaceful and remote, with every comfort. I just am damned bad at the art of sleeping – how I wish it was one of the things I've always been able to do, like crossword puzzles. My only book was an unsuitable one – the second volume of Painter's *Life of Proust*. It is at once too thought-provoking and too finicky. I wonder – is it valuable and illuminating to shred the fine texture of a great work of art and take each thread back to its source or sources? Not an image or remark, much less a character has escaped this patient, loving analysis; in the end I became almost exasperated. It's like laying out the corpse of a beautiful woman and saying, 'You see what an exquisitely turned tibia she had,' or 'Her little fingers were like her mother's.' Would one want to trace all the reminiscences in a work of music, or know exactly what paints Sisley used in small blobs to create an iridescent effect? It is unnatural it seems to me to try and undo the act of artistic creation and put it into reverse. One looks up Elstir in the Index and finds five or six sources in human shape. Yet the true biographer's art of bringing the writer to life seems to me to have eluded Painter, and Proust remains a ghost walking through a dead landscape of disintegrated references.

July 29th

Julian has just been to lunch bringing his brother who is one of the teaching Fathers at Downside – fresh-faced, bright-eyed, loud-laughing, full of vitality, and quick-witted. Was he perhaps a shade too aggressively some of these, as much as to say, 'You see, one can still be a human being although one has renounced the world'? In spite of his intelligence and responsiveness and readiness to make jokes about his calling, or listen to Julian's talk about 'sodomy and stealing in the school', I was aware that deep inside his fresh outgoing personality was a wooden wall, against which one occasionally butted one's head with a dull percussion. All those who have battened down the hatches of faith give this effect of being shut away; it makes them into pretty cold fish. I felt this a little about Anthony Jebb even though he said, with truth I'm sure, that he liked all his boys. He told us how he had often had to break the news of a parent's death, once recently of both parents in a car smash, and how little they minded it. In this his imagination I'm quite sure failed him. Then there was a most revealing story about how he'd succeeded in making the only boy he nearly didn't like, and who didn't like him, run in the half-mile race. The boy hadn't wanted to and had tried to get medical exemption but Anthony had pitted his will against him and insisted; and here something terrifying came out – it was for the *system*, not the boy, he did it; it was also for himself – *he* would be disgraced if he couldn't put in a candidate from *his* house for the half-mile. I was so completely on the boy's side (and I think Julian was too) that I was sorry to hear that, after finally being persuaded to run, he had started by just ambling round the course, but suddenly began running in earnest and came in second. What Anthony failed to see was that the boy had won a victory over himself and this was the only thing that saved his own action from being bullying and perhaps harmful. It was not his victory, but the boy's.

August 3rd

I drove Henrietta and Sophie to Hilton for the weekend. All four glorious girls[1] were there. Fanny has as much character and intelligence as Nerissa, though in a slightly different way. She has taken to music like a duck to water, or like Nerissa to painting, and

---

[1] Daughters of Bunny and Angelica – Amaryllis, Henrietta and the twins: Fanny and Nerissa.

plays with fiery zeal on flute or horn. We had a lot of music. There were fascinating arguments – one about killing animals. 'The desire to kill *waxes* or *wanes*,' said Nerissa leaning forward with blazing eyes, 'but it's absolutely *basic*.' Amaryllis is in a way the least original of the four, though sweet and charming; the faint affectation all professional actresses develop veils her. Henrietta is the warmest and the most full of human instincts. All four girls slept and slept as if they could never have enough sleep and make up their arrears, which I'm sure was true. Angelica cooked marvellous puddings and pies and looked exhausted and anxious, and no wonder. Sophie trotted or staggered about with cries of 'Hal-LO!' or 'Funny!' or 'Oh dear, *dear*!' or more often streams of gibberish. Dear little girl, I find her almost more touching than I can bear. She adores Henrietta and if unable to obtain her entire attention flings herself on the ground in a passion of abandoned despair. Henrietta runs up to her with warm and all-enveloping gestures – I think she's very good with her. But of course someone is needed to take the burden off her. Duncan came on Saturday, so we were an enormous party.

August 8th: Cranborne

The first taste of real summer arrived unexpectedly yesterday. I sat out sweltering away deliciously on the lawn trying to do exercises in Russian, and later walked with David Cecil to the Manor to get a potted cyclamen. Welcome stillness and deep shadow enveloped the beautiful house and garden, with draperies of clematis and late roses covering the old walls.

The ineffably pretty Molly Cranborne[1] was digging among her irises in a baize apron, one of her boys circling on a bicycle, a little girl with a high domed Cecilian forehead ran out of the house.

Francis Wyndham came yesterday – a little piano on arrival, he has now revived and shows all his excellent judgement, and talks delightfully in his curious faintly cockney voice. Laura and Hugh are here also. There are two new Portuguese servants to whom Rachel is heard shouting loudly in pidgin English in the kitchen.

After lunch I took a rug on the lawn and lay in the sun with my head under the speckled shade of a small tree, reading Françoise Gilot on Picasso. Oh, blessed horizontality! I heard a loud hammering noise, transmitted by telegraphy along the flat surface of the lawn,

---

[1] Wife of David's nephew, later Lady Salisbury.

and saw a distant bird tapping its beak and listening. It whisked me back, as did the soothing position I was lying in, to the old days at Ham Spray.

Dickie Buckle, writer on the ballet, came for a drink, a fresh-faced, sailorly man, with a healthy interest in everything. He told us about a visit from Nureyev, 'a very spoilt young man'. He arrived by car at Buckle's cottage, said first, 'It's a *very* long way,' and then (looking round), 'I thought you would have big estates.' Buckle told him he was taking him to see an old lady 'who used to know Diaghilev and Nijinsky'. 'OH, I'm so tired of people who knew Diaghilev and Nijinsky!' But Juliet Duff talked to Nureyev in fluent Russian and completely won him over.

The weekend talk has touched often and stimulatingly on ideas and generalities; but has kept away – by pure chance I think – from moral or political issues. Last night the subject of aesthetes and dilettantes came up. Why were these now terms of abuse? Would one rather be called one of these or 'an intellectual'? Francis Wyndham preferred 'an intellectual' as 'more honourable'. David said he would hate that, envisaging pipe-smoking, hairy, humourless dons at red-brick universities (rather conventionally, I thought), and liked to be thought of as a dilettante. I don't think he *is* one. 'A roomful of dilettantes' Francis thought was 'not the sort of room one would like to be in'.

August 9th

To drinks at the Manor yesterday. Arriving, we saw clean through the lovely house up the sloping French-looking avenue at the back, where the company was assembled. Molly Cranborne wearing an enormous hat; various children; an immensely tall, aged and distinguished aunt, with her wrinkled parchment face, heavy body, low, royal bosom encased in spotted lavender silk, and spindle-thin legs; a retired general and his wife. Gentle, aimless conversation for half an hour in exceptionally beautiful and elegant surroundings; the whole scene seemed to have come out of a Henry James story. Someone was evidently deaf, for there was always someone else shouting.

A walk in the afternoon along green paths winding through a magic wood. Talk about books, Hardy, Scott, various moderns; the aggressive disagreeableness of successful women.

August 10th: West Halkin Street

I feel myself reduced and quaking within the four-square pressure of the external world. Difficulties over the Russian trip; difficulties over Conan Doyle (Adrian Conan Doyle now wants everything put in that was formerly cut out and I was closeted with Jock Murray yesterday over this), difficulties over Gerald's letters which are due back from the typist today but I can't get any answer from her on the telephone.

Georgia has been here, bringing Gerald's typescript. The other typists have maddeningly failed to produce their lot up to time and this afternoon Miss Hamill[1] is coming to carry off the letters. I have been out to battle with shopping and other mechanical tasks, and as usual I feel rather better in consequence.

August 11th

Given a long stretch of time virtually to myself, the possible area of things to think about is boundless, a vast gromboolian plain where (in theory) it is possible to take any direction one fancies. The result of course is that one is lucky to have a single thought. Here I am in the Euston–Windermere train on my way to stay with Tom and Nadine: solitude in a crowd, for every seat is taken. A strong smell of boy comes from a carriage full of campers. It is hot. I've already eaten some stodgy sandwiches in the 'Buffy' car, and done an exercise in Russian. Just now a railway official, gorgeous in gold braid, draped himself round the door of our carriage and asked each of us in turn, 'Where you for, love?' in the most stylish way imaginable. In contrast, the passengers refer to each other as 'the gentleman in that seat'. Like the realms of possible thought, the world of visual sensation is laid out through the carriage window, far and wide, as if specially for my possessing, and I have really felt that I stretched out and took for instance a small secret green pond, quite round and encircled by elms, or a huge bright pink sow lying in a field with her piglets round her.

[1] Chicago dealer in books and manuscripts.

August 13th: Skelwith Fold, Cumberland

I stepped out of my train into sweetness and softness comparable to Litton Cheney's, but spread with something sharper and more poignant. Poetical? Yes, and so was Dorset, but this is different and with a more heart-rending flavour. Nadine's mother, Dolly Hambourg,[1] is here, and at first I thought this was going to be a saddening and confusing ingredient. She must be at least eighty and presents me with my own future in spectral form. But she is a really delightful person, with a very individual saltiness, and her head still mercifully screwed right on. Tall, bent and bandy, with almost blind but rather fine pale blue eyes, snow-white hair netted round a pink scalp; fingers ending in vaguely reddened nails; a harsh pink line where the make-up has not reached her hair-line. Every evening she puts on a *décolleté* and sleeveless black short evening-dress from which her arms dangle with a species of elegance. There's nothing informal ever about her rig, so that I feel my bare legs and trousers to be almost a rudeness. The weather is divine, sunny and warm until evening. Yesterday Tom, Nadine and I walked up a small hill in the intense smell of hot bracken.

August 14th

All yesterday we were soused in sun and natural beauty – today a lid of grey had closed down on us. I grow to like and admire Nadine's mother more and more. She has made her retreat into age dignified and not at all supernatural. Dolly Hambourg is absolutely all there, her personality and critical faculty and dry humour intact.

We took a picnic yesterday to Loughrigg Tarn, and from where we sat on a grassy slope backed by high grey rocks we looked across the lake to a beautiful recently cut field, pale and shining with a gloss like that of short plush, a few perfectly placed fine trees, and in the distance the hazy silhouette of Langdale Pikes. One side of the lake was full of water-lilies, white and yellow, and long waving rushes. A promontory with one tree, one cow and a bright blue boat on it was the place we chose for our bathe. The water closed over us, brown and flat and relaxing. I was loth to get out and went on contentedly flapping about among the water-lilies.

---

[1] Widow of Mark Hambourg, concert pianist.

August 16th

Now there are only two days more here. The silent mist reminds me of the artificial smoke Zeffirelli pours over the stage at Covent Garden; it seeps everywhere and descends suddenly and claustrophobically just when it seems to be lifting. Yesterday Tom, Nadine and I walked up a small hill over cropped turf, through bracken fronds, rocks shining with water and tiny streams edged with strips of yellow and white flowers, flowing down the hillside with a steady trickling sound. Why should this noise delight one so, when it is remarkably like that of someone pissing into a chamber-pot?

August 18th

In my London-bound train. A sweet little nun sat opposite me. She had been visiting her father at Grasmere, liked talking about the mountains and a falcon's nest she had found on top of the 'Lion and Lamb'. I looked at her strong sensitive hands knitting a dark green garment and the gold ring of her marriage with Jesus on her right hand. What shall I find in London, I wonder?

August 19th

What I found was a tremendous lot to do, not the empty stagnation I expected. The contrast between the north country quiet and this hectic, ceaseless buzz is startling.

Various changes have appeared in my future landscape. The visit to Russia now seems probable; Gerald and Gamel arrive in London early tomorrow morning. Henrietta comes to see me tomorrow. Gerald wrote me a long and rather touching letter under the influence of reading all Carrington's to him. 'When I think now of how she loved me and of how little I deserved her love and of how badly I often behaved I feel ashamed.' He goes on to his marriage to Gamel. 'I was never attracted to the middle-class girls one met in the Thirties, because there was always a "lady" hidden in them. I cannot bear the "lady" in any woman, and this is the side of Gamel – growing today – I don't like, even though it is only on the surface.' I have been reading his letters to Carrington with great admiration, interest, occasional boredom, and a sudden snort of laughter as when he describes a Moorish café: 'The tables are full of soldiers

155

playing dominoes, the ground is muddy, the walks wet and sticky, and a baby creeps about in the mud, showing its red, cloven bottom to whoever looks at it.'

Carrington has come to the fore in my life also in that Richard Garnett brought me today the proofs of Noel's edition of Mark Gertler's letters to her and others. I am to correct the notes and make an index for them. There is a strange link-up between the two lots of letters, as it seems Valentine Dobrée had some sort of affair with Gertler and that both were involved in the indiscretion about Gerald and Carrington which finally led to the 'Great Row'.[1] Well, I shall take the proofs down to Crichel for the weekend and brood over them there.

August 21st

Gerald and Gamel suddenly arrived in London yesterday morning and I got them to come to dinner. Neither of them at first sight seemed in the slightest degree ruffled by having travelled all night and having taken rooms in a noisy, unsympathetic hotel. Gerald rang me up in the morning. 'HULLO, Gerald,' I cried. 'Welcome to London!' There was as usual a very long pause and then: 'Gerald speaking,' slow and weighty. How pleased I was to see them! Having been deep in Gerald's forty-year-old letters it was extraordinary to be made aware of the continuance of his essential characteristics. Imagination but no judgement; or rather, those judgements he makes are rooted in emotion. During dinner he began saying how *boring* Shakespeare was. His plays were completely undramatic, no one could sit through *Hamlet*, he preferred Pinter or *Who's afraid of Virginia Woolf?* – they at least were 'contemporary'. I found myself aflame with anger all at once, and attacking him just as he wanted me to, and as I know Ralph would have done, though throughout the previous two hours of being with him (as indeed all the evening) I had felt the warmest affection and delight in his company. Gamel was her usual self. The more she drank the more she tossed off remarks like, 'Don't be funny, Gerald!' and 'You know it's nothing of the kind,' and references to 'I happened to be re-reading Montaigne the other day,' and I was amused when she (the idlest of women) said she couldn't

[1] This was the name given at Ham Spray to the highly charged explosion between Ralph and Gerald as a result of the revelation of a secret relation between Carrington and Gerald. See Holroyd's *Life of Lytton Strachey*, etc.

imagine how anyone could get along without work. Georgia came in briefly after dinner, filling my room with a radiant glow, as had Henrietta earlier in the day. What pleasure both these girls gave me. Henrietta looked perfectly lovely in a very pale pink linen blouse and less heavy make-up than usual, bringing out her delicate skin and lovely dark grey eyes. Georgia had been down to stay with her and Duncan at Charleston and I could feel in them both how the influence of that extraordinary and ever-fresh civilization had pulled against the superficial glamour of the dashing young people who live for their own beauty, sex-appeal and clothes and keep themselves in a state of hectic stimulation with drinks and drugs. I mean of course the young men laden with jewels, the long-haired, lace-shirted dandies of the Ormsby-Gore party, whom Francis Wyndham defended so hotly at Cranborne. I found myself doing the same at Maude Russell's dinner. Yet, yet, yet – I can't go all the way with their empty thoughtlessness, and the prig in my nature resents their lack of seriousness. The curious thing was that contact with Charleston and the country should have produced a rather similar reaction in both Georgia and Henrietta.

Jonny and Sabrina [Gathorne-Hardy] have had a daughter. Henrietta describes Jonny's wild excitement, and told me that when she was making him some supper in his flat and Sabrina rang up he went down on one knee to the telephone. I sent her a large bunch of flowers, and was flattered (seeing that I hardly knew her) to hear that Sabrina had said to Jonny, 'I don't want to see anyone beside you and the baby – not even darling Frances.'

This morning before catching my train to Crichel it was all I could do to sort out the tangles of my various commitments. I must turn my thoughts to Crichel and its problems. Kitty told me on the telephone that Desmond is still desperate to keep Crichel going and that they wanted to ask me to join them.

August 24th: Crichel

I was not prepared for the dramatic tension in this house – it has filled the time and everybody's thoughts. Here I found Eardley and Desmond, and Jack Rathbone[1] – not an easy companion in spite of his warm-heartedness and sometimes surprising good sense, nor even in spite of the fact that he knows his own failings well and

[1] Old friend of Desmond's, sharing their London house.

referred to them at dinner one day ('I'm so gushing'). Did he also say he laid on the flattery too thick and was over-familiar? I'm not sure, but he does both, I suppose from a desperate longing to be liked. I'd hardly met him, so was surprised to be clasped to his heart and kissed on both cheeks, with 'Are you WELL?' I can't help suspecting he has in a way enjoyed his role as Confidant in this Racine play, though I'm sure he wants to help everyone. Anyway, he spent his time taking each of us aside or for walks and thrashing the situation out. My turn came briefly yesterday afternoon. But it was to Desmond, who longs to go on living at Crichel and catches at any straw to make it possible, that my heart chiefly went out this weekend. On Sunday morning I took my Gertler letters outside in the sun, but Desmond soon came and sat beside me, to ask me if there was any chance I would make one of the Crichel ménage. I was so moved by his distress that I had to make an effort not to say, 'Well, perhaps I might.' Of course I know it would never do. I simply couldn't take on the strain of living with three other people, none of them Ralph and one of them (oddly enough) Raymond, for, fond as I am of him, our views of life have diverged and we are both of us inclined to be categorical. Jack thinks that Desmond's family history gives the clue to his present agitation. His father was murdered in Ireland, his mother went mad, his sister was killed by a fall from a horse. He never had any family or home to speak of and Crichel represents this to him.

Eardley is all right. He wanted to leave Crichel even before Eddy died and he is perfectly tough about still doing so. In my private talk with him on Saturday after dinner, while Confidant Jack was having one with Desmond next door, he said to me, 'To be honest, Eddy died for me ten years ago.' He was being honest and this I should have admired and been gratified by. But there seemed something rather cold-hearted in having been able to withdraw his affection from someone he declares he really used to be deeply fond of and who still retained his originality and charm.

Until Raymond arrived back from Mottisfont today I wasn't sure about him. He has picked up a lot since Eddy's death, and seemed self-confident and much less than his seventy years. Had he thought of giving up Canonbury and living entirely here, I asked him. 'I have thought of it, of course. If you and Eardley, or Dadie were to be here, I might; but I'm only prepared to live with old chums.' Then he started attacking Desmond on various scores – always being in a fuss, always late for everything, but furious if anyone else was late.

My part in the Racine drama was confined to listening, and

suggesting (in contradiction to Jack's advice) that a few months should be allowed for Desmond to calm down, go for a holiday, and face his future.

All of them made a great fuss of me, more than usual, and I am feeling well stroked and purring as I head back to London. And in spite of what may seem to be cool criticism, I love them one and all.

August 27th, 7 a.m.

Grey, horrible, cold weather, wet roofs. I have been working all out, unable to stop, much too wound-up and tense, alone a good deal of every day but far from empty-plated. Yesterday Noel [Carrington] came to lunch and we went through various Gertler difficulties. I realize that while I felt I have 'given him' all the letters to Carrington, *he* thought they were legally his 'as next of kin'. The main complication here is that if I was wrong in thinking that all her possessions went to Ralph and thence to me, I had no right to give Gerald *his* letters, which have gone off to America to be sold. The copyright in Carrington's own letters is also in question. It's rather an interesting Trollopian situation. When I sorted out all those trunks at Ham Spray it never entered my head that everything in the house was not mine. Noel has been equally assuming that both letters and copyright are his. Over lunch we agreed this should be straightened out by an expert and this is going to be done. After Noel had gone I went on working steadily till 8 p.m. – perfectly mad. Listened to Stephen Bishop playing the Emperor Concerto and went to bed early with my head buzzing with words, tunes and more words.

I've finished reading Gerald's letters to Carrington. His astonishing lack of judgement comes out over and again. Meeting Lionel at Alec's[1] house he says he seems 'Nice but very stupid. Though science seems to be his business he knows much less than I do.' The truth on its head and several times multiplied.

Yesterday morning I suddenly began to fret and fume over the lack of news about Russia. Rang up the Wayfarers' Travel; I should of course have done it long ago. All is now settled, Kitty and I fly at early dawn on September 8th with the rest of the party who are not going by sea, and do our extra four days at the end of the visit. Everyone is pleased. I've rung up Kitty and it's a great relief to have it settled.

---

[1] Eldest of the Penrose brothers.

As far as the MacCabes are concerned[1] I'm still convinced Charlie won't come and doubtful about Mary. I got a mysterious message from Stokke to say there had been a slight mishap – Mary had lost her passport. And her Russian visa of course! I guess that she's getting out of coming.

August 30th

Neither Charlie nor Mary come to Russia. The passport loss was genuine and strange, but it's not the whole explanation. Charlie says they 'can't afford it and after all, she's now had her fun pipe-dreaming about Russia'.

It is Bank Holiday Monday and I have come back to London after one night and day of chewing the cud of rusticity with Noel and Catharine. On Saturday night Gerald came to dinner with me; we were alone together for four hours and at the end of it I felt thoroughly battered by his egocentricity. 'I've been talking about myself all the time, as usual,' he said rather ruefully. It's not exactly selfishness; it's merely that he isn't in the least interested in any other subject. I occasionally tried to say something – not about myself, heaven knows, but about some other topic. At once his eyes glazed over with boredom. The most *dis*interested emotion he voiced was appreciation of Georgia. We talked a lot about the past – Carrington, Watendlath, the 'Great Row'. Of *course* I believe what Ralph told me absolutely, rather than anything that Gerald says, but my memory is alas unreliable, and the most inscrutable part is the Valentine Dobrée episode. I found a letter from her to Ralph, inchoate and emotional, utterly uncontrolled. I wanted to read it aloud, but Gerald wasn't interested – it was too remote from himself. He is quite indifferent to Hetty[2] now – she was a masturbatory object to him, indeed I think all his sexual activity has been in the nature of masturbation, and it's that that shocks me about it. His latest adventure is with little Teresita, the mere child who works in the house. He thinks she may be sixteen now but isn't sure. He sat on my sofa under the light which shone mercilessly down on his bald head – where a curious long lump like a prehistoric barrow has appeared – describing how he kissed her and put his hand down the front of her dress and gave her presents and she came to say goodnight to him

[1] Charlie and Mary had suggested coming to Russia too.
[2] His latest girlfriend.

160

when he was in bed, and one day he hoped to get her into bed with him – of course he wouldn't '*do anything*' to her. He tells everyone this and I wonder what feelings it arouses in others – whether, as in me, a sort of disgust at the thought of an old man of seventy lecherously pawing a young girl. And there's 'nothing physical' in it, of course!

I do enjoy Gerald's company, but my God, it's exhausting.

August 31st

I have just been to Russell Square to collect tickets and vouchers for the Russian tour. So it seems I am a registered item in this strange parcel. Looking up from my seat in the bus at the grey clouds driving through the blue sky, I thought what a long way away Moscow seemed. Well, calm, calm, I said to myself. And nothing to lose.

My work has more or less closed down. The last obsequies of Conan Doyle are done up in a parcel for John Murray. My brain seethes ineffectively with the Russian I have been struggling to stuff into it. I quail and thrill alternately at the thought of the rapidly approaching unknown. I spent most of yesterday going to Kew with Gerald. His love for plants is one of his most endearing qualities and he was a perfect companion able to enjoy the signs of race in some exotic face (a tropical shrub bearing unmistakeable affinity to a milkwort) as well as their purely visual aspects. As usual the water-lily houses were the most stunning – water-lilies blue, pink and white rose from the steaming water, while all around them were spires of red and blue, or hanging swags of coppery green, strange cucumber-like fruit and purple trumpets. In another house we saw the great waxen leaves of the Victoria Regina with its stiffly curled-up edges veined with red, and a flower like an untidy pink hearth brush, and noticed the taste shown in letting a different small green water-plant fill in every available cranny of the water's surface between the monster leaves. Climbing a white metal spiral stair, we looked from a height on the palms trying to break their way out of the crystal-palace roof; dangling waxy fuchsias; sprays of delicate spotted orchids; grey and crimson leaves; epiphytes sprouting in myriads from mossy stems.

Gerald came back to tea and talked about himself, on the whole sympathetically and a little sadly. He's a perfect chameleon for quick-changing.

September 6th

I'm like a horse galloping up to the starting-post; yet I've deliberately tried to take these last few days lazily. Yesterday I didn't get up till nearly lunch-time, went off to play music with the Penroses in the afternoon, to visit the Gathorne-Hardy family and there collected (over the telephone) a rather desperate Julian who had no one to have dinner with, and who very sweetly and nicely came home and shared my cold roast beef and a bottle of wine. Rather to my surprise he said he had noticed Gerald's aggressiveness to me and that he'd been shocked and embarrassed by it; that Gerald had contradicted everything I said. This shot a pang of uneasiness through me. Had I been insensitive? For I didn't feel it as particularly directed at me. Had I been aggressive – and, like Gamel, contradicted Gerald? I didn't think this was what Julian meant, but he looked at me so gravely under his brows as he said it that I did for a moment wonder.

September 8th

'Your seven o'clock alarm call' hauled me from the lowest depths of sleep. Of course I got to the Air Terminal half an hour too early. At the check-in I was given a sharp look: 'You're going on to Moscow?' 'Yes,' I said proudly. 'Well, I'll label it right through.' (Kitty West and I were going for some reason via Paris.) Moscow, magic word! Beautiful in itself and glittering and spiky with associations. Descending to the 'toilets' I thought with a pang of amazement that this mythical entity, in existence for centuries but for me hitherto only the scene of Russian novels, was now suddenly to become real. It was pouring in London, grey at Le Bourget. Kitty and I bought whisky and chocolate. We looked about for other green Wayfarers' labels and spotted two: a large, smooth, solid American male and a small, middle-aged female like a guinea-pig, an Italian Baroness from Venice. She was inconspicuously dressed and wore a navy-blue bathing cap, yet contrived to suggest wealth; her expression never changed all day, whereas the American (Zerbe his curious name) flashed his teeth at us, patted us, name-dropped hectically, and was occasionally dynamically useful. Through the Moscow door at Le Bourget we stepped at once into Russia – a smallish grey aeroplane

162

bearing the magic letters АЭРОФЛОТ. We had two plain but kind and informal hostesses who brought us vodka and a delicious lunch – caviare, steak, peaches and a glass of wine. Half mine fell on the floor, the trays were so ramshackle. One air hostess opened our bottles of mineral water sharply with her teeth, remarking that it wasn't pleasant to do so. Now real happiness began, as, rising from among the other toads squatting on the tarmac we soared swiftly and were up and away eastwards towards a totally new country. 'Oh yes, this is happiness,' I thought, swamped by excited anticipation and sense of adventure. 'I am off to Russia.' Then a doze. Then Moscow and the first taste of Russian ways of doing things, of something that isn't unfriendly so much as stubbornly inflexible. Our passports were whisked away at the very door of the aeroplane. In the airport, bewilderment. No one told us anything; we saw people filling in forms and did likewise; we queued with others for our passports. A new 'Irish Georgian' appeared, a nice soft-voiced elderly man called Hughes, dressed in comfortable tweeds and clutching a crumpled ball of mackintosh to his stomach. He spoke of wanting to come to Russia because of 'having very little more time', as if he had some fatal disease. We were shepherded to a bus, making off for the 'domestic' airport for Leningrad, through a dead flat plain covered with trees (mainly birches with slender white trunks) and small, gaily painted but rather dilapidated one-storey wooden houses like toys. Darkness fell. At the 'domestic' airport there was something of a frenzy while an intelligent, worried girl had to turn our vouchers into air tickets in two seconds; then we tore across the airfield to where several colossal aeroplanes were crouching, only just in time. I shall never forget the strangeness of being suddenly inside this huge, dimly lit and poorly ventilated crocodile, which seemed to be full of large, powerfully built Russians, with serious faces, returning perhaps after the day's work in Moscow. Less than an hour's flight ended in a stifling fug before the doors opened, and Kitty began wailing a little. We were taken to a room with an elaborate cut-glass decanter and a glass on the table and I took a fortifying swig of my whisky. I am enjoying trying to use my few words and read the alphabet. At last we set off in another bus and drove for miles and miles through the outskirts of Leningrad. 'Here is the Europa Hotel,' said the Intourist guide. The rest of our party were there, having only just that moment arrived by sea, and were swarming like bees round the Intourist desk in the hotel; this they continued doing for some hours. In the middle of the swarm were the bowed heads of our leader Mariga Guinness[1] with her floating dark curls, and a Russian who turned out to be our chief guide, Valentín. Slowly we were sorted out and rooms ascribed to us, passports collected. Tired now, disorientated by the change of time, and hungry, Kitty, Mr Hughes and I went in search of food. It was late but we got a plate of cold meats and salad in a large vulgar dining-room with a band playing old-fashioned jazz very loudly, and couples revolving in the style of a village dance of twenty years ago. We had of course no money, for one can take no roubles into Russia, and not yet any coupons for meals, but in the end they agreed to let us pay next day and we went upstairs to see our rooms. They are magnificent. I have a hall with lots of pegs and a large bathroom leading off it and a big, old-fashioned sitting-room with sofa, armchairs, writing-desk, plenty of lamps and my bed in a curtained alcove. Hurrah!

September 9th

I woke feeling expectant about six (which is four by yesterday's time), nor could I sleep again, but lay reading in my delightful bed alcove with its rough linen sheets buttoned round the blankets so that they won't tuck in. Breakfast of fruit juice, water, sweet buns, toast, strawberry jam, and excellent tea without milk.

The morning was spent on a bus drive round the town 'to orientate ourselves', with many pauses to get out and stroll round and take photos. Immense spaciousness is the first impression – huge squares, broad streets without much traffic, gardens and parks everywhere, buildings on a noble scale, eighteenth-century palaces lining the river banks, all painted yellow, green, blue, terracotta, and picked out broadly in white and surmounted here and there by a golden dome or spire. The centre of the town is intersected by canals, rather like Amsterdam. A gently sunlit day without wind with these gilded pinnacles gleaming palely through it. What a ravishing town! But somehow I had expected it to be grey and all this prettiness of colour astonishes me. One is well aware that the Neva is flowing out between flat islands to the Baltic and that the Arctic is not so far away. People of Leningrad strong and square, women with huge

---

[1] First wife of Desmond Guinness, née Princess Marie-Gabrielle of Württemburg. Between them they ran the Irish Georgian Society.

busts; a fair race on the whole with good complexions; all are adequately dressed – not poorly, but no one is smart. Children warmly clad in caps and leggings of bright colours filled the gardens and playgrounds. Little flocks of tots moved along the pavements in tiny crocodiles holding onto strings. The most exciting buildings this morning were Smolny Church and Convent – a cluster of bright blue buildings with gold onion domes. They were being repainted and the oldest paint was of an extraordinarily beautiful and intense peacock blue.

After lunch exhaustion began to set in – at least among the air passengers. But off we drove in our bus to St Isaac's Cathedral. The official state religion being Atheism (a stimulating thought) most of the churches are treated as museums. But religion is tolerated and some churches are described by the guides as 'active'. St Isaac's is very magnificent with pink and grey marble and stupendous malachite columns, but as a whole vulgar and ugly. A spoilt rich woman in our party called Lady Dashwood, known to Kitty, tried to get us to go home with her by taxi, but I had a map and longed to walk home and so peg out a claim on the city. Crowds were hurrying along the pavements and drawing fruit juice from scarlet slot machines. I thought they looked a good deal jollier, less hag-ridden and apathetic than London crowds, and I could all at once see what the regime is trying to do, by throwing open their glorious buildings to everyone and turning what were once private parks of the rich into public gardens available to all. Our fellow Irish Georgians are inclined to condescend and murmur, 'They have no luxuries of course,' disregarding the public possession of all these works of art, good music, theatre and films. I've certainly had no more sumptuous hotel bedroom in any other country.

Early to bed but far too stimulated to sleep.

September 10th

I'm a little worried about poor Kitty who droops and turns pale very quickly. She tends to lose everything and get into a near panic. I feel quite tough by comparison, though I live in a disturbingly spangled electrical state of overexcitement.

This morning was dedicated to the Hermitage. Kitty and I endeavoured to make straight for the paintings but officials tried to whisk us to the cloakroom to remove our coats. At last I said, 'Ya nyeh kashoo' ('I don't want to') which produced friendly roars of laughter. Discovered afterwards that this is obligatory – as Valentín told us, Russians would think it 'disgusting' to bring dust from the street into houses or museums. They also preserve the beautiful inlaid wooden floors of the palaces by making everyone put on felt overshoes, and to the same category of appreciation of their own treasures belongs the scrupulous throwing of paper and cigarette-ends into special urns provided for the purpose. We saved the Impressionists for later and devoted the morning to superb Rembrandts, Titians, Chardins, etc. In the afternoon taken by bus to the Fortress of Peter and Paul across the Neva. The church is richly and delicately gilt inside and contains the tombs of most of the Tsars; we sat for a while in the sun on the landing-stage looking across the river at the pale gold domes on the home shore. On the way back we stopped for a moment to look at a baroque belfry and its separate church, both painted deep peacock blue. Unlike most of the churches it was 'active', and this may have attracted our Catholic Irish companions. By the canal outside a lot of old folk were sitting, wearing chauffeurs' hats and headscarves of traditional design, others were drifting into the church, crossing themselves again and again, saluting, waving, bending almost to the ground in an ecstasy of devotion. We were all at once in old Russia. The inside of the church glowed with dark ikons, candles and gilt; the bell began to toll, and more and more gesturing, murmuring figures came pouring in. Some men suddenly rushed in at the door carrying what I suppose was a coffin. I felt a scrabbling at the back of my knees and turned to see an old crone in black down on all fours kissing the floor. Our two devoted professors, who come with us everywhere, led us to the 'winter' church on an upper floor. This is a museum, but there were beautiful ikons everywhere. I liked this church, St Nikolai, as much as anything I've yet seen.

September 11th

'Russia – I'm in Russia,' I say to myself every night as I get into bed and the thought intoxicates me. Sleep is the difficulty, surrounded by so much to think about and try to remember. A radiant morning. We drove in our bus to a landing-stage on the river where we got into a sort of spaceship called a hydrofoil, which shot us with great speed and smoothness out into the Gulf of Finland towards Petrodvorets. The sea stretched limitless on our right. A fine Saturday had brought large crowds to the Peterhof, an immense palace dominating fountains and statues in terraces down to the sea, all the statues brilliantly gilded and gleaming in the sun. Just when I was off to look at the lake and the other pavilions, I was caught by Mr Hughes, who takes everywhere with him a book written by himself on the work of the Goldsmiths' Guild, which he touchingly but rather boringly shows anyone who will bother to look. We sat in the sun eating our packed lunches, and afterwards went on to the ravishing Chinese pavilion of Oranienbaum, once the palace of Menchikov, with its painted ceilings, rooms lined in crimson lacquer, beads and pearls, and inlaid woods. It was surrounded by real country. We wandered through damp grass between slender birches and little duckweed-covered ponds. Yet another palace nearby, Catherine the Great's Montagne Russe, was an astonishing bright blue and white birthday cake standing on an artificial hill; she used to have herself pulled down this snow-covered hill by a carriage in the shape of a swan.

Three palaces made a tiring day ending with quite a long drive home. At dinner the Baroness pitched into the regime and commented on the poverty of the things in the shops. I'd noticed that every pretty little wooden house had a television aerial. 'A sign of poverty', she said, 'just like Sicily. They all have them there.' F: 'But surely they won't buy them if they actually lack food and fuel?' 'Oh, yes, they buy them on hire-purchase. And look how shabby this hotel is. Nothing is *first rate*.' I wanted to say how much I preferred the decayed palatial splendour of my enormous room to the wretched Jollys of her own native land.

September 12th

To Novgorod today – but first we visited two more enormous palaces – how can one possibly keep them all apart? By bus to Pavlovsk – built for Paul, son of Catherine the Great – a beautifully proportioned, yellow, late eighteenth-century building (by the Scottish architect Cameron), with wings almost meeting in a circle.

And on to Tsarkoye Seloe to see Catherine the Great's colossal blue rococo palace with bronze ornaments. Raymond's French friend, Philippe Julien,[1] muttered: 'Épatant! Some want to see one thing properly, others as much as possible. I belong to the second category.' And he marched purposefully off, as he always does, sketchbook under arm, hunched, spectacled and mackintoshed, and

[1] Well-known illustrator and water-colourist.

then sat or stood to make quick sketches of whatever he wanted to remember. Catherine's Palace is indeed a *stunning* building, vast and ornate with its golden domes, more the equivalent of Versailles than anything we've yet seen.

Our guides find us distressingly individualistic. We are all in the impossible quandary of trying to store our impressions. Kitty, I and a pleasant couple called Lord and Lady Dunleath walked round the shores of the huge lake and looked at various pavilions. Mr Zerbe is photographing them for another book in collaboration with Cyril [Connolly].

It took us about three hours to get to Novgorod along a perfectly straight road across the plain, lined with small wooden houses painted different colours, and, oh joy! I have a monk's cell to myself with its own fairly squalid bathroom, a wireless and television set also. Sunk into stuporous sleep after an exceptionally good dinner.

Lady Dashwood has left her suitcase behind in Leningrad, and is furious; she always expects privileged treatment. She carries a small folding chair about with her everywhere, as she is suffering from the result of a motor accident in which someone was killed. 'That *awful* Valentín,' she drawled to me. 'He's a toad. SO rude.' I'm rather fascinated by him as it happens; he makes an impression of forceful intelligence and considerable specialized knowledge. I thought, but didn't say, 'It's you, Lady Dashwood, who is the toad.'

Everyone sits with anyone else in fairly amiable promiscuity. I dined tonight with Mary's friends the Vincents. He is an American, she French, attractive and elegant, fond of vodka and brandy. We also had Philippe Julien at our table and were very gay and talkative.

September 13th

Our morning's sightseeing at Novgorod provided new sensations and a rustic interlude. Valentín was in a specially genial mood and announced that he had arranged a trip on the great Volkov lake by steamer for us. It soon became clear that he had an intense love for and interest in the characteristic architecture and art of the Novgorod churches, which have indeed a startling simplicity and beauty. This formerly extremely ancient and beautiful town, and its lovely churches, was almost completely wrecked in the war. One church contained part of a striking fresco by Rublev, painted in reddish brown, of a row of bearded prophets sitting in huge vases and waving elegant hands. Valentín became really eloquent and

168

interesting when he described the special qualities of this dramatic painting. Now we took the boat from a landing-stage painted green and pale blue, to see another church. I began picking what wild flowers I could see and our fellow travellers brought me new specimens – there were blue patches of wild delphinium. We climbed the hill above the marshy plain, whence we looked over the vast lake to Novgorod with its domes.

The hotel gave us a good lunch including a magnificent bortsch with bacon, herbs, bay leaves and plenty of cream. Then came the long drive back to Leningrad airport, and into the huge dimly lit otherworldly aeroplane which would take us this time from Leningrad to Moscow. Russian flying is tough; there were many aching ears and one young man had a nosebleed. There followed a drive through the darkness into the heart of Moscow and arrival at our hotel quite close to the Kremlin, whose domes, topped with crimson stars, shone through the darkness.

September 14th

I felt pretty strong this morning as we set out to the Kremlin – first to the museum called the Armoury, which in spite of its name was full of marvellous things, jewellery as rich and beautiful as any I've seen except at Constantinople, sumptuous horse-trappings, and saddles studded with diamonds and turquoises: royal crowns based on a band of fur, jewelled ikons. And then the Kremlin churches. It was late afternoon now, and the plum-coloured sky behind the clustered golden domes was an incredible sight. The insides of the churches were painted to their full height with dark rich ikon-like frescoes and hung with ikons also. The paintings and ikons have the dramatic and emotional intensity of the Siennese, and express the same deep devoutness as we saw in the gesturing old people pouring into St Nikolai's Church. I long for more time to think and digest than we ever get – it is different from anything I expected. We came away stuffed with visual sensations and a good day ended with a night at the opera, *Boris Godunov* at the Bolshoi, a sumptuous production which closely reproduced the ikons and frescoes we had just been seeing, the gorgeous robes and fur-trimmed crowns.

I am full of admiration and respect for Valentín but he has his tough side. When Kitty said rather shrilly, 'I don't like this sort of thing,' in one of the palaces, he snapped, 'Not so loud, please.' He has been heard to refer acidly in the bus to 'some people who are

169

dropping bombs on Vietnam at this moment'. When I showed curiosity about the insides of the little wooden houses he shut up suddenly.

Lady Dashwood always feels she has a right to be squired by some young man, the younger the better. 'Come and sit by me, darling!' she says as she gets into the bus. Today she had to make do with Mr Zerbe, whose florid appearance and loud laughter at his own jokes has made him rather unpopular. Philippe Julien I think has both enemies and supporters. With his independence and high croaking voice he's quite an oddity among us, but his manners are good.

September 16th

Our bus took us to the Pushkin Museum and Kitty and I spent the whole morning there. The Russians were eagerly queueing to see the pictures on loan from the Louvre, and one everywhere saw serious furrowed faces studying the paintings with deep interest.

Went later with the Baroness in a taxi to see Tolstoy's house. It stands in an old part of the town among old wooden houses, like the little village ones but bigger, and as Philippe Julien said it is 'very touching'. The trees in its large garden made it dark and there were no lights. We shuffled round in felt slippers looking into Tolstoy's study, the Countess's boudoir, the children's rooms with their white beds and rocking horses. There was no entrance fee and the sturdy old women who let us in and kept watch that we damaged nothing shook our hands warmly on leaving.

Some of our party went to look at Lenin lying embalmed, and were full of their reactions – Lady Dunleath told me he was 'disgusting' with a look of horror on her face, 'so small and shrunken, with his hair dyed red, and it was somehow shocking that he was wearing a lounge suit'. Zerbe 'wouldn't have missed it for anything' and 'found it both beautiful and moving', but since the Americans embalm all their dead I don't know why he was so impressed. He is bursting with rather terrible vitality and even writes an occasional column for the *San Francisco Chronicle*.

September 17th

I have been suffering from dysentery and in two minds whether I dare face the long bus ride to Zagorsk. I'm thankful I did – it was one of our most stirring outings. First we took our leave of nice old Mr

Hughes who was flying home today. He had asked me about my family, and hearing of Sophie's existence gave me, most touchingly, a little doll for her. He is an old dear as well as an old bore, but is very modest about his musical gifts – I heard from someone else that he had learnt from Henschel, almost become a professional and sung the part of Christ in the *St Matthew Passion*.

Valentín told us that, having discovered we were 'a very heavy drinking party' he was taking us for a drink at the restaurant in Zagorsk before we went into the monastery, seeing over which was one of the most enjoyable leisurely things we have done. A tiny church enclosed a holy spring and a bearded Archimandrite was rattling among his bottles, dishing out water like a barman. In the sunny sheltered space between these buildings a lot of old people were sitting on benches, munching apples and bread and feeding flocks of pigeons. The air was mild and still, immense peace reigned. We entered the oldest church, one of the most highly revered in all Russia, called after St Sergei, founder of the abbey. It contained the shining silver coffin-like tomb of the saint. Old women with headscarves stood and sang with raucous passion, crossing themselves, bowing and saluting, went up to kiss the tomb or give candles to a handsome old priest with bushy grizzled beard and eyebrows, and a tall black hat shrouded in drapery, who took them and fitted them into a high candlestick. Another priestly figure, hatless and with long black hair parted in the middle, was leading the singing in a fine baritone. Near me a waxen-faced woman was taking bites from an apple and screeching out a hymn at the same time. We wandered out and sat in the sun again, watching the priests crossing themselves as they hurried through the courtyard.

The restaurant gave us a superb lunch and Valentín came round with a bottle of old vodka, a deep golden colour and mellow and delicious. We were all given some; and as a result in the bus back to Moscow nearly everyone slept.

Bung-eyed with fatigue as I was, I couldn't resist fitting in an Oistrakh concert before we caught the night train from Moscow back to Leningrad. We are all being worked too hard; the constant impact of the other members of the group is tiring – one often has to 'make conversation' as if at a dinner party. Our taxi took us to the wrong hall and we tore into the concert hall just as bells were ringing and everyone streaming in. We panted into our seats more dead than alive and abandoned ourselves to the logical, beneficent language of music. The two Oistrakhs played the Bach Double Concerto, then the son played the Brahms Violin Concerto, his father conducting. We found our party at dinner and had time to be for a short while on our beds until the appointed hour when we had to go to the station. Tired to the bone, but chewing the cud of the marvellous sources of my tiredness, I went with the others to the station where a long red train stood quietly steaming. There were two berths in each compartment and Kitty and I soon got settled in one. The Baroness stood on the platform saying she couldn't possibly share with anyone she knew, she must have a stranger. Lady Dashwood stood in the doorway of hers with her hair round her shoulders looking as if she would have a good try at keeping it to herself. Zerbe was in the corridor in an open-necked white shirt, sweating vodka at every pore, and shouting, 'Nobody wants to sleep with me!' Nor did they, it seems. There were roars of laughter from further up the train. We pulled out at midnight, noisily but smoothly, and soon afterwards I knew no more.

September 19th

Many of our party are fervent Catholics and wanted to attend services of two of the 'active' churches. We set off first to the beautiful blue St Nikolai. The upper church was packed with prosperous-looking devotees standing in rows listening to Gregorian chants – well sung in fine voices, but I always find them boring. Kitty and I went down to the lower floor where as before an elderly and plebeian crowd were swarming, gesturing, murmuring, babies squawked and a handsome young priest held up a cross to be kissed. I saw a young woman come up to him with starry eyes of love, and pour out what seemed to be a brief confidence to which he briefly replied. We moved further into the heart of the church. 'What's that?' said Kitty. 'It looks like a buffet.' It was a table covered in flowers among the crowd of worshippers (many of them munching out of paper bags). Then I saw that among the flowers lay the corpse of an old bald-headed man with a bandage over his eyes, while his poor old wife leaned over him in a statuesque attitude of grief. 'I've never seen a laid-out corpse before,' Kitty murmured with an expression of horror. We went out into the sunny garden outside the church and sat on a bench. A nice Russian woman opened a conversation with me. I told her that I didn't understand, but this only produced a flood of more Russian. How I wished I *could* understand! The humiliation of not doing so! I brought out one or

172

two of my few words and just took in that she was referring to the old religion revived, to the Hermitage, even to Tsarism. All I could do was shake her warmly by the hand and say goodbye on parting.

The hour for our Irish friends to depart approaches, and Kitty and I begin to plan our four remaining days. We already feel more relaxed and unhurried, knowing that we shall be able to return to the Hermitage at our own tempo.

Tonight many of us walked through heavy rain to the circus which has a great reputation and a famous clown, Popov. He was indeed very brilliant and I liked some acrobats with a happily bouncing little boy among them. Our architectural professor was sitting in front of Kitty and me – he was anxiously waiting for '*les ours*' to appear. They did, but it was an agonizing sight. A huge troop of them came pouring in on their hind legs, big and small, but all with thick glossy coats so that at first we felt they must have been trained by kindness. They ambled round in a comic and engaging way, but when they began to do their more difficult tricks – climb ladders, swing from trapezes, or whirl a blazing torch between their front paws – it became clear that only extreme cruelty could have made them do such unnatural things and I began to hate the false smile of their hard-faced trainer as he gave them lumps of sugar. Then bicycles were brought in of all sizes, and finally a motor bicycle, and when some of the poor bears fell off with their furry paws enmeshed in the handlebars attendants hurried forward and hit and shoved them so savagely that I heard myself booing faintly.

September 20th

Kitty and I bought a bottle of the rather expensive and too sweet Georgian wine, but hardly any of our departing fellow travellers would drink it. We said embarrassing, botched goodbyes, and went off to bed.

September 23rd

Kitty and I have now had two days of independent life in Leningrad and I'm sitting up in bed on the morning of the last. Instead of floating on the surface of Russian life and being whirled effortlessly about in Intourist buses, we have mixed in it, and sunk into it deeply. We have walked the crowded streets, shopped, travelled in trams. How has my first impression changed, if at all? I don't get any sense of glumness or drabness. Uniformity yes – I suppose it's the price that must be paid for fair shares for all. So far we have met with nothing but friendliness and helpfulness. In the great Dom Kneegi, an immense bookshop full of books in many languages, a friendly man came and asked if he could help us. We were stopped in the street by a girl who wanted to air her English. It was excellent, but when we complimented her on it and asked if she was an interpreter or Intourist guide, she said no, she worked in the theatre, had never been to England, but didn't want to be a guide because 'you had to say what you were told instead of what you wanted to say.' If she hadn't been rather tiresome we could have taken her to a café and she would have told us anything. As for the shops, they are stuffed full of second-rate and rather ugly goods and Russians eagerly buying them. The cold weather had produced a queue for fur hats, which are cheap even on the exchange foreigners get. I bought one for Sophie.

The stalwart middle-aged women in the museums are not only there to protect the exhibits. We found they gave smiling and accurate directions when asked, for instance, in the vast warren of the Hermitage, where Kitty and I spent whole mornings – the first almost entirely among the Impressionists.

We have enjoyed being on our own and mastering trolley-bus routes, the coupon system and so on. I bought a Russian-produced guide to Leningrad and read the bit about Lenin at the beginning with horror – the insane jargon about 'class struggle' and 'dictatorship of the proletariat', the maniacal persecution-feelings about the Mencheviks or other wicked deviators from the strict line of Leninism. All this is very mad, silly and worse, and one can't as a tourist possibly gauge how serious it is. Mariga says the atmosphere has changed enormously in one year. Everyone seems to be at work, and very hard too. I think they are enjoying having more things to buy. Certainly the regime does not appear to live up to the view that material values are the sole or even the most important ones. Theory and practice have diverged. Perhaps a little while ago it would have been rash for me to note down these reflections.

Tomorrow England and West Halkin Street.

5.40 p.m. We have been lucky to have a brilliant blue day for our planned walk this morning. We made our way through noble Arts Square to the Summer Garden, everywhere passing or crossing little canals on the way. It is a flat shady park bordered by the wide Fontanka canal on one side and filled with eighteenth-century statues and groups of organized but happy-looking children in bright-coloured suits, caps and leggings. There were a good many fathers pushing prams. So this is what they do! I'd noticed all the street-cleaning and even ploughing was done by women. Out to the Neva, where many-coloured buildings line both banks. Crossed the bridge to the green Stock Exchange and its two red columns, past the ravishing forget-me-not-blue Naval School, the long disappearing vista of red University buildings; white, green, yellow and again red palaces, all the way to the next bridge, when we crossed back onto the Neva's left bank. We walked for three hours, sitting on a seat in the sun now and again to nibble chocolate, and we couldn't have had a nicer morning.

After a late slow lunch the sun was still shining. I have been taking photos all day.

September 24th

'The last morning' I wrote yesterday. But was it? Last night before dinner we went to collect our Leningrad–Moscow air tickets from the Intourist Bureau in the hall. A crowd of Finns who had missed their aeroplane were booking telephone calls to Helsinki. The young women at the desk are amazingly efficient, multilingual and kind. (It was not so at Moscow.) They produced our tickets and asked to see our passports, which Valentín had returned to us when the Irish Georgians left. One girl with a round dutch-doll's face began to giggle over them, and the others crowded round. They asked us a few questions. Then, 'Your visas expired on the 20th,' they said. 'They'd never let you go out with these.' Kitty wailed: 'Oh, what are we to do? We must go tomorrow. We've got our air tickets to London.' My heart sank like a stone. I knew there wasn't a London flight every day. Perhaps new visas must be got and new photos? The whole country had suddenly turned into a prison. I envisaged hours of waiting before we should know whether we were going or not. 'Don't worry,' they said kindly. 'I think it'll be all right. Leave them with us and we'll see what we can do. The visa office opens at nine o'clock and you needn't start till after eleven.' Kitty and I went to drink reviving whisky in the foreign currency bar. We were both suffering from shock. But I feel more philosophical this morning. I don't see how much worse could happen than our having to stay an extra day or two in this lovely town. The weather has – thank heaven – become beautifully clear and fine again.

I'm dressed and half packed and in a moment I shall go up and see how Kitty is doing.

September 25th: London

Kitty was serene and calm, though she made the very foolish suggestion that we should 'risk it and try to get through on our extinct visas'. We looked in at the Intourist desk and were told to come back after breakfast. When we did so, they handed us our passports all correct. Everything from then on went smoothly. We were well looked after; a car drove us to the airport, where we made contact with a nice couple from Edinburgh. We had several hours at Moscow airport and lunched with them and did a little more shopping – for caviare and toys.

So we left Russia on a smooth and 'taken care of' note. English aeroplanes are certainly better pressurized. Reached my flat at ten-thirty London time (and after one by Moscow time) and to my horror my key wouldn't open the mortice lock. I called on my neighbour, Sir Cecil Trevor, who kindly gave me a whisky and telephoned the police for me. An all-night locksmith came and let me in.

To bed, but still too excited to take easily to sleep.

October 1st

I have passed five hyperaesthesic days since I last wrote, trying to master the unholy state of agitation Russia has left me in, and going back there every night when I close my eyes, with onion domes flitting across my field of vision and a sense that the map of Russia lies all round me.

I have been deeply touched by my kind welcome; it was wonderful to find Janetta already back, and having filled my flat with glorious flowers. Mary too has sent me a bunch, and I have seen them both, and Robin and Susan, and Julian and Henrietta and Sophie, Raymond, Eardley and spoken to many others on the telephone.

But I wish, I wish I were more phlegmatic and less ricketty. Raymond told me that Juliet Duff has rather quickly and peacefully died at the age of eighty-four. I felt sorry (for she was a splendid person), yet envious at the same time. 'She had suddenly begun to seem old,' he said, 'a little while before.' I rather feel as if I was crumbling myself, and dread the process, though I wouldn't dread a quick peaceful end to it all. Not at all.

I had quite decided to take a holiday – for Russia wasn't *that* – and time to sort myself out. But James wants me to do a Freudian index under pressure, and there is the Spanish Armada piece[1] to finish and type.

October 17th

Last weekend, dreading it, I went to Little Barbara's at Rye. I have never got on better with her; we were both on our best behaviour. It seemed to me that I was going chiefly out of affection for Clive – but this makes doubtful sense. Just before I left on Sunday night she took all the wind out of my sails by saying, 'I have enjoyed your coming and I know you only came out of kindness.' I was appalled, and overdid myself in protestations. That one should condescend towards another human being is bad enough, but that they should know it and tell you so is fifty times worse. I got real pleasure from Barbara's 'dinky' little house with its picture windows collecting all the sun and looking over the Marsh, Rye Harbour and the river winding out to sea, from sitting in the sun, weeding the bricks, driving onto the Marsh to look at a solitary little church, and (perhaps most of all) visiting Roger Senhouse's house in Rye. He was away and had left Barbara the key. We walked straight into total confusion – every piece of furniture and almost every part of the floor was heaped high with dusty books mixed with old newspapers and dirty pyjamas. We went on, picking our way with difficulty, up to the top of the house, and it was the same everywhere; books and more books, letters, newspapers, loaded ashtrays, priceless china, pictures, catalogues – not a square inch anywhere where he could lay a plate and cup or write a letter. Barbara says he sometimes invites her to a meal, when he clears a space somewhere with his arm and lays down some delicatessen from the shop next door. In the chief sitting-room the walls were lined with book-filled shelves with pretty plates on top, but it was almost impossible to see them through the chaotic stacks of other books, filling the room, weighing down sofas and chairs. The kitchen stank and the stove had a thick coating of

[1] A translation of a contemporary Spanish document.

black treacly substance. Good pictures hung on the walls everywhere, but many, many more were stacked face downwards. In the bedroom an unmade bed and a great many crumpled suits on chairs and the floor. The garden, about which he talks as if it were Sissinghurst, is a small rough patch of grass with a few nasturtiums, towered over by a tall wall of corrugated iron on one side. He must lead a complete fantasy life here. No one could possibly accept it as it is, and none of his willing female friends are able to face embarking on it. Seven maids with seven mops would take at least seven weeks to tackle it.

Now here at Kitty's – once again marvellous peace, distilling all that is pure, soothing and satisfying about country life.

October 22nd

Yesterday I went with Anne Hill to White's Selbourne to see Mungo Macfarlane[1] married to his West Indian negress. A bus met us and deposited us opposite the pretty little old grey church and village green, so well-remembered from childhood picnics.

Anne and I took our seats, and the physical chill and dankness of an English church and its worship enveloped us. As people came in, conventional-looking men, and women in hats like puddings of flowers, they all knelt devoutly and placed a hand for several minutes over their eyes. What were they thinking of or muttering? I'm sure they were believers. Anne thought, just like children, it was 'Please God, give me a new car.' Then followed an endless and really grim wait in which no one spoke above a mousy whisper and the appallingly ungifted organist miaouled out sickly and non-religious tunes: 'To a Wild Rose' by some Edwardian composer, and afterwards what sounded like mangled Verdi. This is hell, I thought, longing passionately to get up and go. On and on wailed the organ, about to die altogether and then dragging itself back to reluctant, hesitant life. People began fidgeting and craning towards the door where the clergyman was standing with several tall Macfarlane boys, looking out into the beautiful autumn afternoon. Craig came in, with Elspeth on his arm: Ah, at last, here was the bride, a wafer-thin, jet-black figure in clouds of diaphanous white, her pretty black face split by a wide white grin. And everyone looked with a surge of sentimental emotion at the two attendants – a small

[1] Son of my old friend and solicitor, Craig and Elspeth, his wife.

blond boy in a kilt (Mungo's youngest brother) and a tiny black girl with an excited and wicked expression. The service began. I can't say there was anything festive about it. In a lagging half-tone we mumbled the hymns with their maundering refrains and dismal words ('the dullness of our blinded sight', 'our soiled face', 'I walk in death's dark vale') and listened when the clergyman said that the first two reasons for marriage are procreation of children and avoidance of sin. We gave the responses in a low growl as of very old workhouse inmates. When at last it was over Mungo and Monica stepped out of the church, where silent ranks of villagers were standing, and rejecting the car Elspeth had arranged for them, walked proudly together arm in arm across the Green. There was just enough breeze to float her white veils around her and make a stylish show which was curiously moving. It was as if the astonishing and improbable conjunction of man and woman that marriage always is was emphasized by these two being also black and white, and their two little attendants echoed this equation in miniature.

In the marquee the usual embarrassment, forced jollity and genuine relief. Mungo carried off his difficult role with elegance and charm. Anne, when asked later what was the best she had ever hoped for her daughters, said, 'To marry a Macfarlane'.

October 25th

I have a clear day to sort myself out. Since yesterday I have felt badly in need of it. Julia has cried off coming for tea and a drink. Like a fly in a jam jar she buzzes wildly from one side to the other of her life. Last night at a party of the Craxtons to which Janetta took me after a concert, I talked to Sonia and was forced to agree with her that Julia's position was bound to get worse.

Last night's concert consisted of second-rate old and modern works, well played by oboe (Janet Craxton), flute and piano, but I wasn't once carried away by the music. When I watch musicians I like to see them tossed and swayed by their own interpretation. I love the way a string quartet is caught by the rhythm of the music from the first bar in a sort of combined epileptic seizure which doesn't end till the last, whereas wind players distractingly purse their lips, look askance at their reeds and seem to detach themselves periodically from the whole thing. Elizabeth Lutyens, a piece of whose music for unaccompanied oboe was performed, sat at my table at the Craxtons'. What a confident, talkative creature with her long anteater's nose and her spectacles pushed up over her high forehead.

I spent a happy weekend with Anne and Heywood in the gardener's cottage of her mother's house at Snape. Life seemed very simple and basic there, perhaps it would have been grim had we been shut in by fog or rain but we weren't. The divine weather went glowing on and we went for walks along the shingly edge of the sea near Orford. Eddie[1] was at Snape, genial and hospitable, erudite about the churches we visited. I mentioned Julia and he said he'd ask her to stay. However when I told her this she said she'd decided Eddie belonged to those of her friends whose lives 'weren't worth leading'. Whose is? Does she think hers has been? I suppose I *do* think mine has been, though if I had to answer the academic's question, 'Would you do it all over again?' I should hesitate. One thing I am beginning to realize is that a great many people have suffered as battering blows as I have.

October 29th

'Beginning to realize.' Yes, I think I am, and with this my life is suffering a sea change. It is only recently that I've been able even to try and realize, instead of pressing a mask of numbness over my eyes. Well, what do I see? Certain things that were always true, others that amount to modifications in myself and my way of life. One of these is that I am literally now a different person from the one of 1926–60. When you love and live daily in contact with someone your two personalities overflow into each other, the dividing barrier is submerged. Part of me was then composed of Ralph's ingredients, just as part of him was of mine. One would think that all growth has stopped by sixty, but like an old gnarled tree trunk one does continue putting out small shoots each year or embracing the barbed wire cutting into one's side.

I suppose I have been changing in my very bones ever since Ralph and Burgo died, but more, strangely enough, now that the first battle for sheer survival is over. I mustn't forget that this new quiescence and acceptance comes partly from stepping down to meet old age. I'm able to be quiet and self-contained more than I used, I even sleep better; I spend longer hours reading, I can sink myself more completely in the lives of people I'm with, feeling for the moment that I possess no other existence than theirs.

---

[1]   Gathorne-Hardy, brother of Anne Hill.

October 30th

Yesterday I went to hear the Labour candidate at our by-election. Politics is a dingy and materialistic business. The three speakers referred to nothing except wages, profits, houses, production, national debt. It was intolerably boring and depressing, and though I'd gone almost resolved to vote Labour I came away feeling I couldn't support such a parochial view. Not one single word was said about other countries, peace, international problems, non-material values.

Ray Gunter, Minister of Labour, a fat little man like a Nonconformist schoolmaster, stood soapily wringing plump hands and raising insincere eyebrows while he talked either about how much his mother had loved him (and he repeated her words of wisdom) or praised the British People's power to face facts. The business of this country was treated like that of a small shop full of packets of synthetic foods – a grocer's view of politics.

October 31st

Wet Sunday in London. I have Sophie here for the afternoon. She has been quite amazingly jolly and good, and has now after a little touching mooing to herself, gone off to sleep on my bed, at which I feel inordinately proud.

Last night to a splendid performance of *Trovatore* with Julian and Janetta, Giulini conducting with such vigour and enthusiasm that Janetta (who was sitting exactly behind him) was bounced up and down in her seat. From the first bars the supply of excitement was so dense and rich that I expected it might soon exhaust my ability to respond, but the performance was kept at such a high level that it was impossible not to.

Supper afterwards at Boulestin's. Janetta and Julian's relationship develops and strengthens with time. I can't fit it into any known category; the nearest perhaps being devoted brother and sister. Julian told Magouche his feeling for Janetta was as near being 'in love' as he'd known with a woman. He depends on her as well as appreciating and loving her, and desperately wants the other people he likes, like Desmond, to appreciate her too. What exactly Julian represents to Janetta I don't know. She takes him with her everywhere – he is even going out on her week's dash to Marbella. They must meet or telephone at least once a day.

On Saturday I lunched at Montpelier with the two of them plus Sonia. I don't quite know what to do about Sonia – I had almost written her off because of the irritation produced in me by her intellectual pretensions, drunkenness and catty remarks about Janetta. But she has been so kind and constructive to Julia, and I so hate Julia's own style of 'writing people off' that I've resolved to make another effort to like her – also because I know Janetta would be pleased if I did and she has come to live in this part of the world. Julian and Janetta both said afterwards she had been 'rather too noisy' and aggressive.

Talk about the 'tape-recorder' technique in literature. Julian declared himself in favour of it, though the selection must be of a high order. But I don't see that it can ever reach a higher level than photography. Robert (last night) was dead against it even in his sphere of explicit reporting; he says he longs for it as an extra memory, but that some part of one's critical intelligence switches off when it switches on, and the interviewer should keep a living current between him and his subject all the time. With a tape recorder you are dealing with dead material, performing a post-mortem. Julian also attacked writers who chose to display so sterile a subject as boredom. He was interesting about the cult of boredom, not only among uneducated good-time girls but among certain spoilt young rich who make an existence from smoking pot and a peculiar form of elegance.

November 1st

Janetta has just been here briefly and has left me asking myself various questions. No one in the world supports her friends with a stronger and more sensitive hand and she will think imaginatively of tiny details (worrying for instance whether I was getting on all right with Sophie yesterday). Yet when Sonia arrived very drunk to see her last night (with Francis Bacon also drunk and his friend George sober and helpful) Janetta felt she couldn't do anything to stop her or show disapproval, and went on plying her with drinks until at last Sonia rose to go and fell flat on the floor. After she and Julian left me the other evening (after *Trovatore*) they went to a gambling club and spent all night there. I asked about Julian going to Spain with her and she 'wondered why' or 'how' perhaps he was going. She is very fond of him and has boundless influence over him, he adores her, she doesn't hesitate to say her mind to him and yet – I think this perhaps is the crux of it – she won't say anything with *moral* implications.

How far should responsibility for friends go? Is it as important not to use your influence to draw them into habitual extravagances they can't afford (though *you* may be able to) or conversely to speak up for your scale of values however priggish it may seem, as it is to come to the rescue when disaster has struck.

November 10th

Can I keep my London life going at the reduced tempo it is gradually adopting? Well, it's worth trying, for the competitive racket is beyond me; I can't tear along with the speed and noise of Mary's mini, nor do I have the least desire to. I have a new slow, gentle way of getting through my days. Work slows up as a result; I no longer attack it in a frenzy; Spanish Armada finished yesterday – I ought to begin James's Index today – but shall I?

Henrietta has a new boyfriend, a member of Amaryllis's theatrical company, called Ocky. He has been there the last two times I went to Clarendon Gardens and come here with her. I like him very much and hope the attachment may become serious – he is very good-looking, gentle, musical. I hope there is a firm link forming. The trouble is that the whole company is going to America in about a week for six months – and Janetta said that Henrietta wants to go too and they to take her. What happens to Sophie then? Is this going to be a moment when I should step in and take over?

When Bunny rang up yesterday and asked to come and see me I thought he wanted to talk about this project but I underestimated his egotism. He hadn't even heard of it and quickly dismissed it, saying Henrietta couldn't afford it, the fare alone was £170. He had met Ocky and liked him, but I was struck not for the first time by the easy way Bunny takes fatherhood, loving its pleasures and not concerning himself greatly with the responsibilities. He wanted to talk about himself, tell me the plot of his new book at length, expatiate on his hatred of London and distaste for Angelica's 'squalid little Islington House. I spent a night there, but I never shall again. There's nothing to put your clothes down on except the floor, which is inches deep in dust.' Just like the last time, he talked and talked about himself and asked me no questions. What indeed could he ask? My role is to be 'a good listener'.

November 12th

Campbells, Tristram and Raymond to dinner; they stayed till nearly one, so I suppose were enjoying themselves, and I was too, though Raymond has a curious way of taking the conversation from the general to the particular. He was however in delightfully resilient spirits. Susan was at her nicest and not at all harping on domestic problems and au pair girls. Henrietta came to see me before dinner. I asked her if she was happy, said I thought and hoped so. She said 'yes' she was; and then, after a pause and *sotto voce* – 'Wildly happy'.

November 14th: Oxford

Walking round the old-fashioned streets of North Oxford with David Cecil yesterday morning, we discussed the creeping paralysis of boredom – the symptoms and dragging steps of the 'beats', and their long hours spent killing time gossiping round a table and smoking 'pot'. The Battersea girls whom Nell Dunn[1] writes about kill time between washing their underpants and going out on their boyfriends' motor-bikes; in the elegant world of the frilly-shirted, bejewelled, rich young men and their girls they kill time by preoccupation with their appearances and clothes and again with drug-taking; the older rich spoilt set moves feverishly from Nassau to other fashionable playgrounds with its nursery of games and toys.

November 18th

I had darling little black-eyed Sophie for the whole afternoon. From the moment that she came shouting downstairs to greet me till the time Henrietta picked her up about six, she was as good as gold, cheerful and – what I particularly liked – obviously finding my flat and me familiar and reassuring.

Henrietta's new love Ocky has gone to America with Amaryllis's company. I fear she is missing him terribly and I thought she seemed sad. She spoke of perhaps going to America after Christmas.

November 20th: With Jim and Alvilde Lees-Milne in Gloucestershire

I don't know the name of the house I'm in, nor even of the village. Ben Nicolson and I arrived last night in the misty darkness, and after

---

[1]   Writer and playwright, daughter of Mary McCabe.

driving some seven miles through rustic lanes and swathes of thicker mist we got to this majestic-looking stone house. I had been feeling anxious about the visit – I can't think why.

November 21st

Desmond joined us yesterday at tea-time, and my pleasure at seeing and talking to him was an indication of my not being at home completely in these surroundings, but subtly aware of alien values. It is all just a little too conventional and safe. There are a lot of priceless objects lying about – lapis lazuli stamp boxes, glass-topped tables full of diamond-studded fobs. When we were alone in the drawing-room Ben picked up one of four rather attractive figures on the mantelpiece and said, 'I wonder if they know these are obvious fakes.' Desmond and I questioned him as to what the indications of their fakedness were and he did succeed in making them look false to me, purely by suggestion. Later I heard him asking Jim some question and getting the reply, 'Oh, they're Tang. Four thousand (or four hundred, I forget which) B.C.'

November 27th

Drove with Eardley through the darkness to Crichel. I feel perfectly at my ease with him, yet once arrived, with Raymond, Des and Cressida Ridley he fell silent.

I took to Cressida very much at first meeting and felt perhaps she was a kindred spirit but she is not an Asquith for nothing and I notice in her a tendency to 'inform', even Desmond about music. Desmond played us a remarkable and intensely gloomy quartet of Shostakovich's last night.

November 29th

I keep to my first impression of Cressida – she *is* a kindred spirit and an immensely likeable person. I've had enormous conversations with her and agree over almost everything – the class war, the blacks, religion – and in a curious way her mind takes the same routes and goes at the same pace as mine. I'm a little concerned by Raymond and wonder if I irritate him. He often contradicts me flat without supporting his views in any way. Then I become indignant and ask him why he holds them and he merely repeats himself. Every day I resolve to be milder and more respectful to this dear old friend. There's no end to my good resolutions, but nor is there to my failure to keep them.

The ingredients of life here are as before – walks with Moses, music, reading and arguing about grammar (too much of that).

December 4th: West Halkin Street

An evening here dedicated to listening to the records of *Simon Boccanegra* with Julian and Janetta.

We had a rather delicious little dinner and bottle of Derek's claret half-way through the opera, and Janetta told us the sad story of Sonia's birthday dinner party for Deirdre Connolly.[1] Raymond was one of the guests (a slightly unwilling one as I happened to know). As he left he thanked Sonia warmly for the delicious dinner and then said, 'Aren't you a lucky girl to have this lovely house?' She was drunk as usual and blazed out with: '*Lucky?* – a *house*! You don't think *that* makes any difference when all the time . . . etc. etc.' I don't exactly know what the words were, but they were delivered with a shriek and she banged the door angrily on him. It seems that Sonia was not really upset at what she'd done, but only said: 'After all, I've never liked Raymond.'

December 16th

I've just had an entirely young lunch party – Henrietta, Sophie, Nicky, Nerissa, Julian. Nerissa spoke bitterly of Angelica waking her up in her basement flat by coming (as arranged) to see her, and looking at her pictures and liking all the wrong ones. Nicky said what a nuisance it was for a French young man she knew, who had been given a marvellous car and not insured it and driven slap into another, smashing both, and then run away, that he was now in trouble with the police, 'poor fellow'. We were supposed to sympathize. Henrietta talked the other day about various kinds of dope she had taken.

[1] Wife of Cyril.

December 22nd

Henrietta rang up, full of all the sweetness and generosity she can surprise one with, accepting what I said in a recent letter about values and going so far as to say she thought I was right. I almost burst into tears. I have seen her twice since then – yesterday in her own warm, rich-coloured sitting-room, with the handsome badly made curtains, a broken, unmade bed, Sophie padding round in bare feet and Nerissa lounging on the bed. Today she has been to see me here, and oddly enough I once again feel she is using me as moral litmus paper in spite of the dusty answer I gave her last time.

This time she asked what I thought about drug-taking. It is much in the news; it is the fashion among the dashing, picturesque young, who search for new sensations because they are deadly bored and their lives as well as their heads are empty. I didn't know how to answer her question. I was dismayed. I can't always be saying, 'Don't' but I can't to this say, 'Do'. She pressed it rather urgently – perhaps there were wonderful sensations one ought to try? I think I wedged in some antibodies of a sort – saying that it was of course exciting to experiment in the world of new sensations but it was a mad world, a world of the bored and futile, and of the lunatic asylum.

December 25th, Christmas morning: Litton Cheney

Here I am again slung aloft in the tiny spare room, between two solid walls and two that are almost all window through which I look out on a faint blue sky criss-crossed with bare boughs and fine twigs and can just glimpse the pale green tilted fields below.

After an evening with Cressida, talking for hours on end non-stop and really covering the range – religion, ethics, politics, human relations – I drove down to Stokke on Thursday morning. Oh, poor Mary and oh, the sadness of that house – it's *not* imagination, it's a thick exudation, felt and smelt as soon as one enters the front door. The fact that the 'girls' (Charlie's daughter Nini and another, a Russo-American called Masha) had decorated up the hall with holly and quantities of red satin bows and covered the hall table with carefully 'wrapped' parcels and more satin bows, and that a Christmas tree stood mournfully in the corner (only a few of its electric lights working) all increased the deep gloom pervading the

187

house. Mary tried to jolly everything along, the girls mooned and loafed and went off to make Christmas puddings. Masha was a great lump of a girl, wearing a white Irish sweater grey with grime, and splitting tweed trousers on her shapeless legs; she smoked endless cigarettes, held in fingernails sharpened to a pink point, and her dark brown hair was streaked with yellow dye. Charlie was like a time bomb whose charge was very near explosion point. He would rush in at the door like a bull and ask who had left the bathroom tap running, or merely fulminate against the Christmas preparations, shouting ironically and rather comically of the tree, 'ISN'T it delicious? I could eat it – and I *shall*!'

Then yesterday, Christmas Eve, I took a slow cross-country course by by-roads across wild and remote regions and beautiful, deserted country. Yet my few short stretches on main roads told a different story. I really loved picking my way from Collingbourne to Everleigh to Fittleton and Amesbury, Gillingham and Cerne Abbas over great rolling khaki-coloured downs decorated with sepia or indigo hangers and copses; a slight rain falling, warm. I arrived in the moist dusk to find this house beaming at me from rows of candles in every window and similarly glowing within. In sharp contrast to the dismal festal apparatus of Stokke, this is genuine and heartfelt if childish and innocent. Last night after dinner Reynolds read aloud *The Tailor of Gloucester*, with fourteen-year-old Emma sitting beside him smiling with shining eyes. He read very well, and it was easy to swim along with the current.

Now I've just been brought my breakfast tray, and an enormous striped football stocking stuffed with bath essence, quince jam, matches and so on! Soon afterwards came Emma and Phillida with the contents of their stockings on trays – a profusion of things, precious and otherwise. Now they have all gone off to church and the bells have stopped their loud pealing only a few feet away from my eyrie, and I feel delightfully alone.

December 26th

The Christmas spirit was sustained to an almost fanatical degree all yesterday. I longed for it to blow its fuse and let us all flop, but the major parcel-giving was reserved till after tea and Winnie the cook and a splendid daily (Mrs Olive Myrtle by name) joined in the Christmas dinner. It's lucky that the weather is fine, and yesterday Reynolds and I took a long walk by lanes edged with cascades of glossy hartstongue ferns, across the shallow valley to the hills beyond and back again. Janet makes one anxious by her tension and the trouble she takes. She's just been in to say how she hardly slept at all last night. Reynolds is charming, serene and unselfconscious. There is also staying here Janet's sister Gabrielle, head of the WVS of all England, and her husband George, a prep-school headmaster.

Edward is the odd one out of the family. He has plenty of emotions and a great many undisciplined thoughts, and these erupt and gallop away and are expressed in uncontrolled expressions, and excitable remarks. He makes himself agreeable to me and I respond to my utmost.

Humphrey, pleasant-mannered, much more self-confident, nice-looking, about twenty-three I suppose, is patently 'all right.' Phillida, twenty-one, romantically charming and pretty, has her ear cocked for the telephone and young men ringing up in the background. Lastly, Emma with her thick straight dark hair and sweet smile and voice.

Now today, when I see a beautiful day and frost-sprinkled fields, we have all got to drive to Budleigh Salterton to visit Reynolds' sister. I would much rather not go, but I detect from careful sounding that I'm expected to. So I must now get up and buckle on – such as it is – my armour.

December 27th

The day was of such crystal loveliness that I enjoyed the drive and most of all our stop at Lyme Regis to walk along the Cobb in warm soft sunshine, look about and remember. Every place we passed through had recollections of the past – Bridport where Ralph and I spent a week deciding to throw in our lot together; Budleigh Salterton itself reminded me of our visit to Devon during the war, and there was even a Mrs Partridge living next door to Reynolds' sister who may well have been Aunt Amy.

Sylvia Townsend Warner and her lesbian companion came to tea, and afterwards a tall dark clever-looking admirer of Phillida's for the night. I've had a long talk with Janet's WVS sister and her husband severally, and now they have gone off and so should I. Tomorrow I shall be back on my own rusty old rails.

1966

January 1st

Isobel and I went to *Boris Godunov* last night at Covent Garden and enjoyed ourselves greatly. The performance was long and at about eleven-thirty she and I were returning through Trafalgar Square in my Mini. Massed crowds of youthful figures were all around the fountains and streaming across the roads – the intense blackness of their leather coats making them look slightly sinister, but more so were the watchful figures of large policemen and, under Admiralty Arch, a police ambulance and two police cars drawn up as if to charge, or as if a war, not jollity, was about to begin.

Coming back from Oakley Street I was curiously tempted to return and see what happened in the heart of London when midnight struck, but laziness won, and I met several cars with drunk drivers wandering over the road. 'Poor things', said Isobel, 'they have so little fun, no outlet – so little *room*.' This morning I read in my *Times* that thirty-two people had been charged for drunkenness or assaulting the police, and in Trafalgar Square there was a 'clash between bathers and others with beer tins and rolls of lavatory paper'.

Thinking of Julia and of Mary, I wonder about the egotism and demandingness of love. Of the two it's Mary who most enjoys giving, and is not solely concerned with asking. I shall know more about Julia after she comes to see me today.

January 9th: Iden

Poor old Dick Rendel[1] has died after an operation for cancer and a week of hideous anxiety for all concerned. Jill[2] rang me up early on Thursday morning and told me that Judy[3] had asked for me to go

[1] My brother-in-law and nephew of Lytton Strachey.
[2] His daughter.
[3] His wife, my eldest sister.

190

down, and if I might perhaps take her abroad somewhere. I have been here at their cottage for two nights with Judy, and Jim[2] (who flew over from Australia but is going back in about a week), and it's sheer agony. Judy is very good and brave, and I think only takes in the half of it so far, but last night, after a numbed patch, realization began to dawn on her. I talked to her in her bedroom for some time and then crept through to sleep in Dick's old room – a tiny cubicle, without so much as chair, table or electric fire, just beyond. I hear every sound in her bedroom and I can't get to my room without disturbing her. Last night I felt completely desperate, what with sympathetic pain for her, and puzzling over the problems of the future – is she to go to the village funeral tomorrow? How is she to go on existing alone here? The family have cast me for the role of support, thankfully and as if they were calling in an expert on bereavement as they would a plumber. I may be one, but this only makes me know only too acutely what she is suffering.

Then my new translation came yesterday: I made a very slight start and it is interesting, but also fairly tough philosophical sociology. I need reference books; I need privacy for about four hours a day. Here in this gnome's cottage there is only the dining-room, a sort of passage through which everyone comes. With my torturing thoughts for Judy, how can I concentrate on work? I feel I ought to take everything over, including the shopping and housekeeping, or always be prepared to do so. But there are questions, questions. I can't stay here for ever – each day is torment. But what happens to her when I go? My present plan is to go to London and get more books and clothes and then return for another full week which I hope I can endure. Judy has left her Librium pills at Hastings and won't fortify herself with whisky. I think my line is too realistic for her. The funeral, even if she doesn't go, is going to be a horrible strain and relations will flock here expecting meals. Could I take her right away – and where? Who will take over if I do stay until Monday week? Jim takes the line that she will decide what to do in her own good time; that Jill fusses her. This is true, but Judy needs help and who is to provide it? I don't want to desert her – I wish to God I was not just starting a new book, always an anxious time for me. And there is another complication which I shy away from: Janetta has had a letter from her doctor saying she must come home and have a

[1] His son, Professor of Genetics at Sydney.

hysterectomy – she will be arriving next weekend. Julian is back from Spain and told me two days ago. I want to be at hand when this happens.

January 11th

I see the encephalograph of my mood has been following its usual 'spike and wave' pattern.[1] As is my habit, I plumb the depths, find them intolerable and stagger up to the surface. (Interesting that I first put 'deaths' instead of 'depths'.) The day after I wrote with such despondency I somehow pulled myself together, forced myself to get going with my new book, talked to the family about my inability to stay here for ever, and managed to take over the cooking from Judy without much effort. Jim is a constant solace to me – in his way extremely clever, loving argument and talking about general ideas, he provides a constant challenge, which I enjoy meeting, and can meet on the whole. Of course I couldn't on his special subject of genetics, but there I don't try, I just ask questions. I like him very much – he is gentle and considerate with Judy and a stimulating element in the house. Perhaps there's a trace of the Rendel–Strachey vanity, but his interest in reality neutralizes it.

Then yesterday was the funeral. Tom and Nadine came down for it and lunched here, the house filled up at tea-time. Judy touchingly put a black velvet ribbon in her snow-white hair but made no bid to go to the ceremony. She and I sat by the fire and talked. I hope I'm doing the best I can for her and not being too bossy. I found, as I always have, the congealed family atmosphere after the funeral intolerably suffocating, and the Kentish cold has now set in with acute severity.

I slept very badly last night and I feel pretty *triste* and *morne* personally, and dread Jim's departure on Thursday or Friday.

January 12th

God grant we don't get snowed-up. After bitter winds and iced ground, it is now beginning to fall. I'm in a little train rattling to London 'for the day'. I thought with longing of a night in my own bed and returning tomorrow, but it seems that Jim has to be in London by one o'clock tomorrow to catch his aeroplane to Sydney.

[1] Sign of schizophrenia.

Yesterday came the letter from Janetta which Julian had told me was on the way. She and Georgie will be back on Monday probably, and I've told Judy I must return then. I thought it best to say quite plainly that Janetta was the person I was fondest of in the world and who had done most for me and utterly propped me in my times of trouble. I think Judy accepts this fully, and there seems to be an idea that her friend Dorothy Carter will move in when I leave Iden. Yesterday morning Jim went to London and Judy and I had several long conversations. She said that she felt physically ill and weak, and I said I thought that absolutely natural, and that after Burgo died I felt my legs were giving under me all the time. She burst out, 'Oh, that was so *awful* – and I feel we did nothing for you.' No, they didn't, but nor I suppose did I want them to.

January 14th

Escape to London and as I bowled towards Buckingham Palace I thought, 'This is where I belong and I love the old place.' But craters open. Rang Margaret to try and arrange some music for the future. Had great difficulty in getting her, and she was upset because after our last musical session with Shirley[1] Shirley wrote a letter to her boyfriend saying, 'My mother is *appallingly* bad: I can't think how she has the nerve to play at all,' and left it open and face upwards on the sitting-room table. General embarrassment. Poor Margaret said she adored playing, found it the greatest possible outlet, and was she really too bad? Well, of course she is, and of course I didn't say so.

January 20th

I returned to Iden, where six days have passed and many thoughts also. Now back in London; my affection for Judy has deepened, perhaps through sympathy for her sufferings, the dissolution of all inessentials in the furnace of pain. Julia's last letter was exasperating, as only she can be; totally unsympathetic to other people's troubles. Judy ought to 'dig herself up' and realize she must fling herself into some activity. In what way has she – Julia – 'dug herself up' and thrown herself into activity? On the contrary, she has groaned and moaned and been a constant worry and responsibility to her friends for three whole years. I'm amazed at her reaction about Judy – it

[1] Her daughter, viola player.

almost seems like jealousy that anyone else's troubles should be considered and cared for. I rang her up to see how she was. She'd had an exceptionally amiable weekend alone with Lawrence, but she hastened to put herself in the breadline for sympathy: 'However of course I feel dreadfully ill and unable to cope with anything still; one can't suffer the torments of the damned for three years with impunity.' Why then, should others be able to snap out of their torments in three days?

Janetta came back on Sunday and I went straight there after my return. Magouche had well-meaningly asked an enormous welcoming-party there, to be cooked for by Janetta, including Julian and Georgia, Ed, Georgie and Rose. I would have given anything to be alone with Janetta and not in this rather noisy, scatty hullabaloo round which hung the fever of Marbella-like paper streamers after a night-club session on New Year's Eve. Georgie was in tearing spirits and has advanced a good way towards nubility.

January 22nd: At Celia Goodman's new house, Cambridge

Silently compressed in the grey-whiteness of windless thaw. Last night the Provost of King's, Noel Annan and his wife, also Tom and Nadine came to dinner. Celia says Noel Annan is a great friend, one of those she came to Cambridge for, yet she hasn't seen them more than once since she arrived in August. And now he is moving to London to be Provost there. Gabriele Annan is an attractive and intelligent German: when I praised her, Celia bridled rather. What of Annan? Very Cambridge, relaxed, smooth, urbane, with a loud free laugh and frequent 'don't misunderstand me''s.

He said nice things to me, such as that Michael Holroyd had said 'how sweet I'd been to him': made himself very agreeable, had taken the trouble to know who my 'daughter-in-law' is, and so on.

This morning Celia and I went for a drink at the Provost's Lodge, where everything was sumptuous but safe. What a breath of fresh air Maynard[1] must have introduced in his day. I looked at a rather vulgar portrait of him, which however revealed the sparkling intelligence of his eyes, and thought how he shot ahead behind the high-powered engine of his mind, cutting a swathe through the conformist waters and caring not at all for public opinion or the trammels of success.

[1] Keynes.

194

Noel Annan spoke about the Lytton–Maynard correspondence, which is at King's under some decree that it shan't be read. I almost blurted out that I'd heard it read that icy weekend at Charleston some while ago – and then realized in time that this is a deadly secret. Holroyd dined with me two nights ago and went through the Ham Spray albums; I'm pretty sure he told me then that *he* also had read the above letters, but the Provost of King's had not. I did ask Annan if Holroyd saw them when he came to King's and he said, 'Oh, no. I've not seen them myself.' The trouble about such secrets is that they appear to me so needlessly treated as such that I forget that that's what they are supposed to be. Holroyd asked me some questions about Carrington's affair with Beakus Penrose[1] and her pregnancy by him and her unhappiness, and I realized that I can't ever see any good reason not to answer such questions truthfully.

January 27th

Oh dear, oh dear, oh dear, Julia and I have quarrelled again, no other word for it; and the truth is that when she said, 'Then we'd better not meet,' I felt nothing but relief. I don't know how I shall feel about this crisis later, but I have woken this morning still feeling calm.

How did it happen? Did she arrive with a sediment of hostility? The first thing she talked about was the shamefulness of Roland Penrose's[2] allowing himself to receive a knighthood. I said – what I think – that this is to set too much store by titles; they are unimportant frills and furbelows added to life, or rather like clapping when a singer has done well in the opera. 'Well, you and I never agree over anything,' she said rather tartly, and so I steered quickly away from this dangerous corner and all was amiable for several hours.

I mentioned Janetta's coming operation. She never asked a single question about it – nor said a word, not even 'Oh!', yet she took it in, as I saw later. She asked me not one word about myself.

Disaster was brought on when she began to say she was 'bored by' or 'didn't care to take part in' any conversations with people who were not experts, i.e. knew all about technique, history, etc., in any of the Arts, – books, pictures, music, the cinema, television. At one moment she said that she was too sure of her opinion to want to hear

---

[1] Youngest of the four brothers.
[2] Second of the four brothers.

other people's. She implied that such people as Magouche and Janetta had nothing worth saying about art, and of course I felt she was implying the same about me.

I remembered how much I had enjoyed long and delightful conversations of this very sort with her – one about Proust on a walk at Lambourn, another about the Grünewald crucifix came to mind. I felt hurt and also amazed by her condescension and arrogance. I should have let the subject drop, but I couldn't think how, and I suggested that art could lead into other spheres of ideas, anyway that ideas were the best thing to talk about, and to cut off art was to lop off a whopping great hunk. She merely replied, 'I'm only saying what *I* enjoy.' When I started describing the sort of conversations I liked, and how much (for there's nothing in the world I like more), she answered crossly and at cross-purposes, thinking I was still discussing *her* likes and dislikes. I felt there was nothing left to talk about – we had talked for hours about *her* life; was this the only thing she wanted to talk about? I literally dried up, chatterbox though I am by nature. Nothing seemed worth projecting in the direction of this dry stone wall.

Then when she was going I said something more about Janetta's operation. When I thought of Janetta's enormous kindness and sympathy to Julia, the way Julia had quickly brushed both aside seemed to me quite insufferable. Egotism, arrogance and condescension are a heavy price to pay for stimulating company and originality, and they dominate her at present – even if this is ascribable to temporary insanity – to a degree that positively floors me. I still feel them thundering in my ears like the clatter of passing express trains.

When I told her about Janetta, 'Is she worried?' Julia asked. 'Well, what do you think?' And my fatal final shot was, 'You're really TOO unsympathetic about other people's troubles. And it's not for lack of sympathy yourself.'

January 31st

No, I still feel no regrets. In a terribly chilly way I almost feel my affection for her has gone, and almost (too) my respect. But I expect both will revive.

The day after our brush I was in the London Library helping Janetta choose books about the Moors in Spain to take into hospital and I suddenly glimpsed Julia's pinko-mauve woolly cap waiting for the telephone to be free.

Janetta's operation is now well and satisfactorily over and I am to pay her a first visit.

February 1st

I found her lying in a blue dressing gown talking to Jonny, looking pretty and marvellously herself, her room banked with flowers which contrived to look hideous as hospital flowers do. I went about the question of the result of the operation as deliberately as possible, saying how glad I was to hear from Magouche of the 'satisfactory result'.

To the Bonnard exhibition, my second visit. Very rewarding – the first having given me an over-stretched sensation, this time I felt I'd seen them all. What an observant but above all feeling eye. Each picture gives a fresh shock of transmitted awareness of colour, light and form – not line, which seems to me deficient. This time I looked at the drawings to see if he had it – but no, he hadn't. However, the rich voluptuousness of his vision of ordinary life, children, gardens, nudes, cats irresistibly overwhelms one.

February 5th: Crichel

Drove down here with Eardley yesterday. Dreadfully tired, I longed to go to sleep and suggested to him I might. Desmond was amazed at my temerity and thought I might well have been told to get out of the car. Apparently Eardley *hates* people to go to sleep in his car. Anyway I didn't, and we had delightful talk of the exploratory kind we always do, (more really than is possible here when everyone is present) though I don't suppose Julia would have approved of it. At the moment, having recovered from her dictum, I feel subjects for talk are boundless and that it's an exhilarating activity. Last Thursday night, having invited the Pritchetts and Lennox Berkeleys who didn't know each other well, I did wonder a little anxiously 'what we should talk about'. There was no difficulty whatever, and the evening was a success, I think. Julian came in after dinner and stayed for a while after they'd gone. He started on rather a strange, obsessional, 'darning' tack about Jonny's visit to Janetta which I had interrupted. (It was my first visit to her and I remember saying more than once, 'Oh, don't go, Jonny, I don't want to drive you away,' and he said he simply *must* go, and left.) It seems that as soon as I was seen at the door Janetta quickly said to Jonny: 'You will leave me

197

alone with Frances, won't you?' and he was deeply wounded. Julian laboured this over and over, and wouldn't hear of it being simply that she was tired and dreaded two people at once. She is now doing very well and comes out next week.

Frances Phipps is here – I'm not sure that it will be the easiest place for getting in touch with her. We do best quite alone together.

February 7th

After a morning when I tried to work in the drawing-room while Frances talked without stopping, Desmond kindly rescued me, and helped me withdraw to the dining-room. I've done poorly on the work front. After lunch yesterday Frances's pretty blue eyes went suddenly out of focus and she began to talk of Eddy, and how she 'hated gossip' but his Irish friends and his sister Diana had been much upset because Crichel was supposed to be saying that he drank too much whisky (hence, had 'taken to drink') and therefore written a bad will. How to sort any sense out of it, though, with Frances's voice denying that Eddy drank too much whisky and saying that if he did it was 'not fair' and 'mean' to say so. Perhaps idiotically I felt I must stand up for realism and facing facts, and that one could (and even should) criticize while still loving one's friends.

February 10th

I seem to have been too long in a constant state of tension, physical and mental. How shall I get out of it? At nights I'm aware of my mind racing like a feverish squirrel into various corners, taking a quick anxious look, and on to the next thing. I feel tempted to disappear to a country inn for a week but of course I should be dismally lonely. Last night I had another dinner party (I plan no more for *weeks*), with Robin Fedden, Magouche, Boris and Maude. This morning both Maude and Magouche rang me up and talked at length, largely about the other.

It seems extraordinary that I have found no time to record a visit from Bunny, during which he told me with considerable emotion that his estrangement from Angelica had reached such a point that she had written saying she wanted a divorce. He showed me her letter; it was affectionate but firm. I suppose he has been ruthless to others in his day, still I don't like the idea of this blow so late in his life. He was extremely spirited on the whole, declaring that he

198

refused to be self-pitying or deterred from getting the most he could out of his few remaining years. Happiness and unhappiness are the liquids, the distilled water in people's batteries. Joan Cochemé came yesterday and we spent a pleasant quiet evening together. I greatly respect her Scotch sense of responsibility for the people she loves.

February 12th

Went to the House of Commons for the first time in my long life yesterday, with Dicky Chopping, to hear the debate about homosexuality. We would never have got into the Strangers' Gallery but that Dicky sent a note in to John Smith, our new Member for Westminster, and he came out and let us in. There we sat in the gallery of this Gothic brown interior looking down on the green benches where a scanty, frightfully bored-looking crowd sprawled among their order papers. At the end, like an idol, or a very elegant porter in the sort of chairs they used to sit in in smart halls, was the dapper bewigged figure of the Speaker, one black silk leg cocked over the other. I have long wanted to go to the House and was delighted to be there, but it was an unremarkable and unstimulating sight, more like a board-meeting than the centre of our government. Nobody said anything of the smallest interest, but there was much talk about the 'brilliance of the speech' of the honourable Member for Hartlepool, also of these 'unfortunate people' (buggers) as of creatures horribly deformed but perhaps needing pity. Roy Jenkins spoke in fine ringing tones, clearly and to the point. Another Labour Member was disastrously slow and woolly – one hadn't the ghost of an idea what he was trying to say; most of them mouthed, put their fingers in their waistcoat pockets, spoke of the 'other place' and showed every sign of enjoying themselves and never wanting to stop, just as their hearers showed every sign of intense boredom and usually flocked out noisily whenever a speech began. There were a number of shocks of long, greying hair; the square pale clever face of a Foot (I think) stared up at us women, Queers and Indians in the gallery. Among a row of peers in the front of the gallery sat Patrick Kinross and a small restless white-haired man, whom Dicky pointed out as 'Boofie' Arran who had brought in the Bill to the Lords. I think I owed my deliverance before boredom had really set in to a schoolboy and very characteristic impulse of Dicky's. Lord Arran left. In a trice, 'Shall we go?' said Dicky, and pelted after him. He caught him up on the stairs and panted out: 'I'd like to thank you for bringing in this Bill!' (I thought he would say something more personal and he told me he'd meant to add: 'As a lifelong, married homosexual'.) Lord A. looked a little surprised but not displeased. 'So you think I did right? I've LOATHED every minute of it.' Now appeared a figure in knee-breeches and a white finely pleated shirt without a collar, black jacket – heaven knows what he was (Black Rod?). Standing with one well-turned knee bent across the other he began a stagey, almost shouted conversation with Arran, largely for the benefit of Richard and me or any other audience. 'I used to be in the Navy, and in my view there were three things you should never have on your ship – rats, buggery and thieves – I couldn't make up my mind in what order . . . But now if you and I wanted to go upstairs and misbehave ourselves, I can't see any harm in it.' The logic was far from plain. Dicky's revealing features were rivetted excitedly on this pair of show-offs, while I lurked slightly uneasily behind. Then we got into my Mini and drove through the gathering darkness to Wivenhoe.

We heard later that the ayes for buggery had got it. Modified jubilation. I wonder very much whether quite a few who get a kick from being outsiders and rebels won't feel a sort of disappointment, and perhaps have to try some new eccentricity.

I tried this theory out on Denis at breakfast next day. He agreed. Is it just an age difference that so distinguishes Raymond, Eardley and Desmond, who don't talk all the time about homosexuality, any more than heterosexuals do about their sex life, from Dicky and Denis and some of their friends who can never let the subject drop?

February 13th: Wivenhoe

Icy cold, grey sky and bitter wind. The Store House has been transformed with infinite attention to detail from Denis – and is much less pretty in some ways than it used to be. The sitting-room walls are covered in ordinary brown paper, china and books have disappeared, a giant wooden play-pen encloses the foot of the stairs. They have installed powerful central heating which is curiously cheerless, producing a bursting sensation in the head (especially as the windows were kept fanatically shut), and no comforting glow. At times I was driven to ask for the electric fire to be put on. Denis was in his brisk sailorly mood all Saturday morning, constantly running out into the village on some errand or other.

When the telephone rings he always rushes to it, and answers in level tones, inviting all and sundry to 'come round'. Yesterday afternoon therefore two 'old Queers' arrived not long after lunch. They were old friends from Denis's past, and both very rich, and live in quilted and frilled splendour in Montpelier Square. At once Denis got overexcited and began offering them champagne. Their refusal was an obvious acceptance and three bottles were brought and drunk. Denis then rang up the pub or shop and asked for some more – and one more (all they had) did arrive. The next three and a half hours were pretty gruelling. I sat next to one of the visitors who was quick-witted, direct and funny – so I did my best, and to such effect that my arm is now black and blue with roguish 'go on' pats. Champagne kept being swished into glasses and overflowing onto the floor. It felt like a drinking-bout even to me who was not having a drop. I saw Dicky was infuriated by the whole proceedings which were causing him to be surly and inhospitable. He was very tired, having been in London examining would-be art students all week. The conversation kept returning compulsively to buggery; if it got on to anything like the present government or Rhodesia, the visitors' views were appallingly retrograde. Then the telephone rang again and Denis snatched it up. 'Why don't you all come round,' in ponderous tones, and with a truly devilish expression: 'Eric and Rex are here.' Eric and Rex made another attempt to go and were pressed to stay to dinner or for the night. At some point Eric began planning a dinner party – the women to be me, Janetta and Leslie Caron[1].

I decided I couldn't face the new arrivals, said goodbye to our companions of the long boozy afternoon and went up to my room, whence I distinctly heard the obviously boring conversation below. These long hours of unreal talk to perfect strangers had left me exhausted, my brain spinning and pulsating.

February 19th: Hilton

Sitting in the battered, cold charm of my bedroom working at my translation, I have been letting my mind wander off from time to time towards the sad breach between Angelica and Bunny, which has turned the house all at once into a dry husk. I drove Bunny down here yesterday afternoon through steady rain, the planetary landscape of the Great North Road dissolving in damp whiteness round us. He

[1] Their neighbours in Montpelier Square.

201

found a letter from Angelica (who is at Leeds helping look after Quentin's children while Olivier recovers from an operation), and after reading it showed it me with a sad face and trembling hand. He had asked her before insisting on legal steps – separation or divorce – to think well about the difficulties it would put between their continuing friends, and owning the same objects – I'm not sure if he added children.

He said that she had written to him that she didn't know 'why she was so unattractive to people', and that the irony of this (as he wrote back) was that she had always been attractive to him. There was a special sadness in his writing to her about 'taking care of each other when we're ill' – a thought he must often have. When one is over seventy, how cruel to be left suddenly without support – ever again. Meanwhile he valiantly takes on the cooking and housekeeping and female duties in the house.

February 20th

When we arrived only William was here. Yesterday morning there arrived Nerissa and Fanny with her French horn. I love this family and feel deeply engaged with them and their happiness, as I do perhaps with no other. I worked all yesterday morning, then the sky cleared and a sweet aroma of spring flooded the air. Walked into the garden, glass of red wine in hand, and inspected the dwarf irises, aconites and snowdrops and all the sprouting bulbs that Angelica had lovingly planted there, leaving labels to indicate what they were. Did she then hope to peg herself to the Hiltòn soil, or was she trying to do some last improvements for the family's sake? Her lack of interest in this house was noticeable a good long while ago, and Fanny told me the Bechstein piano had hardly been played on for ages – it is woolly and dim as a result. We had some music; me playing piano, with William on his oboe, and later with Fanny on her horn. She is the one who has astonishingly burst into flower, and who is now so alive and thinking so violently that Nerissa seems dreamy and somnolent by comparison. Nerissa took me on a lovely walk through the muddy fields and we talked about painting – among other things why she hated Poussin, and I tried to tell her why I greatly admired him. In the evening we had an energetic, philosophical set-to, starting round the dinner-table with Fanny taking the chief part – moral values, religion, biological survival, the difference between man and animals. It surged about, broke here and there in

Above: Julian Jebb and
Jaime Parladé near
Cape St Vincent.

Left: Henrietta with
Sophie.

Left: Bunny and Angelica Garnett arrive to stay with Eardley Knollys and myself at Orta, Italy.

Below: An Italian picnic: Joan Cochemé and Eardley Knollys.

Left: Eardley and Mattei Rader lunching outside our house at Orta.

Left: Anne Hill making mayonnaise.

Right: Kitty West by the lake at Tsarskoe Selo.

Left: The Irish Georgian group touring Russia: Lady Dashwood and, in the foreground, Mr Zerbe in Leningrad.

Below: On the bank of the Neva.

gusts of laughter and never got overheated. Moreover it was obviously greatly enjoyed by one and all. At one point Bunny got a book and began reading some Metaphysical poetry aloud – as he read Henry King's on the death of his wife he almost broke down, and I felt it expressed almost too poignantly his sadness at the loss of his own.

February 25th: London

Yesterday I met Raymond at the Bonnard exhibition, and pushed him round in the wheelchair he had reserved for the purpose.[1] It was a pleasure to find how much we agreed as to the pictures we liked or disliked, and I enjoyed this my third visit, though Raymond was rather a heavy baby and the wheelchair not altogether tractable. The figure of Lawrence looking much older, stooping and grey-haired came towards us. With visible excitement he said how incredible he found it that Bonnard had never painted while looking at the object. He goes to America for a month tomorrow with the Turner exhibition. Resentment has definitely got the upper hand in my feelings towards Julia, most un-pacifically. I think of her as a bully, and still have no desire for her company. I feel exhausted by adjusting to her and always anxiously considering her feelings and reactions. When Sonia was going to the cinema to see a Fellini film with Julia the other night and expressed doubts about it, I said without thinking: 'Oh, Julia's mad about Fellini. She's sure to enjoy it.' 'Oh, I'm not worried about *Julia*,' Sonia said, 'It's me I'm thinking about.' And I realized how Julia has for so long automatically inhibited my 'thinking about me' when I'm with her, and how at last the worm has turned.

Bunny has just been to lunch. He tells me Angelica rang up this morning and said that she had been persuaded by Rosemary Peto and another friend to put aside any idea of divorce for the present. With rain streaming like the saddest of tears from the pitch-dark sky he talked on and on, and I gradually put together the grounds of difficulty between them. They are as I supposed physical. I tried to suggest that their relationship might be well worth preserving even without the sexual element, although he himself had said that the necessity to communicate his feelings and experiences was something he greatly

---

[1] He was recovering from an operation.

missed. But he seems to feel his physical rejection too bitterly still – and doesn't want to see her for the present. We talked of Henrietta also – she rang me up yesterday under the influence of hashish which had made her feel so mad that she hoped never to take it again. If she really doesn't it will have been well worth it.

March 4th

A delightful visit from Henrietta and Sophie yesterday has greatly reassured me. Sophie was ebulliently gay, tore about, went to sleep when asked, and referred to me as 'the Frances'. I had a long talk with Henrietta in which all her occasional nonsense dropped off and nothing but sweetness and sense remained, as well as a great deal of honesty. We talked about Bunny and Angelica – she doesn't think Angelica has any other person in her life, but that she does very much want to shake off Bunny, William and Hilton. She blamed them both to some extent – Bunny for teasing Angelica, Angelica for rebuffing Bunny, but I think she was more on Bunny's 'side'.

I went a few days ago to a party to celebrate the Spenders'[1] silver wedding and Matthew's[2] twenty-first birthday. The ICI galleries in Dover Street were crammed to bursting with a lively crowd of all ages – from the glamorous young to Diana Cooper and Iris Tree. At one end in the obscurity jazz music was thrumming, and dancers were pounding obsessionally up and down. This and the vast horde of guests made it only possible to talk if one put one's mouth to an ear and bellowed into it – none the less I had several quite intimate conversations, enjoyed myself very much, feeling like a corpuscle in the blood stream of some huge animal organism and stayed till about one o'clock when the old were fast thinning out. It seemed very much an 'occasion' and a memorable one, faces were alight with friendliness and intelligence. Having wondered if I would 'know anyone' of course there they all were – Robert and Cynthia, David and Rachel, Rosamond Lehmann, Mary and Charlie, Koestler, V. S. Pritchett, the Ayers, the [James] Sterns, Julian, Tristram, Georgie. As Robert said, 'The people we know are very nice.' I caught sight of Julia among the throng and at one moment I went to talk to Cynthia not noticing that Julia was on the other side of her. She moved very quickly away.

[1] Stephen and Natasha.
[2] Their son.

I have thought a lot and painfully about our fractured friendship. I don't really yet feel I would enjoy seeing her again on the old terms. Though I kept such a frantic guard on myself before, it was to no purpose. I would though like to be 'on terms' of some sort, all the same.

March 9th

Excited by an invitation to go with Raymond to Asia Minor in May; I feel as if a bit of luck had dropped into my lap.

Raymond and I have just been to Cambridge to see *Measure for Measure* – lunch with Dadie first and drinks afterwards with him and Noel Annan in his rooms. Very like all undergraduate performances – beautifully spoken, stiffly acted, leaving one with the recollection of some moving situations and memorable phrases – like '*desperately* mortal'.

March 24th

A long period of hard work lies behind me. Today I posted the last of '*Communication*' to my typist. Tidying up proofs of Conan Doyle; I spent all this afternoon 'trying to relax' and utterly failing. One of the stress-producing things was that yesterday Henrietta came to tell me that she and Sophie were going to set off today with Nicky and Serge [Brodskis][1] in the wreck of Janetta's old car which breaks down incessantly. Where to? To France, Spain, Morocco – and perhaps Uganda! Janetta, Bunny and I telephone each other aghast – poor Janetta because she realizes they all expect to go and stay with her in Spain and she doesn't want them.

March 28th

I have been weltering in the gore of my own life, a very odd experience. Last week Michael Holroyd brought me the second volume of his life of Lytton, asking me to read and correct any factual inaccuracies. Of course I plunged in at once, deeply interested, at

[1] Her first husband.

205

first with a sort of horror, then with amazed admiration. For I think the impression he made on me of being a realist is accurate and that he has to an astonishing degree kept close to the facts. Perhaps he has probed too unmercifully, even the bedrooms and beds are explored for data; but he has relied enormously on written materials. The story of Lytton's last illness and death and Carrington's suicide made moving reading. I liked very much Lytton's comment on dying, when near his end: 'Well, if this is death – I don't think much of it.' Also how when incredibly weak he still talked philosophy and wrote poetry. When he complained that poetry was becoming difficult the fat plain nurse said, 'Any poetry that's written round here will be written by me.' Lytton in a very faint voice: 'My hat!' I also liked the remark of one of the eminent doctors who attended him: 'I should quite dote on that chap if I saw much more of him.' The portrait of Ralph is, as I'd expected, rather unsympathetic. But the only really inaccurate portrait of a *situation* is of the Gerald–Carrington–Ralph row, Watendlath and after. I shall try and put him right on that.

But – what astonishes me is this young man's power to make me see Bloomsbury with slightly fresh eyes. The impression of life, originality, working out their own standards, intellectual integrity, and fearlessness is still there. But – in Lytton at times, though he was not a good letter-writer and therefore shows in them his least serious side – a certain silliness emerges, a tendency to dismiss everyone and everything, however slightly outside the inner circle, as 'odious' and 'horrid' or 'infinitely dim'. Dogs, and children too of course – but not the rich upper class, to whom to some extent he capitulated.

April 3rd: Crichel

Besides the three present inmates we have here Pat Trevor-Roper[1] and a young man who is intelligent, beautiful and well informed, called Andrew Murray-Thripland. Raymond is enchanted by him, Desmond also, Eardley a little growly. I had quite a long talk with him alone yesterday, discovering that he had been to Eton and then read philosophy at Dublin, then became a press correspondent in the Middle East and is now a stockbroker, but he means to give in his notice tomorrow. I like Pat Trevor-Roper very much. He's a quick, eager, clever man with a perfect passion for facts and information. Raymond is in his element, always coming up with some odd piece of

---

[1] Eye surgeon. About to take Eardley's place in the house.

knowledge; someone runs next door for the OED or the Encyclopedia every few minutes, there are comic arguments, as when Pat declared that up to a certain date no doge died a natural death and Raymond challenged him. Andrew is absolutely up to the level of it all, well-versed in Gibbon and knowing at once what Roman Emperor had an aunt called Livia, as well as a lot of unrelated facts. It is lively and amusing, but I miss more general ideas as usual, though at the moment – rather weary-minded – I'm hardly able to produce any.

But I love being here and it doesn't discontent me at all being odd man out. Yesterday afternoon Eardley, Moses and I went a very long walk, cold and beautiful, all round Crichel lake. The trees are only just coming out here and there, large ash buds bursting from mainly bare twigs, whereas the fields are fresh green and we walked between great tufts of enormous primroses. It was bitterly cold and the lake quite rough, dry straw-coloured rushes rattling and creaking in the wind.

We had a general election last week and, as everyone knew they would, Labour got in with a large majority. Bunny dined with me and he and I went to look at the results on telly at Montpelier Square with Julian, Georgie, and Georgia, Jonny and Sabrina, Tim Behrens and Ed Gilbert. Except for Julian and me, *everyone* had voted Conservative (including Bunny) and some for trivial reasons. I was pleased that Bunny took to Julian.

At dinner Bunny told me Angelica is now wavering about the divorce but he is hesitant. 'I love her and I want to express my love.' Does this mean that he simply won't have her except on his own terms?

April 4th

Discussion of Turkish plans with Raymond last night – he wants to leave it all to me. Desmond again spoke of my going to Guatemala with him in the autumn. I am flattered but bewildered: though fond of Desmond I'm not sure if I know him well enough. Nor is he perhaps used enough to females. I don't want to struggle too hard not to seem like one. Eardley is very silent, under the weather of a cold, still looking rather craggy, and shutting himself behind disapproval of the critics from his position as creative artist. Raymond wearing his own suit of armour (being well informed about everything) with confidence, and laughing merrily and competitively at the least slip anyone makes. They are all extremely kind to me, and I love them severally and collectively.

Back to London today – it has been mortal cold all the time and no gleam of sun. Lying in bed before getting up I wonder what is happening to Julia and think how to arrange the jigsaw of my life. For the next few days it will remain so. Then I hope to get my translation finally off to Weidenfeld and creep down to spend Easter at Stokke.

April 9th: Stokke

Yesterday was Good Friday, and I drove out of London down the familiar Great West Road after breakfast. A long jam of holiday-makers' cars all round Reading filled me with shame and disgust. (What am I doing? Why be a party to it?) To refresh and purify I turned off the Bath road down to Kintbury, determined to take the Ham Spray lane, and run the gamut of all those old associations. Stopped for a moment at Kintbury to wash off the ignobility of packed cars by walking along by the canal and picking a bunch of the most ordinary flowers: butter-bur, marsh-marigold and even dead nettle looked sparkling and brilliant this gentle softly sunny morning. Very little change as I sped along past Ham Spray gates in a cloud of memory, missing both Ralph and Burgo with sudden acute pangs. On Thursday my translation was tied in brown paper and posted off to Weidenfeld. This therefore was the first day of freedom or would it be vacancy? For London is pretty empty – Janetta and Magouche both away, Julia in her tent like Achilles.

I don't know what lies in store today, Easter Saturday. I've been down to the kitchen, collected a breakfast tray and eaten it happily in my bed. Oh blessed solitude, and how I am enjoying my new leisurely tempo! There is to be a dinner party here tonight, I believe.

Talking to Mary about various words for sexual intercourse, I said, 'When I was young we talked of "copulation",' and she gave a slightly distasteful wriggle and said, 'There's something elongated and Modigliani about it.'

April 10th

At the Tycoonery,[1] I remember with astonishment, Serena actually ate her dinner in a different room because we were thirteen. Embarrassing

[1] Stowell House, home of Sir Philip Dunn, Mary McCabe's first (and again her last) husband who was often known as 'the Tycoon'.

for me as the extra one, the guests' guest, and making me feel I had stepped into a very alien world, was 'slumming' in fact, to use the arrogant Ham Spray expression. Last night there was a dinner party here, and I sat between the Gateses, father and son. No slumming there. Sylvester Gates is a very clever, hard-headed man, if a little glossy. Our views met at plenty of points – anti-Christianity for one. At one moment there was an outcrop of silly jokes which I thought might go on forever – elephant jokes, Polak jokes, and I'm not sure Charlie didn't hurry away to get some more jokes which he never got a chance to read aloud to us. They were *dreadful*. Otherwise Mary's dinner was exceedingly gay. The Jellicoes – now married and Philippa pregnant; Jim Douglas Henry, rather drunk. After the rest had gone he, Mary and I were left and Jim and I had for half an hour an absurd half-drunk argument, launched by him at me in a shout and at close range. How was it that although ever since the Industrial Revolution man's environment had steadily got 'better', he was no happier? was what it amounted to, and no one could mistake what he was saying, nor fail I should have thought to accept my answer: that this proved that happiness did not depend solely on material things, but that love, friendship and peace of mind were more important still. I could have said (but didn't) that some of the so-called improvements resulted in the atom bomb. Anyway it mattered little what I said as I was accused by turns of 'logic-chopping', being 'feminine', and taking my facts from the colour supplements. We both shouted but didn't really lose our wool nor fail to see the comic side of it all. He used words in an odd way – I was not allowed to speak of mind and matter or mental and material – but he allowed 'objective' and 'subjective', and the only thing I said that he heard was that these were not so much fields of thought as *ways* of thought, and I'm not even sure that's true.

And Charlie? He failed to stick out the dinner party and rose before the rest of us had finished from his head-of-the-table seat between Philippa and Pauline Gates, and quite politely said goodnight and went to bed. It can't have been much after ten, and can there be another host in England who would do something that so obviously showed his boredom with his visitors – leaving the two chief lady guests who had dressed in their best and driven a long way to visit him?

Last night I took myself to *Elektra*, the last performance. I remembered going to it only once before with Ralph, Burgo and his friend Michael Shone. One is curiously detached when seeing anything by oneself – both responsive and free from any necessity to react in a special way. A good performance, but I've decided I don't really like the work and never want to see it again; it's too turgid musically as well as emotionally.

On the way back from Stokke I called on Alix and James for an hour. Their great and splendid dignity reassured me. I think Holroyd has perhaps failed to catch it in his book.

April 15th

Last night Michael Holroyd came to dinner to collect his life of Lytton volume 2 and my corrections and some Gerald–Carrington letters. I had spent the afternoon re-reading part of his book in the light of my feeling (from visiting Alix and James) that he may have underestimated the 'nobility' of old Bloomsburians. It is a question of stress – they were also of course a little absurd. But what I decided from a second reading was that the most damning impressions came from their own mouths. Lytton in particular went all lengths to depreciate and make fun of the members of his own circle (unbridled cruelty about Clive, E. M. Forster 'a mediocre man who will come to no good', 'dullness exudes from Desmond[1] in a concentrated stream'. Lionel Penrose has 'entire absence of brain', Julian Bell 'half-witted', Logan Pearsall-Smith is 'senile'). This is made worse by his own great susceptibility to flattery and appreciation especially from rich duchesses. Indeed, success mellowed him as it usually does. Michael was aware of this and thought it should not be concealed. Our evening left me still liking him and respecting his judgement. I think he also respects mine, and he came nearer talking about himself than usual – he is going on holiday to Spain next month with a rather hysterical girl in her car. (He can't drive.) His girlfriends 'are inclined to be neurotic or schizoid'. He is obviously heterosexual and gravely hampered by lack of cash. I do hope he makes some money out of this book.

The Horror of the weather! All yesterday it snowed and blew leaving cars and street coated with what looked like lumps of coffee-sugar.

I gave Michael a few letters between me and Carrington to show that our relationship was more complex than he had realized and far from purely hostile.

*

[1] MacCarthy.

Julian has just been to lunch and gradually he induced me to talk about the past and give an account of my life. The guilt that doing this always arouses was temporarily assuaged by seeing without possible mistake that he was deeply interested; but it has surged over me again. With all the desire to be accurate in the world does one perhaps distort?

April 16th

Ahead of me lies a longish patch of solitude which – out of some desire to test myself – I have made no attempt to break. Waking late this morning, I have remained in bed devouring *The Times* from cover to cover and savouring my leisure. By tomorrow evening, when Robert's face is due to be the first to loom through the desert, I expect the taste of time passing will have gone sour. Anyway I intend to try. Last night with Georgia to a modern French film, beautiful to look at but senseless, brutal, superficial and chaotic in what it set out to do. Georgia knew about the director as a human being and interpreted him for me – he is stupid, that's the trouble. And therefore, given his immense facility with visual material, inevitably pretentious. The whole thing a succession of '*actes gratuites*' or '*gestes arbitraires*', as she pointed out, taken from pop art, woven out of machines, comics, fast cars, bleeding corpses, indiscriminately and charged with the potent dynamite of boredom.

8 p.m. So far, so good. Excursion to shops this morning, and this afternoon I did what sheer curiosity has long impelled me to do – went to a clairvoyant seance at the Spiritualists Association in Belgrave Square. Disappointing and pathetic, a very small gathering had turned up in the 'Conan Doyle Hall' – one jet-black man in a duffle-coat, two saturnine middle-Europeans, one elderly charwoman, three other men and me. A woman 'of the house' sat beside the medium and a man came in late at the back – both of these were clearly kind of stooges and provided a good deal of confirmation with enough very slight deviation for the medium to make play with.

She (the medium) was an elderly stout party, a pyramid of dense black with a quite jolly pudgy white face and white hair; she got excited as she talked and in a curious way didn't strike me as a deliberate cheat. Besides the two stooges, she 'talked to' three of us: the charwoman, me and a well-educated middle-aged man. Was the charwoman a stooge? – she really didn't seem so, but garrulous and nearly mad. Anyway, she nodded and said, 'That's correct,' to a great number of very exact details about 'Aunt Lily – your mother's sister. Uncle Jim, a dog called Princess and a dog called Gyp – both in the spirit world – and a very BIG tabby cat, quite a monster.' 'Yes, he was a Tom,' put in the charwoman. 'He used to rattle at the window,' took up the medium; 'do our pets live, I'm sometimes asked. Yes, I can tell you, they do.' Then she turned to me. 'I'd like to talk to you, darling.' She was quite at sea and I hadn't the heart to tell her so except once. She started with my being much mixed-up with Roman Catholicism, living in a Roman Catholic country perhaps. Then got on to a man, she thought my father (fathers and mothers are more popular than husbands and wives because everyone has had them) who was very upright and you were proud of him. A flat and futile experiment which I have little desire to repeat.

I went to bed early but lay awake until nearly two, reading and thinking about a new book about two young men of promise who were killed in the Spanish Civil War – Julian Bell and Frances Cornford's[1] son John. The revival of the old themes of war and peace, violence and passivity was strangely disquieting.

April 19th

We creep about, day by day, in unspeakable darkness, cold and damp, God help us all. It doesn't give one a chance – except to show fortitude and endurance.

My evening with Robert was so delightful that I remember nothing of our conversation, having been too deeply engaged in it. We talked of psychoanalysis though; he now goes only once a week. Like me, he believes in the theory but is doubtful about the therapy – though he described how after one session he suddenly felt detached from his own tormented unconscious, and looking at it as if from an astral plane without being agonizedly involved. He said also how usually the awareness of the infantile source of his states of mind failed to clear a path in that subterranean turmoil, and this I can very easily imagine.

Dined last night with Raymond and the Pritchetts at the Travellers' Club ostensibly to talk Turkey, but in fact we talked mainly about books and other things. Dorothy wheezy and unwell, complaining of insomnia. V. S. P. has a curious coldness, possibly of an over-sensitive man who doesn't want to be upset by other people's

[1] The poetess.

horrors. He talked of 'sympathy' as something to be regretted and weak. I don't really feel sure that if one were sinking in a slimy river he would pull one out. But who would? Robert of course, Janetta, and Julian; Mary would have a try.

April 20th

With Mary to a party at Murray's for Paddy Leigh Fermor's book – enjoyable. A roomful of interesting literary faces, and such a very handsome room, too – Robert, V. S. P., Raymond, the Berkeleys, Patrick Kinross. Normally I shrink before such things, but if I get there I am glad I've gone: it's entirely a matter of confidence. Poor Mary is low and looking worn. I fear gnawed by unhappiness about Charlie and uncertainty for the future.

This morning on the spur of the moment I rang Angelica because there's been no news from Henrietta. She was expansively friendly and forthcoming – and after quite a long talk raised the question about the 'Dy-vorce' as she calls it, between her and Bunny. I said my say, as to not liking the mechanical interference of the law in tender human relations. She told me she was now definitely against it, but it was Bunny – perversely – who was insisting. What a mess! She explicitly said it 'had been going on for some months', which looks as though their trouble was recent, and also that 'she didn't want to marry anyone' – or perhaps 'there was no one she wanted to marry,' not quite the same thing.

Though preparations for Turkey have advanced, Raymond told me on the telephone that his back was hurting him again and I suddenly feel the trip will not come off.

April 21st

Another odd experience last night – a dinner with the 'Anti-Shakespeare Society', invited by Lionel and Margaret Penrose. A large gathering of solid, intelligent-looking middle-aged and elderly people in evening dress, including the Duke of St Albans and Lord Wakehurst, both directly descended from Lord Oxford who is the favoured candidate of the society. When I told Sir John Russell, a hatchet-faced legal light, that I too was descended from Lord Oxford (which is true), he looked at me in ludicrous amazement.

There was a strong element of *snobbery* about the supporters of Oxford, though I don't know if they thought Shakespeare's two noble descendants – both of whom made speeches – were worthy offshoots. The Duke, a pink-faced youngish man with an unbridled smile, excused himself for not bringing up a portrait of Oxford from his country seat, but gave no reason. The 'man Shack-speer' or 'the man of Stratford' was mentioned several times with smug and pitying smiles. I asked Lionel what on earth all the eminent scholars who thought Shakespeare wrote Shakespeare had to gain by their beliefs if they weren't true? And he muttered something about vested interests, Establishment and scholars always being heated. I forgot to bring up Ben Jonson to Marjorie Sisson who is an Oxford addict and was sitting next to me. Indeed, not a single argument was produced except for Sir John Russell declaring that *The Tempest* was obviously not by 'Shakespeare' (it was written after Oxford's death), one reason being that the 'cloud-capped towers' speech plainly showed that he didn't believe in an afterlife, while the author of *Hamlet* did. One speaker alluded to Shakespeare's ambivalent sexual tastes, and Mr Christmas Humphreys briskly waved aside any idea of his being 'cissy'. In fact everyone was completely woolly-minded.

April 26th

During most of my drive to Lambourn and the Carringtons last weekend I was wondering whether to take my courage in both hands, ring up Julia and ask her to have a walk, so putting an end to the indigestible and undigested lump of our disagreement. When it poured all Saturday afternoon I admit I felt a certain relief that no decision need be come to. On Sunday, however, blue sky and warm wind put another face on things and I had sufficiently rehearsed what I would say – that I wondered if she would care for a short walk; she could think about it and ring me back. It was Lawrence to whom I gave the message, as Julia was in the bath, but she soon rang up and said she would like it very much.

I am very glad the deed is done. It has cleared a patch of guilt on my theoretical 'pacifism in private relations as in public affairs'. I knew it was right to make a move, yet wounded pride and other ignoble feelings, perhaps just dread of p and q-minding, held me back. There was quite enough to say about people and events without going into dangerous territory or making any allusion to our last meeting, and we both with one accord avoided red lights. The nearest was when I asked if she had seen Sonia since she came back from staying in Spain with Janetta, and if she'd enjoyed herself. Julia said hurriedly that Oh yes, she'd seen her, and she said she'd felt very sorry for Janetta. She never realized before how unhappy she was. Obviously Sonia's visit wasn't a great success, and her hostility to Janetta is pretty plain in this comment. I dropped the subject quickly.

The other dangerous corner was when, heaven knows why, Keith Baynes[1] was mentioned, and Julia said, 'Oh, I know for a fact he died fifteen years ago.' As I'd seen him off and on until two years ago and firmly believe he's still alive I was starting to say, 'Oh, I think you must be thinking of someone else,' but the red light switched on and I switched off.

I leave the next move to her. Total impression – Julia unchanged in every particular, a fascinating if difficult companion. Perhaps she is getting used to her situation?

May 1st: Cambridge

Staying with Celia Goodman; perfect summer weather with the freshest green leaves, white furbelows of cherry blossom, and lilac coming out. Sun pours in at the windows. University life with its drawbacks and advantages surrounds me – the safe, flat landscape, the clever highly-qualified people we have visited and been visited by. We had Scotto-Russian Professor Postan, a lively gossip who liked to talk of Bertie Russell and his cortège of adoring American Trotskyites, his vanity and his anti-American obsessions. Celia told me Arthur Waley is dying of cancer of the spine, discovered after a motor smash. With typical gallantry and goodness she lives up to her views by paying him harrowing visits. She described his present mistress[2] lounging naked in a dressing gown with her grey hair falling round her shoulders, saying what a fiend Beryl[3] had been. Talked of the arrogance and cruel remarks about their own friends indulged in by Old Bloomsbury, wondered what was the reason for it. I've thought much about it lately, and it has been a relief to turn to Desmond's[4] letters, running over as they are with the milk of kindness and human sympathy to the verges of sentimentality.

Back in London. Still grilling hot. Took a pie to eat for lunch in the

1 Painter of the London Group.
2 Later his wife, Alison.
3 de Zoëte, who had lived with Arthur for many years.
4 MacCarthy. His children had invited me to edit his letters.

215

Square where the sun had brought out many other picnickers and sunbathers. Colin Haycraft has rung up apparently delighted with my translation – but I have to go to see him and 'check a few points'.

May 6th

For some time I've felt great reluctance to write a word in this book and the mere thought of it produces a dull wooden thud like a croquet mallet striking a peg. I'm not sure why – I've been 'getting along' quite all right but in a curiously unreflective way that I don't at all relish. Again I think of mallets and pegs – the apparatus of some fairground game, in which I bounce uncontrollably from obstacle to obstacle, not mistress of my fate, unthinking, and slightly unfeelingly.

Since I finished my last translation I have been going through the Desmond letters with a red pencil and I'm simply not sure what sort of a book they would make – whether perhaps something a little insipid emerges. Prolonged contact with anyone through their letters, diaries or memoirs is a stringent test, almost like marriage. But I do like his unmalicious sympathy and understanding. I've had no shortage at all of things to do and people to see, and the trip to Turkey now hurtles towards me and absorbs all plan-making instincts.

I've just remembered an interesting story told me by Professor Postan at Cambridge. I asked if he had known John Cornford, killed in the Spanish Civil War. 'Yes, he was a pupil of mine and a most remarkable, brilliant and formidable young man. An odd thing happened not long ago. I was correcting some history papers for a colleague who was ill. I didn't look at the names in case I knew some of the students, but I suddenly had an extraordinary sense of *déjà vu* – the turn of phrase, the ideas were familiar. Could the student have cribbed from something I knew? I looked at the name – Cornford; the paper had been written by the *posthumous* son of John.'

May 9th

Back in my nest after a short ice-cold weekend at Thorington with the Penroses. That paper-thin old house let in the shrieking wind which hurled rain against it all Sunday, and I felt anxious for the thinly-dressed wife of an American paediatrician who spent the day with us, and heaped more logs and coal on the fire whenever Lionel wasn't looking. As always I loved being with the Penroses though, in

216

spite of material discomforts – apart from stimulating talk, their geniality, appreciativeness and tolerance are at the moment what I particularly like. How though can so clever a man as Lionel think Shakespeare's plays were written by a syndicate?

Bunny had tackled Lionel on the Shakespeare question at a Cranium dinner[1] and he rather accusingly suggested this was my fault. 'Why, of course I told him about the Anti-Shakespeare dinner,' I said. 'I didn't think there was any secret about your views.'

Side-stepping among the values of the Penrose family I inevitably check them against those of other friends – Janetta, Magouche, Julian, Henrietta; and the Penroses get top marks for constructive kindness, music, intelligent thinking. Shirley and a nice plump girlfriend were swotting for exams with unheard-of persistence and enthusiasm (medicine and Greek philosophy respectively). Lionel would look up from a sheet on which he was writing mathematical formulae to join in the general conversation. He seems to have discovered something new about Mongols[2] which excites him greatly – there are, he now thinks, two sorts; and another discovery concerned miscarriages, which have never been properly investigated. But analysis of two hundred showed that fifty were abnormal as to chromosomes.

Barely keeping warm by sitting on top of the log fire and wearing two jerseys and a flannel shirt, I never stirred out all yesterday but on Saturday I walked off along the green lanes alone, beside the stream and up the hill to a bluebell-carpeted wood. A magnificent swan sailed silently along the narrow strip of water and hissed menacingly when I stooped to pick some *cardamine amara* by the water's edge. Further on his wife proudly arched her neck over her nest. I enjoyed my bath of greenery.

Shirley described with obvious horror the ghastly things she has to do in her medical training – particularly in practical physiology. They have to anaesthetize a cat, cut it up and attach all its various blood-vessels or nerves to tubes. I may have got this wrong, but it called up a sickening vision. 'Are the cats killed afterwards?' someone asked. 'Oh, good *God*, yes!'

The two quiet Americans spoke gloomily about President Johnson and Vietnam – saying that he was absolutely devoid of imagination, and also of international feeling or even curiosity.

---

[1] A dining-club dating from the late twenties.
[2] Now always referred to as Down's syndrome.

217

May 12th: London

Raymond has just rung up to say he has German measles! I feel incredulous, yet that 'it had to be.' He told me he had it as a child and the present diagnosis was made by a 'very young locum'. Anyway, it is such a trifling complaint that one would be prone to ignore it. But the sound of his deep voice, anxiety-soaked, ringing up with reiterated alarms has begun to unnerve me, and I feel if some other less anxious person would take his bookings over I should be almost relieved. But who? Bunny? Anyway I suppose he will want to postpone, not cancel our journey. All my present activities – my Turkish lessons and so on – have had the stuffing knocked out of them. I had begun reading the history of Asia Minor, and in every sort of way letting myself gradually down the steps into the swimming-bath of next week's journey. Thank heaven frustrations and disappointments seem to matter less than they once did.

May 13th

What a day yesterday was, poised half in England, half in Turkey, not knowing how to spend my time nor able to leave the flat in case Raymond should ring up. I begged him to get a second opinion, in case there might be some mistake in the diagnosis. He promised he would, and said he would ring up again about noon but when he did, he had done *nothing*, and still accepted the obviously charming young doctor's verdict. Again I urged him to make quite sure – he declared he felt quite well, except for the rash, and had no temperature. At tea-time he rang again, his voice an octave higher. He had with some difficulty got hold of a doctor from the Fever hospital who said at once, 'Oh no, that's not German measles' and declared it was a vaccination rash. So we're off after all!

Last night I dreamed most vividly that Ralph came and walked beside me along a road I was following. I was intensely aware of his presence and personality and I turned to him and said, 'Oh, how COULD you leave me like this all alone?' The sensation of violent pain and indignation woke me up.

May 14th: Crichel

Oh dear – not out of the wood yet by a long way. Shall we, shan't we go to Turkey? I don't know, but at the moment it looks very doubtful and Raymond seems a most unlikely and (it must be said) rather undesirable travelling companion.

Yesterday afternoon I drove down here, heard tapping in the drawing-room, and found him at his typewriter. He at once said he felt far from well, was still covered with the rash, and showed all the symptoms of abandonment to a literary man's dejection. In the course of the evening things got worse. Eardley arrived starry-eyed from having bought a little country house with Mattei Radev. (This was a fresh blow, as I think Raymond had always believed he might stay on here.) After hearing about it Raymond went up to his bath, but returned to dinner in a much worse, a really deplorable state – preoccupied, self-centred, impatient. There's no question, I now see, of his being pressed to go unless his rash is *quite* gone in the next two days – and this I begin to doubt. At dinner he was pitiful, had forgotten to brush his hair, interrupted Eardley's and my remarks with impatient strings of 'Yes, Yes, Yes', burst into thunderous blimpish disapproval of the Labour Party, of Harold Nicolson's bad spelling and all 'young reviewers who didn't read three or four books round each book they reviewed' (as he did for his dull piece about the Zulus last week), and was inclined to contradict everything anyone said in a very dictatorial fashion. I encouraged him to go to bed, sat talking to Eardley for a while and then went up early myself – and brooded.

Well, I've reached several conclusions. I must at once make clear to him that of course there's no question of our going till he feels perfectly well, and perhaps give him the chance to back out altogether. How I wish my companion was to be Eardley or Desmond. I don't want to nanny Raymond through Turkey and I'm reminded of how Ruth Lowinsky complained of being made to wash his underpants! I'm ashamed of my fickleness, for of course he is now one of my oldest friends and one whom I see from old diaries used in the past never to fall from grace. But in the last ten years or so we have grown in different directions. I do feel sorry for him, and I'm not as heartless towards him as this outburst may seem to show – and I realize very vividly that it would be much too cruel to try and persuade him to come to Turkey if he is not feeling well. That's absolutely final and I shall hang on to it for all it's worth.

Mrs Spicer has just brought in my breakfast tray. I gather Raymond is no better and is not dining out at Michael Pitt-Rivers's this week. 'It *is* a shame. He does *try* so hard. He *tries so hard in the world*, Mr Mortimer does. You know, he's a sweet person.' And so he is, of course, and does.

May 15th

Raymond followed hard on Mrs Spicer, and as a result of a bad night and no diminution of the rash and my determination not to raise obstacles, an hour was spent postponing our departure for one week. I think it highly likely he'll be perfectly well by Tuesday, but what does it matter? Now I've changed gear and don't care a bit, and he is enormously relieved, so it's well worth it. Pat Trevor-Roper and his friend Andrew arrived for lunch and confirmed the genesis of the famous rash – he was also much impressed by it. Poor Raymond – I've been hard on him. How could he feel 'himself' if his body is in such a state of protest?

May 16th

I drove back to London this morning, and now lie with my swollen and aching leg up, cursing smallpox inoculation in general. I left Raymond as spotty as ever and not (I feel) tremendously sanguine, though the presence of charming Andrew made him put as good a face on his troubles as possible and even look better. I asked Pat if he thought it would certainly be gone in a week, and he said, 'Oh, yes,' but I thought I glimpsed a reservation in his eye, and he said rashes were always slow to go. Yesterday was brilliant and beautiful, today also; we played croquet and lay on long chairs in the sun. I went a long walk with Eardley and Moses (too long, I fear, for my leg). The feeling that Eardley is a real friend gives me great pleasure. When we are alone I don't 'think what I'm going to say to him' at all – nor I believe does he. I'm interested in his thoughts, we pursue anything that comes up (like associations in pictures), we drop a subject and come back to it. I can't help contrasting him with Raymond, who is a good man, and who 'tries hard in the world' but has less resilience or power to shift his angle of vision. I'd better go on while I'm about it and criticize Raymond's way of stating categorically something which he's quite unable to support in any way. A tiny example – we were talking about Falstaff whose 'nose was as sharp as a pen and 'a babbled of green fields.' The latest interpretation, Raymond said, was 'a table of Grenville (or Grenfell)' meaning a picture of the Admiral. But 'How? Why?' I asked; 'it doesn't appear to make sense.' 'I can't remember, but it seemed very convincing and is now generally accepted.' Then at dinner he declared that Pragmatism amounted to much the same as Christian Science. Again I asked how in the world he made that out? All he will say is, 'Well, isn't it?'

May 17th: London

My leg is just as painful and turning somewhat blue, so I'm quite glad not to be going today. Meanwhile I loll on my bed, surrounded by books and papers and have long talks on the telephone – an immense one with Frances Phipps who is dining at Buckingham Palace tonight. She goes with an admirably detached curiosity about it all, and I shall ring her up tomorrow and see if she's engaged Harold Wilson in talk about Vietnam.

Last night Julian took me to *Ballo in Maschera*, which I simply loved. There's not a dull moment in the score – or only about one. Afterwards back to Montpelier Square where we found Nicky drooping over the television, and looking handsome but dejected.

May 18th

Paul Hyslop[1] telephoned. Raymond was better, but had 'sounded cross' because Paul hadn't sent our air tickets back to the agents – I should think so! We can't get the new ones till he does. Then he said flatly and so far as I can remember in these very words: 'If Raymond *dies* while you're in Turkey you don't need to bring him back or do anything special. I thought you'd better know; he wouldn't want it.' Oh, what a cheerful holiday this promises to be! I wonder if the message originated with Raymond?

May 20th

Dined last night with Magouche and Robin Fedden, and was taken on afterwards to Joan Rayner's,[2] where were Connollys, Betjemans, Patrick Kinross, Johnny Craxton and so forth. I was sitting between Cyril and Deirdre and put several feet wrong with Cyril. One sees at once when one has done that, as he delights in showing disapproval. On the other hand if one is lucky enough to amuse him (I did once though I can't remember how) he wrestles desperately to control his smile.

[1] Who shared Raymond's Canonbury house.
[2] Later Leigh Fermor.

I'm wondering a little what I'm in for in the way of Turkish muddle. The only arrangement Raymond has had to make – getting our tickets to Izmir – has been bungled: first they went to the *Sunday Times*, then Paul failed to send them back to the agents. Now mine has still not come, though they say they posted it yesterday, and Raymond's has gone again to the *Sunday Times*.

May 22nd: Hilton

A wild wind is blowing the clouds across the top of the dovecot and has turned my fatalism about Turkey to hectic agitation.

Bunny and Angelica appear to be as sweetly and happily united as anyone could wish. What is to be made of it all? There's not even the feeling of guardedness that might be expected after overcoming (as I suppose and hope they have) a major crisis.

Nerissa walks about like a tragedy queen, in tattered jeans and a large velvet Rembrandt tam-o-shanter, or sits drooping her long hair over her knees, and seems at times to utter audible groans at the boringness of our conversation. We were talking harmlessly after lunch about national characteristics – the ugliness of the French and the way middle-aged Spaniards suddenly 'gave up everything'. Nerissa was obviously exasperated and burst out: 'I'm amazed how you all make such *wide* statements that they can't possibly be true, and look so pleased about it.' 'But good heavens,' said Bunny, 'if I were to say most English cats are black or tabby, would you object to that?'

After I'd written the above, Nerissa melted into total sweetness, no longer needing to show that she found us all irritating, for some reason concerned with her boyfriend. But I was touched by the fond pat she gave Bunny as we left this morning.

So off Raymond and I seem to be going, though I feel as if I had been cast somewhat for the role of Dr Moran, whose detailed medical account of Winston Churchill's last years has been appearing in the Sunday papers and exciting a lot of interest.

Raymond rang up and added to the funeral note by saying he had been to Craig Macfarlane to make a new will also, he had 'felt awfully queer after lunch – it quite worried me.' 'What sort of queer?' 'Oh, just dizzy and strange'. Then belatedly, 'But I'm quite all right now. I'm sure I shall be in *top form* tomorrow.'

May 24th: Athens

Thank heavens that with the passing of the years I seem to have lost all sense that there's anything odd or frightening about flying – although I know it would take very little indeed to resuscitate it. Eardley drove Raymond and me to the airport and left us there in what Raymond said he felt to be 'a specially horrifying form of Dante's Inferno', while to me it looked rather more as the central Post Office must to a parcel. I felt confident I should be dispatched and arrive at the right destination but all the alarms that have preceded our departure, and my awareness of Raymond's anxious forebodings, resulted in my 'not greatly caring' whether I did or no. We were passed through the sorting compartments effortlessly, except for occasional, convulsive checking-up of vital organs (spectacles? passport? ticket?) and soon we were sailing along with uneventful smoothness through the layer of haze which seemed to be hanging over all Europe. A sideways somewhat horrific glance at Mont Blanc; the Gulf of Corinth sprinkled with islands like a paperchase – and Athens. How strange that a place only once briefly visited, and that exactly thirty years ago, should immediately present a familiar face. I find it as I did then for the most part unattractive, too white, too monotonously spread over the plain, except for its astonishing focus. I'm trying not to wave my antennae too obviously towards Raymond. He very sweetly bought me a bottle of lovely Dior scent at the airport as if in apology for his *faiblesse*. In the aeroplane there was a good deal of whisky-and-pill-swallowing; but I think he's relieved to be here. He has a surprising and touching way of talking ('making himself agreeable') to all and sundry including unlikely housewives from the Midlands, whom I can't help feeling he mistakes for 'cultivated people'.

It was six by Greek time when we got to the hotel, and he went at once to rest, arranging to meet at seven-thirty. I couldn't for a moment consider staying in my room all that time but set out walking through the small streets between the Olympic Palace and the Acropolis – a very nice part of the town, full of tavernas and shops where carpets were being cleaned and picture frames made, wine and vegetables sold. Soon I found myself on the lower slopes of the backside of the great object itself and began climbing by twisting lanes of small white-washed houses, with old black-clad women immobile on kitchen chairs, cats and pots of flowers at every corner. Except for the fear of keeping Raymond waiting I would have gone on to the top, for the light was fading and the town was slowly melting in a pink misty glow below me. I returned, feeling I'd visually (but not at all historically) nipped and possessed a minute fragment of Athens without wasting a moment. Had a swig of whisky and felt ready for anything. When Raymond appeared we more or less retraced the path I'd followed, passing a mysterious sign reading BOTTOM in different coloured lights (one of Eddie Gathorne-Hardy's night haunts?), and sat down in a restaurant with a garden under the deepening sky looking up at a delicate crescent moon and the silhouette of the Acropolis. Kind and handsome waiters looked after us. We ordered moussaka. Was there any fish? 'Only screams', they said diffidently (shrimps – or rather prawns). This made a delicious meal with some warm, white unresinated wine. Raymond was aghast when three young men stood up before three microphones holding very shiny electric guitars. 'They're preparing to *tor*ture us,' he said in his profoundest basso – but they sang traditional Greek songs in soft voices and a restrained style, and I for one enjoyed it. Raymond was anxious to be back in the hotel by ten (nine o'clock English time).

May 25th

Hazy hot-looking morning. We took a taxi up to the Acropolis. It was crowded with holiday-makers, many white-headed, picking their way with stiff legs over the rough platform of stone. The complete image, both visual and auditory, including the loud American voices and groups of lively, very black-haired Greeks, was suddenly *there*, as something I had never forgotten; the nobility, purity of line and Godlike arrogance, the very pale curdled cream of the stones. Perhaps the Erechtheion gave me less of a thrill at second sight, and what I'd remembered as rows of Vanessas,[1] smiling enigmatically and tilted slightly forward in the museum didn't turn out to be quite that, but were beautiful none the less, and remote, and smoothly polished as if they'd lain under the sea. Out again into the powerful but not crushing heat. The silvery stones we walked over were sprinkled with red poppies and yellow crucifers.

After lunch a small nearly empty Turkish aeroplane chugged us at what seemed a snail's pace over the dusty brown coastline, the Aegean, and then the identical dusty brown coastline of Turkey to Izmir Airport. Raymond picked up a plump and pretty American girl

[1] Bell.

who turned out to be a member of the Peace Corps – a voluntary do-gooder, all honour to her. I heard him telling the passport man clearly, slowly and amiably: 'I am delighted to be here. I am sure I shall enjoy myself very much. But I am OLD.' This went down extremely well and he got a lot of 'patting and holding' as he calls it. Intense scrutiny of passports. Bus life very Turkish – it bounced and rattled, though the road was good, and the driver kept half leaping to his feet to try and close a trap door which had mysteriously opened in the roof. The country we drove through might have been southern Spain except for less attractive cottages. Olives made pools of shadow for sheep and cows to lie in; gentle hills – a *kind* landscape. Izmir was at once more oriental, with its minarets, bazaar-like shops, piles of amphorae, and vine-covered alleys crowded with people carrying baskets.

But my first walk in the town hasn't greatly charmed me. There are quantities of huge-winged American cars, some belonging to the American Army and often driven by negroes, others surprisingly converted into Turkish taxis. The extent of the American occupation begins to arouse Yankophobia in me – one hears the twang on every side, particularly from horrid little shaven-headed juniors. Then a peasant woman swathed in a black veil comes by leading by the hand a little girl of about six wearing the prettiest Turkish trousers under a tunic.

Is Doctor Moran taking enough care of his patient? I do hope so. Raymond retired for two hours while I took my walk and was in bed again before ten, from which I conclude he is very tired indeed. I question him often about his back, feet and sleeping, and he answers in great detail; so he must be very preoccupied with them. I really see rather little of him – but he was cheerful during dinner, eaten in our hotel restaurant: a huge plate of kebab and yoghurt. Afterwards we walked through the warm night to the sea. This very comfortable hotel can only have us for three nights and we want to stay four. We shall have to think again.

May 26th

My room looks out on a waste land of trees and logs – part of the Park of Culture that has run to seed. This morning there is a peasant woman there with her head and shoulders swathed in a bath towel and a sheep browsing on the end of a lead.

I was wakened by the telephone saying 'Günaydin' to me, and

225

managed to ask for breakfast in my swotted-at Turkish. Raymond had made an appointment with the Consul, and we set out thither along the sea front – it turned out to be a long way, and taxing to poor Raymond, who sighed but pegged on valiantly. The Consul, Mr Wilkinson, a rather charmless man with false teeth and a dark brown wart on his nose, addressed me several times as Mrs Mortimer and was friendly and helpful. A visit to the tourist agency to get Raymond's press card and a tiny cup of dark mud in a café took up the rest of the morning. Plan-making over lunch. Raymond remarked that 'we were not likely to differ much.' I hope not. The fresh, warm, salt-laden air and the benignity of the sun dissolves and relaxes my anxieties and I see that in this kindly indolent land one could soon give up doing much except sit on a divan eating sweetmeats. There are extraordinary dishes on the menu, translated as 'Bulbül Bird's nest', 'Lady's navel', and 'The Imam has fainted'.

After my 'Bulbül bird' I lay on my bed and began to read my Penguin Herodotus with pleasure. Afternoon drive to the Agora, our first glimpse of I suppose many columns and fragments of antiquity. My response was mildly pleased; I was more delighted by our subsequent walk through the crowded streets of the bazaar. Tomorrow is Turkish Independence Day and a national holiday, so the town is already hung with crimson flags with crescent and star, while each little booth displays shiny shoes, coconut-covered cakes or artificial flowers, and barrows are loaded with juicy cucumbers and black cherries.

Raymond has looked less anxious today and seems better, but we have taken tickets for a trip to Pergamum tomorrow and in preparation he had bolted to bed soon after nine-thirty. Before that we drove to a restaurant on the hill and looked down on Izmir's twinkling lights, drinking raki.

May 27th: Pergamum day

The Consul warned us of Turkish unpunctuality and sure enough both breakfast and the bus that was to take us were late. The latter was a small battered *dolmüs*, full to bursting with very fat red-faced Germans, to Raymond's horror and almost equally to mine. He and I were on the back seat – the worst, and there were anyway no springs to speak of. Bouncing out over the appalling *pavé* roads of the suburbs was a gruelling start to our excursion and I felt very anxious for Raymond's powers of endurance. But we are now safely home and he says it was 'much less exhausting than he expected', and he has been in splendid spirits all day. Once out into the country the road improved and I gazed eagerly about at this first sight of rustic Turkey. Camels – several strings of them – slowly moving along with expressions of vast disdain, another group including young ones collapsed into heaps for a rest; buffaloes, storks; workers in the fields using implements with such short handles that they were bent with their bottoms higher than their heads under the noonday sun – the women wearing full trousers and a scarf or tablecloth over their heads, men with heads swathed in turbans, or Colonel Lawrence fashion. The Turks do seem rather a melancholy and defeatist race, as Patrick Kinross said, and though this was a national holiday there was very little gaiety. It was two hours' drive from Izmir to the Acropolis itself, astoundingly poised on the summit of a conical hill out-topping its neighbours and with the theatre plastered against the steep topmost slope, looking as if the audience must topple from their seats into the plain. The prevailing colour of the stone was a curious dull bronze, like the dancing-shoes of my childhood, and exceedingly dark red poppies grew among the stones. Our guide's yells in deafening German, followed by hastily epitomized English were not inspiring, and for some reason the ruins left me rather unmoved in spite of their splendid situation. But I enjoyed the whole day, perhaps most of all the drive through the wide valleys and gently sloping hills.

Back in Izmir, we found Independence Day being celebrated in a jolly but stodgy and family way; Ataturk's statue was piled with wreaths and the streets were full of people carrying or dragging their children. Meanwhile the sky turned a lurid purplish red with black tadpole clouds, all reflected in the quiet sea, and a few piratical-looking ships became silhouettes of innumerable lights. Raymond and I sat down at one of the restaurants on the sea front. I was delighted with the valiant way he had stood our long day's outing and didn't want to discourage him from going to bed soon after nine, which seemed to be what he wanted. So I walked back to the hotel with him and went out again not long after, curious to see what was going on. The crowds were thicker now and I felt a little sheepish about my solitude and glad when some Turkish girls sat down beside me. Soon everyone began to crane forward and stare down the esplanade, and the insistent, ferocious sound of drums beating a slow, ponderous rhythm grew gradually louder and nearer, until up came a procession of soldiers or sailors all dressed in white; short, square

227

and strong, with shiny white crash helmets fastened by broad bands under their chins. The most extraordinary thing about this frightening display was the way they lifted their short, snow-white legs in time to the shattering drumbeat, not in a goose step but with '*knees high*' (like Strauss's Electra) and then stamping masterfully on the ground. I felt these strong, square men were longing to go and kill someone, and that the roaring and clapping of the crowd was purely warlike.

May 28th

Today we had to move for our last Smyrnian night to a lower-grade hotel. In the morning to the archeological museum – but I have to confess that these headless deities and fragments of groups don't greatly thrill me. Peered dutifully at tiny objects of metal, clay or gold, wondering what they were used for, and walked out into the flat and flowerless Culture Park with its hideous modernistic buildings, feeling unstimulated. Thence with relief into the life of the town; bought postcards and sat drinking limonata in a café. Was reproved by Raymond for being so unhygienic as to lick my stamps. After Raymond's nap we set off in a taxi to Teos, a fishing village picturesquely embraced by the ruins of a Genoese castle, from the walls of which hung a beautiful prickly plant with large pale flowers and cascades of purple stamens – the caper. Women in brilliant trousers stood staring at us from under an ancient gateway and some children burst into rockets of laughter at our comic appearance. How odd, I thought, we've hardly heard any Turkish laughter till now. Yet they break easily into gentle and friendly smiles tinged with melancholy. They seem well disposed to the English, preferring us to Germans and Americans, but fatalistic and without much energy or enthusiasm. Our little mustachioed taxi-driver brought out a tiny Turkish guidebook in order to enlighten us quite incorrectly about what we were looking at, and thumbed it over hopefully, muttering about Dionysus and Anacreon.

The classical site of Teos, a mile or so further on, was rural and enchanting. We drew up at the edge of a field, and there through the old olives and a forest of flowers (mullein, anchusa, umbellifers and these very dark red poppies) we saw a few stout incomplete grey columns. A bronzed man appeared with a little boy and soon afterwards, stepping proudly in her trousers and bare feet and carrying a short-handled hoe came a handsome little girl of about

228

ten. 'Mehraba!' they said, and 'Mehraba' I replied, and then explained that I was English. 'Ingiliz-im, anlimiyorum' (I don't understand) and 'Vah Vah' (my favourite phrase = What a pity!) . . . The ruins were a total jumble, but made really beautiful by the wild flowers springing up all round them and enveloping them. When I started to pick them the children brought me more and more, and then leaves, berries, sticks, wheat, anything, till my arms were full. There wasn't another soul in sight except this charming little family, until a youth rode up on a donkey, to whose 'Mehraba!' Raymond replied, 'How are *you*?' in his best cocktail-party voice. A white pony was browsing among the stones. Lovely drive home in the golden afternoon light – the quadruped-like workers were still hacking away with picturesque but terrible industry at their fertile fields.

May 29th: Villa Park Otel, Antalya

I see I shall have to go on about Raymond a bit – the usual obsession with one's fellow traveller. It is not yet ten, and he has gone off to bed, leaving me high and dry, though the town is *en fête* in a purely Turkish fashion (hardly any tourists here) and tinned music is blaring from several loudspeakers so as to make sleep, one would have thought, impossible for hours. He told me he takes a sleeping-pill about ten, even after having an hour or two's sleep in the afternoon. Can anyone need so much? Then in the small dining-room he eagerly turned from me to talk to two quite nice Swedes and a pretty ghastly American, and of course it is the usual thing – travellers' tales of things seen or about to be seen. He does it I think consciously and almost perhaps on principle. He's mentioned it being a habit: 'I talk to everyone.' But I must remember he's an invalid and not strong at all, and I must look after him in his fragility. He dutifully writes dozens of postcards, sighing and groaning, and denying that he enjoys it.

This morning our nice little taxi-driver called to take us to the air terminal. The aeroplane was almost empty and we sped pleasantly and briefly over quite high mountains streaked with snow. Our hotel here consists of two villas on the edge of the park which ends in cliffs overhanging the sea and looking at the most sensational mountains across the bay, tier upon tier of them, with dromedary humps.

The town is exciting and beautiful and while Raymond dedicated himself to the ritual siesta I went out in the full heat of the afternoon to have a look at it. The mountains were rising out of swathes of mist like a beauty in a Victorian photograph. Leaving the park I turned to the small deep harbour full of pretty fishing boats and with a tiny mosque on the quay built over a spring of fresh water from the Taurus. Streams from these mountains flow through the town (one down the main street between two rows of palms) and fling themselves over the cliff into the sea. Steeply sloping up from the harbour is the oldest part of the town with crumbling brown walls, some tall trees with enormous leaves and the fine big houses of the Seljuk quarter, their gardens overflowing with roses, stocks, bougainvillias; they have enormously wide eaves and projecting upper stories – sometimes bellying out like giant wash-basins with their curved undersides painted with delicate patterns. There were wooden lattices so that the women could look out without being seen, and at the height of the afternoon when every café and lane was full of pleasure-seekers I several times looked up and saw a female face. An old woman smiled and waved at me; a young beauty with her hair bound in a silk scarf leaned her gold-braceleted arm on the sill and looked out wistfully. The festive crowds are all Turks yet the mixture of clothes is surprising. I saw veiled women swathed from head to foot in black, or others in Turkish trousers walking arm in arm with friends in short skirts and high heels. An old bearded man was carefully carrying a bright green chameleon on a stick, and snake-charmer music poured from loudspeakers.

May 30th

It took me half an hour's telephoning to get my breakfast this morning; when it came it consisted of quite good tea with lots of hot water, a piece of goat's cheese, olives, toast and some sort of preserved fruit in syrup. I read my Herodotus with it and reflected about the ancient world and the way people feel about it. He is a very lovable writer, realistic and practical and infinitely inquisitive. I'm sure he wouldn't have been in sympathy with the religious awe and humourless intoxication with which people like Freya Stark respond to the classics. Yet in spite of amazement at the learning and civilization of the ancients, I'm appalled by their brutality – nothing but impalements, hostile expeditions and executions, mingled with the boring utterances of the Oracle of Delphi. I like Herodotus best when he is describing the habits and customs of some foreign race like the Scythians, often hilariously, and one can't believe a word of it. The semen of the Ethiopians, according to him, is black!

The tourist agent arrived as he had promised, but his amiability began to sour under Raymond's criticisms. He's obviously used to a diet of flattery and satisfaction, and Raymond told him our rooms were much too dear for their simplicity, that one needed skill to be a hotelier, and that Turkish hoteliers had no idea of the needs of western Europeans. I'm horrified by this attempt to impose our English standards on a strange, still unspoiled country whose charm partly lies in its primitiveness. I neither want it to be quickly corrupted, nor to view it from the safe distance of an international hotel, like a hunter watching lions and tigers from his platform in the jungle. I said this, hoping to start a conversation, but he only said, 'Yes, perhaps'. And so it always is. The town has few taxis, but a lot of very pretty crimson victorias drawn by two horses. This morning we took one of these to the 'best' beach, a long stretch of shingle, overlooked by the glorious mountains and with a bar, restaurant and bathing boxes. We both had a delicious bathe in warm clean sea, and lay in the sun for a while drinking Turkish vermouth.

We have arranged to join a concerted bus to tour the three great classical sites of Perge, Aspendos and Side tomorrow.

A Parisian couple was in the hotel dining-room, and Raymond swivelled round in his chair and addressed all his conversation to them in a boasting match which shrivelled my desire to utter. The last man sent in to bat for our side is generally 'And then from Izmir we went to a *rav*ishing little place called *Téos*'. Their last player was the splendour of the grand Büyük Efes Hotel, in praising which they revealed that they were snobbish, smug, typical rich people. Nor did they respond to Raymond's hopeful references to Michelangelo and Anacreon.

After Raymond had gone to bed I couldn't face being imprisoned in my room to the melancholy accompaniment of hours of fair music from the park, so I walked out into the night and took a ticket for the variety show in the marquee there. After three Turkish Beatles singing into microphones in a variety of languages, a wonderfully beautiful girl came in and did orgiastic oriental dances, ending by working herself to a climax with her private parts presented to the audience and her body leaning backwards parallel with the stage. 'Miss Strip-Tease' followed: a slip of a nymphet dressed in gauzy Victorian clothes, who minced immaturely about the stage taking them off one by one, stretching a gawky arm towards some man in the audience and piping 'Yes?' This seemed to me totally unsexy, but the audience loved it and roared out 'Yes!' Then a large chubby negro sang some songs with traditionally flapping arms, and a conjuror dressed as a matador flew round the audience abstracting their wrist-watches; but by now I'd had enough.

May 31st

I wonder what Raymond is writing in his diary? I'm afraid there are no remarks about me as tart as mine about him – I almost wish there were. He's too kind and nice, and anyway I'm quite sure is only noting down '*rav*ishing temples' and good or bad 'little 'otels' and restaurants. I can't stop thinking about his character, and more especially about the way his mind works. I remember Eardley once saying to me: 'I don't like going about with Raymond – he will *tell* me things all the time, and I don't *want* to be told.' And it's quite true: the suppressed schoolmaster is all-powerful in him. On the whole, unlike Eardley, I rather enjoy being 'told' but I can't bear it when he 'tells' the Turks what's wrong with Turkey, for their own good as I think he believes. Then I'm amazed by his idea of what conversation is – purely the interchange of information, hardly ever a delightful dovetailing and communication of impressions. He will be kindness itself if I say I have indigestion or a blister on my heel, but I would so much rather he was interested in my thoughts and prepared to reveal his to me. He seems to have almost given up thinking, though he loves using his eyes and imparting information. When this palls he picks up a book and acquires some more. Travel is a great revealer – it revealed terrible things about me to Julia, as I must never forget. I think with gratitude that Eardley and I have been better friends since Orta than before.

We started off this morning in our minibus, with our amiable pair of Swedes, two Turks and an intelligent charming boy as guide who was going to be an archeologist, spoke French and had pretty teeth. It was a glorious outing enjoyed by us all. Our guide neither roared at us nor hurried us, and as the day was to include a long pause for lunch and bathing at a little beach near the innocent village of Side, he stopped the bus for me to buy a bathing suit at a larger village shop on the way, and helped me to wave aside two or three expensive ones in garish artificial silk with false breasts and buy quite a nice striped cotton one. To lighten the load, I leave my bag at home and put camera, money, etc., in my Spanish basket. Raymond comes free-handed and is inclined to add Guide Bleu, his bathing trunks and cigarettes to it. I'm guardian of the Common Purse also, which is quite a responsibility, but I hand it over for him to make the manly gesture of paying.

We lunched after our bathe at a restaurant on a platform over the sea, off stuffed peppers (called '*dolma*' after the stuffed buses) and fish. I talked to a grey-haired Turkish ex-airman who had quite a lot of English and found him a really nice human being – interested, intelligent, humorous and friendly. So I was dismayed later on to hear Raymond lecturing him about how badly the hotels were run and how good modern ones catering for Western needs and tourism in general were what Turkey needed, how the pillows were too hard and there was TAR on the beaches. (He has mentioned this often in tones of catastrophic doom.)

Into the town for dinner this evening at a quite good restaurant, bleakly fluorescent and full of Turks. The English translations of the Turkish dishes on the menu sent Raymond into wild giggles. Instead of 'Houri's navel' we had 'Woman's thing' and there was 'Cauldron Ox bottom', 'System to Holland' and finally 'Krasky' and 'Krisky'.

June 1st

We decided to take today easy. The hotel has a very small terrace with about half a dozen quite comfortable chairs and some tables. I found Raymond finishing his breakfast there when I got up after mine (in bed as usual). The day was fine and the air delicious, but he disappeared soon afterwards to his dark back bedroom and spent till noon groaning over four postcards. As if playing a sort of game, I've set myself to get him to discuss some general subject or talk in some other way than just purveying information. Last night in the restaurant he followed this thread for so long and with such animation, poor fellow, that I'd finished my first course before he'd begun. For there was nothing for me to say. Then I wrenched him away to Crichel and its future, which 'took' for a while. He's anxious, probably with reason, about Eardley's departure. We talked of Mattei and he said he liked him and thought him intelligent. 'But there's one thing that worries me. He's got very little general knowledge, about history and literature.' F: 'But do you really think that matters? Someone like Julia who has practically none is a delightful companion because she's so original and responsive.' R: 'Yes, but you know, I mean, I mean, one's little jokes about Bloody Mary may not be understood.'

In the afternoon I started what I thought a good subject – respectability, *à propos* of Henry James's *Siege of London* which I've been reading. He beamed kindly and even looked interested, but wouldn't say a thing. Yet with all this there's something so touching, so angelically kind about the dear fellow that of course I feel very guilty at thinking or writing such things.

A bathe this morning and lunch at the beach restaurant. After we had failed to get a taxi or *dolmus* to drive us there, the driver of a small lorry said he would take us there for half the taxi fare. He was a big, black, jolly man with a lot of gold teeth and for some reason I was temporarily inspired to understand quite a lot of what he said. I've found Turkish, comical Black Sambo language that it is, surprisingly easy to get a smattering of, and my hundred or so words have been invaluable and added enormously to my enjoyment. Our return taxi dropped me in the town, where I wandered through the Bazaar while Raymond went back to bed.

June 3rd

Woken early by a complexity of noise – insistent *roucoulements* of doves, distant snake-charmer music, heavy steps in the corridor, inexplicable thuds and clatter from the basement regions. This is our last morning at Antalya. Yesterday morning to the museum housed in the Seljuk Mosque, a fine building with six domes, whitewashed inside – the rather stout minaret is one of the great beauties of Antalya. We saw quite a lot of fine things brought from Perge and Aspendos, and the custodian took me aside to point out a figure of Priapus, illustrating by gestures towards his own grubby person, in case I should miss the point, with such enthusiasm that I thought he'd have it out in a moment. Then into a more modern, active mosque. We took off our shoes but saw that we should have washed our feet also in the troughs of water provided. The floor was closely covered with small prayer mats so as not to leave a crack between, and the impression made by what was going on inside was sluggish, soft and dreamy; some figures were slumped on the floor, cross-legged and with heads bowed as if drugged or dozing. A maniacal mumble came from a man reciting the Koran in a corner. No music nor service; a meanly narrow staircase led up to a sort of pulpit. This religion seems to have nothing grand or spectacular like Catholicism, nor any of the dramatic ecstasies of the Russo-Greek church. It merely suggests fatalism and inertia. There followed a walk through the Seljuk

234

quarter and back to the hotel, to find the tourist agent and the two Swedes discussing the possibility of going to Termessus this afternoon. I have a childish longing not to miss this mountain outing and I said I'd definitely go if we could make up a four. But the female Swede was loth and two newly-arrived Finns were uninterested. Nothing to do but forget about it, therefore.

As if he had been having a look in this book, Raymond had no sooner climbed into the two-horse carriage which drove us to the Seven Mehmets for dinner last night than he began talking about diaries (he is reading Gide's) and volunteered his own thoughts about them. Was he introspective or not, he wondered, and decided *not*, also that his character had changed very little in the last forty years. He went on to talk of manners and education, of the arrogance of Stracheys and Stephens, and finally he asked me how Ralph got to know Lytton and some of the events that followed.

I don't suppose I shall ever come back to Antalya, or see Termessus. I realize we've reached the half-way point of this Turkish holiday.

Kuşadasi: 10 p.m. Here we are in a motel standing on the end of a promontory and entirely full of Germans. The day has been very hot and a thunderstorm is just breaking – perhaps that was why the small Dakota which brought us back to Izmir Airport from Antalya tossed us so wildly over the mountains. The detachment so necessary to flying is quickly fractured when one is made to feel one is inside some living thing – bird or moth – battling its way against conflicting airstreams, rolling, dipping, plunging through the clouds over the crests of the jagged mountains. I usually keep my imagination well stoppered when flying, but it leapt from its genie's bottle and I had the same feeling of being utterly at the mercy of unfriendly elements as I do on a rough sea. I don't think any of the passengers were particularly happy, and an American girl got out saying, 'Well, thank heavens that's over!'

Our faithful taxi-driver met us at the airport and drove us here in the darkness. I feel this motel to be extremely antipathetic – but must wait for tomorrow to judge it by the light of day.

June 4th

The weather for once looked black and scowling and when I tried a Turkish phrase about it to one of the houseboys, he said '*Çok fena*' (very bad) and imitated rain falling. But after a few thunderous rumbles it cleared enough for us to venture out. Useful interview with the travel agent who was full of ideas. It looks as if my Mecca, Bodrum, would be out. The agent 'didn't advise'. It was a long way and a bad road. Walked out to the port and stood admiring a big dark blue caique with a fairhaired man sitting on deck, with his back to us. 'It might almost be Michael Pitt-Rivers,' I said (we knew he was sailing somewhere in these waters). A moment later the figure turned with a cry of 'Raymond!' and proved to be Michael's boyfriend, William Davis,[1] a charming but younger replica of Michael himself. We went on board and drank some deep pink Samos wine with him, sitting in the sun on deck and enjoying our first social contact since we came abroad. Then reeled off into the town to look at a large and handsome mosque, and home to the motel for a bathe and lunch.

June 5th: Otel Imbat, Kuşadasi

I've just had breakfast on my private balcony at this much grander new hotel, sitting in the shadow but looking out on the milky blue sea with a few clouds making pearly reflections and the distant hills of Samos behind. It is a brand-new, hideous but comfortable affair in a superb position among olive groves, with cornfields sloping to the sea. When we asked where one bathed they said, 'The beach will be finished in a day or two.' We looked and saw men putting down sand on the shore, which soon turns into a sort of mud. But our rooms are large and sunny, with shower and lavatory; and you have only to walk out of the front door to be in the country. Walked with Raymond to the nearest headland, picking flowers and feeling a welling-up sense of peace and happiness.

The Pitt-Riverses had asked us to dinner and we were received by the charming William. Soon Anthony and Tanya Hobson[2] bobbed up through the hatchway, then Michael from the hammam in the town, and his aquiline-nosed actress mother. We all sat on deck drinking whisky for some time. The Hobsons brought an exciting message – Jock Jardine of the British Council at Ankara had been there during the day. He was driving to meet Eddie Gathorne-Hardy at Izmir, and they will be at our hotel tomorrow night. He offered to

[1] Painter.
[2] My second meeting with a couple with whom I later became great friends.

236

drive us to Miletus and Didyma on the following day and said they were going on to Bodrum and had booked rooms there. Why didn't we do so too? Hopes aroused, but as it may well turn out to be impossible, I don't want to get too involved.

We all dined in a restaurant on the Quay. I sat between Michael and William, but as Michael directed all his conversation to me I couldn't talk to William as much as I'd have liked. Michael was amusing about the Hilton Hotel at Athens, where he said you could live an entirely self-contained life. 'You want to post a letter?' he told his mother. 'There's a post office. Buy films? Cash a traveller's cheque? All here. You needn't go out *at all*.' Whereupon an American fellow traveller chipped in to say he'd been staying there a fortnight and had not gone out once. 'Well, why not stay at the Hilton in London and turn on the television?' I asked. 'Oh, the Athens one is best. If anyone feels they are going to be ill they should fly immediately to Athens.' Then we got on to religion, the problem of choice, Free Will and determinism, Buddhism. As I know nothing about it I can't tell if he's right in saying that Buddhism is founded on determinism – or rather fatalism which is quite different. You must accept what destiny hands out, and so intervention is always bad, even to stop a father cruelly beating his child. This hypothetical cruel father occupied us enjoyably for some time. Now it was nearly eleven – late for Raymond – and a heavy shower was heard pattering on the roof, so we took a taxi home to bed.

June 6th

We were sitting in the hotel lounge this evening when Jock Jardine appeared – a lean, hatchet-faced, obviously queer man in shorts. Eddie was 'resting' he told us, and it was some time later that he toddled in with his distinguished performing-bear-like gait. They are on their way to Antalya in J. J.'s car, and it soon became disconcertingly clear (over rakis) that it was far from certain we should get even to Miletus and Didyma with them, much less to Bodrum, which is about 300 kilometres and we should have to hire a car back. Eddie *seemed* to be delighted to see us, but I very soon realized that it was he who was obstructing Jardine's friendly offer, out of sheer selfishness. He's afraid of being squashed in the car, or of my expecting to have the front seat. He even said to me as we were fencing round the subject of Bodrum, 'There wouldn't be room for your luggage in the boot, my dear.' I think he'd told Jardine not to

237

take us anywhere, but as we had practically accepted his lift to Miletus and Didyma it was almost impossible for him to refuse.

At dinner Eddie consolidated the outline of his grotesque selfishness by complaining because Anne and Heywood have come to live in his mother's house in Suffolk, which Heywood has now bought and made comfortable with central heating. 'I can't see why they don't go on living in the Lodge, my dear; it was agreed they shouldn't come into the house until Mamma dies. They say they can't afford it, my dear, but I simply don't believe it, my dear.' The Lodge is a tiny labourer's cottage for which they have to pay quite a large rent.

Jock Jardine has found us a taxi to fetch us from Miletus and take us to Priene. I abandoned Bodrum as soon as I saw Eddie *didn't want us*, but it is pretty disagreeable not being wanted on tomorrow's excursion, though he tried to put a good face on it. I couldn't resist a slight tease about the 'famous Gathorne-Hardy selfishness' and got a crocodile smile in return.

June 7th

After all, we had a wonderful day yesterday seeing such incredible beauties that I feel tantalized by my desire to capture them in the only way open to me – with my camera. I had a colour film in it, but doubt if I've caught the soft glowing greens and blues of the Meander valley – or plain rather, for it is very wide between Miletus and Priene; or the hundreds of storks' nests, some with baby storks in them (sometimes three or four nests quite covering a small roof); or the pair of storks copulating with clashing bills on top of one of Didyma's tallest columns; or the groups of camels by the roadside; or the little parties of children with brown faces and tawny hair (the little girls look ravishing in their trousers); or the great caravanserais of exotically dressed toilers coming back from the fields (the women with check tablecloths over their heads, and trousers made of beautiful faded and often patterned materials with a preference for magenta, dull green and peacock blue); or the sheer loveliness of the poplars turning silkily in the breeze. The fear that all these magical impressions (now clear in my mind) will instantly begin to fade, torments me.

We set off at nine (of course I saw that Eddie had the front seat) and followed a beautiful winding road across the plain, and along a dusty track to Didyma. Here there is just one 'sight', the colossal temple to Apollo. The few standing columns are fabulously tall and

238

the walls and foundations on a stupendous scale. The flights of steps for the priests to go up are vastly wide as well as high; the walls made of massive stones (white, or blackened as if by fire) so beautifully fitted together that letting one's eyes slide along the surface is an excitement in itself. There were tunnelled passages with the builders' initials engraved on them, and bits of sculpture or ornament pristinely sharp and clear. This must be one of the noblest Greek temples after the Acropolis at Athens. As we were leaving we met the whole Pitt-Rivers party arriving.

Back next to Miletus, of which I remember best the profusion of ruins invaded by the waters of the Meander, and a tiny museum. A boy brought us coins he had picked up, and wicked old Eddie tried to cheat him of a few lire for them.

Now we parted from Eddie and Jock Jardine and got into our waiting taxi to drive back across the plain to Priene. We lunched close to the entrance to the ruins. Oh, what a beautiful place! We both capitulated to it completely I think, as we climbed slowly up a road of enormous stone slabs grooved with chariot-wheels, and found ourselves among the intact foundations and walls of the Greek town (little altered by the Romans).

Home to Kuşadasi, and dinner in our hotel. Raymond was very excited by a group of English people at the next table; he felt sure they were 'academics' because of the copy of Herodotus that lay on their table, and leapt up eagerly to engage them in conversation. I, trailing sheepishly behind, was landed with a tall erect lady with a grey screwed-back bun, who at once told me they were 'members of the Inter-Church Congress' and were 'following the steps of St Paul'. Raymond had been laying himself out 'agreeably' to a lady carrying a copy of Lord Moran on Winston Churchill and was thunderstruck when I told him what sort of angels we'd been entertaining unawares.

June 8th

Various Turkish types: the voluptuously oriental (mainly female); men like Groucho Marx with eyes too close together, swashbuckling moustache and an eager ingratiating way of leaning forward as they walk; square strong men with thick black hair, like Mattei.

Tourist boasting is a popular sport; 'What! You *didn't* go to Priene? Oh, what a pity! It's quite the most romantically beautiful place we've been to.' Though it often springs more from self-aggrandizement than 'desire to cause pain' it usually succeeds in both departments.

June 9th: Samos

Getting here – it is in Greece – proved unexpectedly difficult. Our taxi was slow to come; with what now seems incredible nonchalance we wandered to the tourist office to get our tickets a few minutes before sailing time, only to find that we couldn't pay with Turkish money, but only with Greek and we hadn't nearly enough. Meanwhile time was passing and our taxi-driver was adding to the hysteria by hooting steadily on the horn. We screamed, and were at last handed our tickets; then we charged off to the boat, with bags, with whisky bottle and basket of wet bathing things, and Raymond with his heavy leather case of medicines. At last we panted on board our little vessel – the 'Afroditi' bound for Samos.

There were only three other passengers, all German. The boat was run by three Greeks – the Captain, the engineer and a boy with blue eyes, a beautiful profile and a charming smile, who looked after us solicitously, brought us blankets and cardboard receptacles if he thought anyone looked like vomiting. One of the Germans retired to a cabin and did so. The sea was beastly rough and we rolled and pitched like mad for nearly two hours before reaching calm water in the lee of the island. I felt theoretically 'all right' in so far as that is consistent with loathing every moment. Raymond, on the other hand, was in his element, happily dashing up and down the tiny heaving decks and stairs in a way which terrified the cabin boy. We had been sitting on plastic chairs with our feet braced against the rail, talking intermittently to a doctor from Stuttgart, I with my eyes fixed on Samos, counting the moments until we should get into sheltered waters, when the Captain in voluble Greek ordered us below into a minute stuffy cabin (the upper one was occupied by the sufferers). Not knowing what to expect and fearing the worst, down we went. But soon afterwards the sea grew calmer and we ascended again and watched the sun setting behind the silhouette of Samos. At last the twinkling lights of Pythagorion came into view. All round us the machine-gun rattle of Greek pounded our ears; we clambered into a taxi and drove across the island to the further port of Vathi.

Here I am now sitting on the balcony of my room in the Hotel Xenia, continuous and cataclysmic noise having woken me at five-thirty.

June 10th: Samos

Raymond has taken a new lease of life because he finds himself in Europe, whereas I am homesick for Asia and (ludicrously enough) for a country where I can *just* make myself understood. Not that this island isn't beautiful – it certainly is; but I miss the potently Oriental strangeness. In spite of the lack of water and general ramshackleness of our quite expensive hotel (the grandest in the island) Raymond feels he is in 'civilization' again, and I see he must have been more afraid of Turkish outlandishness than I realized.

Well, here we are on the return voyage to Kuşadasi, and the sea is fairly calm and blue, the sky serene.

June 11th: Back at Kuşadasi

We had been invited to have a drink with a certain Rosie Rodd (briefly met at the port restaurant when the Pitt-Rivers boat was in) and she called for us here in a little car. A tall handsome woman of about fifty, a friend of Mary's and sister-in-law of Nancy Mitford, she is now living in the openest sin I ever saw with an American soldier about half her age. Raymond had been alarmed by her dominating voice on the telephone, but we found her lively, warm, enthusiastic and quite without malice. She drove us along a narrow stony lane and stopped beside a tall Aleppo pine at the door of a tiny love nest bowered in English garden flowers and looking through the olives at the blue sea. It consisted in one not very large room crammed with a confusion of Victoriana, Wedgwood teapots and *trouvailles* from classical sites. Rosie Rodd opened a door revealing a mere cupboard with a double bed in it, and another (pitch dark) which was the bathroom. We sat outside and drank whisky, with a pug puppy gambolling round our legs. Rosie addressed the American lovingly as 'sweetheart' or 'darling' and was anxious to bring him into the conversation. He remained fairly silent however, though he never said anything stupid, and looked at us with dignified pale blue eyes. She has the untouched confidence, overflowing chatter, and scattiness of an ex-deb, but I liked her courage, enterprise and vitality. From among the splash of her talk, we learned that 'Ken' had been stationed in Turkey, 'sold someone a tape recorder illegally' and as a result been tried several times and condemned to ten months in a prison on the Black Sea, and then 'banishment' (she tossed off the word as if it was a normal one) here at Kuşadasi. But he was loved in the village, and adored the Turks in spite of all and spoke good Turkish. She obviously expects to be 'loved in the village' too and implies that she is. They call her 'Lady Rodd' and when her lover had to go away for a while the milk boy asked if he could sleep outside her door to protect her. She's an amateur botanist and bird-watcher and told me about places I long to go to and even suggested that she might drive us to Lake Bafa. I should *love* this, but after the disappointments of Termessus and Bodrum I don't want to hope for it too much.

I've just had a letter confirming her offer and it's a golden opportunity but Raymond is full of muffish hesitations. Her car isn't comfortable enough; she wants to take us too far. His Asian-phobia is back and he has lost his Samian enterprise.

I've just found a dear little tortoise ambling about the floor of my room. We have seen several quite large ones on the roads. Rosie Rodd says there are bears, panthers and hyenas in this country and that the jackals come and eat her peacocks.

June 12th

Our voiceless taxi-driver called in the afternoon to take us to Ephesus. It is indeed very splendid, suggesting, more than any other ruin we've visited, a city of vast size (as it must have been with a quarter of a million inhabitants), yet the imagination falters before the effort to fill in the gaps. It's easy to approach these classical sites in a schizophrenic mood, torn between the purely visual – accepting them as beautiful chunks, or fragments of stone garlanded with flowers – and a hesitant attempt to envisage the past. On the whole I stick to the first, partly out of laziness, yet I am interested in their history.

Raymond seems a little tired this evening. I do hope he isn't depressed, or anxiously dreading our outing with Rosie Rodd tomorrow – though it's by no means certain if we go, and if he doesn't feel up to it I must renounce it too – I can't desert him. He says he's lost his appetite and is 'longing to be back in his dear old rut where everything is arranged as he likes it'. It's odd that he loves travel so much when the smallest inconvenience, such as the bumph refusing to come easily from its roller or the lid of the lavatory refusing to stay back, irks him so dreadfully. I believe he travels conscientiously to collect information and things to talk about just as he conscientiously writes postcards to collect love.

7 p.m. I'm lying on my bed looking out at the fading sky and pink tops of the mountains, hearing the jaunty Frenchified hoots of the taxis and the confused hubbub of conversation rising from the street far below, and thinking that I know now I've lost my heart to Turkey. As much as to Russia? Not quite. But it has lived up to the impression I glimpsed when Ralph and I went to Troy thirty years ago.

We are back from our day's outing with Rosie Rodd. Ken didn't come and perhaps it was just as well, as she told us a lot about him. I liked her even more this time – for her determination to live life to the full, her courage in flouting conventions and telling us that Ken is seventeen years younger than her, her lack of fuss about her appearance, her enjoyment of flowers, animals and scenery and her general curiosity. She told us some grim facts about the Turks, confirming my impression that they are an odd mixture of kindness and brutality, and says when they've drunk a lot of raki 'knives come out at once'. Bastinado is still practised – as, for instance, on suspects when her jewellery was stolen. If a child runs straight in front of your car and is killed through no fault of your own you go to prison for fifteen years. I'm deeply grateful to her for making possible the beauty and pleasure of today, her generosity to perfect strangers certainly contrasts with Eddie's stinginess. She drove us very steadily and safely once more across the lovely Meander plain, passing a procession of proud camels, loaded with flowering broom and led by a little donkey. They made a halt close to us and we stopped and took their photographs. The camels turned their long necks and munched the yellow flowers on their backs, and the camel man offered us a genial handshake and 'Mehraba!' The animal and bird life is a great feature of Turkish travel. For the first time I saw several roller pigeons – brilliant blue with terracotta backs, and there were armies of storks marching across the plain, egrets, cream-coloured cattle, mares with their foals. We turned off the Miletus road along the side of the vast salt Lake Bafa and on through a wild unpopulated region, where everyone was wearing nomad's dress; we saw their tents and nomad women wearing gold fillets round their heads. Stopped to eat our picnic, where the almost complete skeleton of a dark grey Corinthian temple faded into the olive-covered mountain behind. Raymond and Rosie had been hard at it gossiping away about mutual acquaintances. 'Oh yes, *she* was an Antonelli . . . and when

243

did *he* marry? *She* had an affair with my friend Maurice Druant. He was supposed to have behaved very badly . . . Then do you know my friend Rory Cameron?' etcetera.

June 13th

We went to have our last dinner at the port restaurant and when I asked Raymond how he was feeling, he said 'Rather tired – you see, I've not had my afternoon sleep'. Yet he had two good hours to repose from six to eight. It *is* rather old-maidish. I minded this the more because it was the one day we've spent completely according to *my* taste – in wild country, with a picnic, breaking the routine of rests and postcards, and I felt he was grudging me it. I'm afraid our tastes have become too different for us to be completely comfortable travel-companions. But I'm sure he came away in a state of panic, half expecting to leave his bones in Turkey, and he apologized this morning for being 'appallingly hypochondriacal'.

June 14th

Arrived in Athens, Raymond set aside his Asian angst and became spirited and lively. We found letters and messages at our hotel, and the unexpected and lovely surprise that Janetta was arriving tonight to meet Paddy and Joan, and all would be staying at the Olympic Palace too. I had left a note in Janetta's pigeon-hole and until she opened it she had no idea we were to be in Athens. We went up to her room and sat having the most *human* conversation for weeks.

It was arranged for us all to dine with Paddy and Joan, and Peter Mayne, a novelist. Raymond was made desperate by the familiar, inevitable delays. Out of his 'delightful rut' and not in control of times and arrangements he could no longer keep up his manners, and hardly talked to Janetta at all at dinner. Paddy took us to a garden restaurant some way from the heart of the town and the conversation was lively and much concerned with words. 'Ribcage' and 'foolish' were tossed about by Paddy and Peter Mayne – an odd, not uninteresting man much given to 'patting and holding'. I asked him about the sex life of the Turks. 'Do you really want me to tell you? Well, they're extremely *tender* and affectionate. Also – and I should know – they've got the smallest cocks in the world.' I said to Paddy that I didn't feel I could believe a word Herodotus said after reading that the Ethiopians had black semen. He almost choked, turned pink and then went off like a rocket: 'Black semen – yes – black semen. I'd forgotten about that. Rather like those advertisements of STEPHEN'S BLUE BLACK INK – do you remember? – they used to be in railway stations. A *great black splodge*.' (Nudge, nudge.) 'Or perhaps it would be just a black dribble.' And went on for ages – ridiculous, fantastic, and endearing. I felt pleasurably intoxicated by the company, talk and animation. A discussion began as to whether we should all go and watch a rehearsal by Nureyev and Margot Fonteyn (who is a friend of Joan's) who are performing in Athens. But it was obviously long over. Or 'go on somewhere', and if so, where. I was touched by Paddy's eager, obstreperous devotedness, leaving all decisions to Joan, only wanting her to decide and looking at her expectantly like a curly wet dog that has just fished a stick out of a lake and bounces about as if to say, 'Only tell me, mistress, where to put it and I'll do it at once with joy.'

I noticed that Raymond had begun to wilt at his end of the table, and I was anxious to rescue him, but he wouldn't help. So as not to break up the rest of the party it was vital to be quick and firm about leaving. In the end – and it was only about twelve-thirty – we all tried to get into a taxi which refused to take us, it being against the law to take six. Raymond grew suddenly hysterical and stood with arms hanging shouting – 'This is absurd! We must get into two taxis. I want to go to bed! I'm absolutely BROKEN.' He, Peter Mayne and I got into one and drove home.

I told Janetta of course about Eddie, and she said it was absolutely characteristic, that when she'd had him staying with her for weeks in Spain he'd hardly let her drive her children on expeditions 'for fear of not having enough room'. Also that he's always terrified of not having the front seat, and once she, Jaime and he went on a little sightseeing tour and she and Jaime were never allowed to sit together, as he always wanted the front seat.

Newspapers. We fall on them – but nothing whatever appears to have changed in our absence.

June 15th: West Halkin Street

The solitude of my flat, my life, struck me like a slap in the face. No flowers, no papers, no Mrs Ringe, nor has she come this morning.

My post provided nothing consoling. I was glad to hear Mary's friendly voice from Stokke, and Bunny saying he would bring my Mini up today. The empty space of my flat in which I was floundering drove me to pick up Freya Stark's *Ionia* (which had seemed unreadable before I went to Turkey) and go back over my travel-tracks. The photographs of some of the ruined cities had been taken before archaeologists had reared a column or two on end, so that there was merely a jumble of grooved cheese-like segments. Ephesus was such a one, I think. And what a difference those few up-ended columns made, merely by suggesting the portentousness of the whole. All the difference so important to human sanity between jargon and sense. A jumbled ruin is like a visit to a lunatic asylum. Exactly what sets a site alive depends on a lot of variables though – the broad Arcadian avenue with its massive paving slabs leading down to the silted-up harbour made sense for me, and so did reading in the guidebook that (unlike most ancient streets) it had lighting. I know there's a lot I want to think about, which (had Raymond been someone else) we should have talked about in Turkey.

June 17th

Two days have taken a little of the ache out of the bruise of my return and I've seen several friends – Bunny, Julia and Mary. Bunny brought the news that Henrietta and Sophie were back and I went to see them yesterday. I was let in to the pandemonious, sluttish, charming flat by Nerissa and little Sophie, and Henrietta ran up the stairs soon afterwards looking brown and excited in a pink frilly blouse and short evzone's skirt. My mingled pleasure and anxiety for them both, the desire to ask questions and yet not probe too much, and to attend to both of them at once, led to a confused state of mind that got me (I fear) nowhere. Sophie is taller, very *rubia* from the Spanish sun, pale, with a guarded anxious expression in her dark eyes – all right though I think. Henrietta looked tremendously blooming. Why then do I worry so about her? I expect I shall continue to do so unless or until she marries some delightful person who will be kind to Sophie. Bunny came yesterday with my car, rosy and beaming, and talked to me exclusively about Wales and the fish he'd caught (or not caught) there last weekend. I could hardly believe he wouldn't ask *one* question about Turkey but he didn't, and I volunteered nothing, waiting to see if he would. He still didn't. Perhaps no one is really interested, but most ask out of politeness.

Julia had rung me up on the morning of my arrival and this so encouraged me that I got her to come to supper the following day. She seems to me to have become more realistic about her own life, as well as more sanguine (which she may not realize). Our conversation went so well and without friction for four hours non-stop that I was amazed when a single spark did suddenly fly. We had been talking about the Hills, generally prime favourites. J: 'Of course I don't really know Anne, and I was very shocked by something she said about fox-hunting; when I said how horribly cruel and revolting I thought it, she said she wanted it kept on because of it being *traditional*! That seemed to me so utterly awful and stupid. But you won't agree with me I know because you're in favour of bullfighting as you've often told me.'

F: 'But Julia, I've always been dead against bullfighting.'

J: 'Oh, no. You were quite cross with me I remember and said I oughtn't to eat meat if I was against it.'

F: (trying to mollify) 'Oh, well, I think it's probably inconsistent of us all, me included, to eat meat. But I believe it's the cruelty that matters – not just killing. I envy the animals that.'

Julia's voice was high and she was preparing to insist on my love for bullfights, but I managed to steer the subject away and I think all is well for as she left she said she hoped I'd come for a weekend some time.

June 24th

The inevitable speed-up; cramming the stocking as full as it'll go. Murray have sent me the Conan Doyle book to index; I'm back to the last sessions of my orchestra and a concert next week; and have had music with the Penroses and Angelica.

Yesterday Duncan came to see me to discuss the agitation he felt over what Holroyd has said about him in his life of Lytton. He left it for me to read, and I devoted last night to it – after dashing round to see Janetta, just back from Greece.

This horrible little list of Stop Press items must do for the present. I've also seen Eardley, Julian, Georgia and Heywood, and got enormous pleasure from all their company, so that the friendless feeling of my return is dwindling. And I always feel different about London when Janetta is in it.

June 30th

Angelica wholeheartedly supported Duncan, saying, with an adamant, disapproving expression on her face, that one couldn't publish such things about living people. I pressed her a little further – was she in favour of suppressing all Lytton's feelings about Duncan and indeed about the other people in the book, like Roger Senhouse? Had she read the preface starting with James's announcement that Lytton was a homosexual? Did she think one could possibly write a life of him without revealing that fact? But I suggested rather tentatively that the parts about Duncan could be cut, removing anything he found objectionable or too physical, or about his own feelings. It didn't seem to have occurred to her that it was hard on Holroyd that everyone had handed him all the letters and material, and after he has toiled at it for years on end, they scream and say, 'He can't publish THAT!' What surprised me about Angelica's response was that instead of saying 'Duncan finds it too painful,' which would be hard to answer, her first remark was, 'Duncan has a lot of conventional friends who'll be horribly shocked.'

I can't sympathize with pandering to conventions – but the subject is complicated and difficult. I don't see any sense in biographies that suppress or distort the facts, and I should have thought the days of Lytton and Duncan's love were long enough past to be harmless. Also this attitude of Angelica's reminded me of the absurd pretence of Charleston that Angelica was Clive's daughter – kept up long after everyone knew about it, just as of course practically everyone knows Duncan is predominantly homosexual. There was always that foot fumblingly advanced by Bloomsbury towards the conventional or aristocratic enclave, their Victorian childhoods perhaps coming to the surface in a way totally inconsistent with their defiance of *idées reçues* – God, patriotism, and monogamy. As I'm wholeheartedly in sympathy with their setting up their own standards, I hate their not having the courage to uphold them publicly. To me anyway it's an important discrepancy. Perhaps this very thing makes me disagreeably aggressive sometimes, as when Jack Donaldson said at lunch that he 'was completely behind the American action in Vietnam' and I couldn't let it pass without expressing my strong disagreement, and saying that it seemed to me the most squalid war there'd ever been. But even though I'm ashamed of getting overexcited and losing my calm, I think one must stand up for what one believes. This, along with the futility of war, is perhaps the central belief in my credo. I admire people who stand up for homosexuals being free to carry on

248

their love-affairs, and it seems to me it's now very old-fashioned and ostrich-like to pretend that no one knows that they do, and always have done so.

July 4th: With the Cecils at Oxford

Matthew Spender came for a drink, and I found him quick-witted and interesting as well as charming to look at. Another young man in jeans arrived and swallowed two neat whiskies, after which he drove Hugh off to confide in his troubles about a girl. At nights I lay in my truckle bed with its worn and mended cotton sheets listening to enthralled communication going on in the passage and from room to room. I never knew such delightful and complete confidence between parents and children. Voices have to be raised because of Rachel's slight deafness, and her voice impregnated with sympathy and interest is raised too because she had a deaf mother herself. Irrelevant thoughts drifted through my head: the way one battles against old age, decrepitude and death as if it were possible to defeat them; the click with which one's vision of the world changes, as though a new slide had been slipped into the magic lantern — one moment's tortuous complexity becoming (for instance) in the next a sort of jungle richness.

A quotation from Isaiah Berlin on Alan Pryce-Jones: 'He's like a wafer. You may want some. You may even order some, but you never want one all by itself.'

July 14th

The Holroyd business has been a continuous obsession. He came to bring me back some photographs one evening and I felt uneasy at the thought of the chopper ready to fall on his head, so when he mentioned Duncan I thought I'd better say, 'I did gather he was rather agitated.' Holroyd was obviously surprised, hadn't thought he'd mind, but was expecting possible trouble from Roger Senhouse. And will get it it seems, for, from what Raymond and Angus Davidson have told me, Roger too is upset. His affair with Lytton has been gone into in great detail by Holroyd, including their complicated life of sexual fantasy. Holroyd said to me that he was prepared to refer to Roger anonymously, and perhaps this would have been better. I lay awake till two one night thinking about it — I'm enormously interested in the different reactions, particularly

249

among the homosexuals. Having known and been friends with so many for so long, I'm more than faintly surprised at their secretiveness just when their position seems about to be legally ratified. For in conversation they are usually confident and jolly about their 'persuasions'. Yet they evidently cherish the belief that half their acquaintances don't know about them, and I've often thought they enjoyed play-acting at being 'normal'. Yet it's hardly possible to remain a bachelor these days and pass off as such. Angus was very old-maidish and prissy. '*I* certainly shouldn't like anyone to read some of Duncan's letters to me,' he said with his eyebrows going up into his hair.

James, having talked so hysterically about the book on the telephone ('Had I seen the bit about Ralph and me?' he asked among other things. And what am I supposed to mind?), has now calmed down to a state of reasonable fatalism. I spent a night at Lord's Wood with him and Alix and was made to read some of Holroyd's literary criticisms of Lytton's books, which I found pretty unreadable. James now says no one will read the book so it doesn't matter. He seemed to be in complete agreement with me about anti-Bowdler principles, and this was a relief to me for I feel quite strongly about them; but he thought the people in question (Duncan or Roger) must have the last word. The person who emerges most strangely from all this is Bunny, who has violently entered into the lists in favour of wholesale suppression. He and I had a fairly heated conversation on the telephone about it. I said of course that no one wanted Duncan to suffer a moment's pain on account of the book – but from there we got to discussing what should be the basis for suppression. 'Well, a lot of people would be very shocked,' said Bunny. 'For instance, you should just have seen the people Angelica and I lunched with on Sunday! They would have been horrified.' F: 'What sort of people were they?' B: 'Colonels and conventional old ladies'. F: 'I really don't think one should set one's standards by those of Colonels and old ladies! And I'm particularly surprised because if I may say so, in your autobiographical books you haven't been at all reserved.' B: 'No. I know; but I've made it a rule not to make revelations about people who are still alive, or have relatives alive who would mind, like Lydia about Maynard.'

Since then I've wished I'd told him how many people have said to me that they were appalled at his publishing Ray's anguished, intensely private and personal letters when she was dying of cancer, and (what's more) that, though I was amazed at his wanting to do so and found them very painful reading, I defended him *on principle*. Alix agreed with me that this was the most disgraceful revelation she'd ever read in any book, and I suppose that I and the rest of my family might be thought to mind as much as Lydia about Maynard. Knowing myself as unable to keep anything to myself for long, I expect I shall come out with this to Bunny sooner or later. He had gone down to Lord's Wood two days before I did and amazed Alix by his red-faced truculence, and talk about libel actions.

Another aspect of this subject: Julian gave me a very amusing account of an all-bugger weekend at Crichel, six of them. He said he was quite shocked by the amount of anti-woman talk there had been, particularly from Pat Trevor-Roper, who said female minds were inferior, they didn't deserve a better education. Perhaps it's a good thing I never considered joining that ménage?

July 16th

In the train on the long journey to Dorchester, gliding between grey banks under a grey sky.

Last night Robert came to dinner, after packing Cynthia and the children off to stay with Poppet[1] at Ramatuel. After a long darning of Georgie's prospects and plans (she is leaving school this term) we got into exciting and deep waters of all sorts – values, their nature and origin; whether they could all be related to one's sense of being part of a whole (the universe) which in spite of its horrors and terrors was wonderful and adorable; progress, was there any grounds for believing in it? Politics, war, poverty. There's nothing quite to equal the pleasure when two people together weave a cat's cradle of ideas. We were never really in opposition – not at all. And Robert had a lot to tell me about poverty – as he had interviewed seven 'poor' families for the *Weekly Telegraph*. All of them had television ('we couldn't get along without it') and seven or eight children. I suggested that both were really luxuries as much as a fast car. He didn't say that any of them were short of food, but they had sunk into anxiety and debt.

July 19th: Litton Cheney

Greeted by Janet Stone, whose pale orange hair was set off by a pink silk scarf. None of the children were there save Emma with an Italian

---

[1] Pol, daughter of Augustus John.

girl of twelve who spent much of the time in her room weeping from homesickness.

The green lanes arched over by enormously tall trees and with all their banks frilled with as many rows of hart's tongue ferns as a Spanish dancer's dress; the constant sound of running water; glimpses of tilted fields far away near the sea; great comfort and hospitality carried to a fine art; too much social life though I liked the people we saw – the very nice Hubbards[1] to dinner on Saturday, Pat Trevor-Roper to lunch on Sunday, all made a lovely weekend.

I am much less liable to panic or 'go blank' in the middle of conversation than I used to be; but I listened with almost total incomprehension while Reynolds talked about Hermetism and Lullism and Giordano Bruno. It all seemed mumbo-jumbo and I realized I was attending to Reynolds' sparkling brown Basque gaze rather than his words. Next day he gave me a book about it all to read, and I see I was right. It *is* mumbo-jumbo.

July 20th

Mary has just rung up suggesting that I interfere in an unhappy love-affair, and arousing my feelings that it would be unwarrantable arrogance – almost morally wrong, anyway useless. Yet I don't think one can lay down such general rules. I do however feel that to say to someone 'You're behaving badly to your best beloved' or whoever passes as such, is absolutely foredoomed to fail. If he doesn't treat her more kindly without being shamed into it, if she can't make the necessary adjustment to make him, what earthly hope is there for them? You can't get love at pistol-point, nor sensitivity either. What's more, the anguish of the injured party usually makes their love stronger, according to the fiendish mathematical law which governs human love and sends one bucket unfailingly up as another descends. When I think of the troubles of Robert and Janetta in the past, I do see that Ralph and I may have then done our level best to intervene in the interests of both. But what good did it do? And they were (both of them) the best loved and closest of our friends. The whole idea of intervention revolts me and I find it difficult to say why – 'clumsy', 'lacking in delicacy' are the phrases I think of. I simply can't imagine ever having wanted anyone to 'speak to Ralph' on my behalf. It is so essentially and vitally a matter between the two people

[1] John (painter) and Carol.

concerned. Yet I see that to someone wholeheartedly believing in 'ambassadors' it seems chilly and unsympathetic to refuse.

Went with Desmond to a concert at Guildhall – lovely Mozart, beautifully played. Though there was no conceivable rush or difficulty, he was in a frenzy all the way there and back: 'Oh DEAR! now I've gone wrong. Oh, this is AWFUL! We'll be crossing the river in a minute!'

July 21st

The weather is appalling. Torrents of rain, blasts of gusty wind, dark grey skies; and *pour comble* an economic crisis, with new 'restrictions' which I know I shall be quite incapable of understanding. On every side shipwrecked marriages, together with a few small boats pitifully putting out to sea. I took a party to Handel's *Jephthah* at Glyndebourne yesterday. Julian, Georgia and I went down by train and Duncan met us there. The heavy pall of grey sky faintly exuding damp made the whole place look unspeakably ugly and the figures who drifted along the grass in their evening dress under umbrellas were few and far between. But we managed to find a little cubby-hole under an archway with four chairs to eat our picnic and be quite jolly in. I sat in the train reflecting on the difference between Julian and Georgia's generation and mine – *their* bubbling high spirits, imitations of upper-class imbecility and giggles made me feel grey and old.

Gerald writes that Julian begged to be sent a copy of his proofs,[1] and 'since then – about February 1 – I haven't heard a word. His letter may have been lost, but if he did not write I find his behaviour inexcusable and would prefer not to see him again. For if he disliked the book he should have said so. Not to have done so was to suggest either that it was so shamefully bad that it couldn't be mentioned or that he took such a low view of my character as to suppose that I could not take an unfavourable opinion.' Then he says, alas, that this is on his mind and perhaps I can relieve it. I therefore started to tell Julian last night. He looked desperately stricken, afraid, and almost angry and said: 'Yes, I get the message.' Nevertheless I dislike, though I suppose I understand, this unforgivingness of Gerald's, and after saying that he could take any amount of criticism he rather pathetically recipitulates the favourable opinions of V. S. P., Jonny,

---

[1] Of his novel *The Lighthouse always says Yes*.

etc., and says that the book was killed by two unfavourable Sunday reviews and by the fact that 'it has become impossible for a novelist of over fifty to get through the barrage of the young reviewers . . . Honor Tracy declares it's envy and jealousy . . . '

July 28th

Last night in bed I lay in the darkness in a spectral haunted mood; a tiger seemed to be ranging with long restless, prowling strides through the jungle of my thoughts, back and forth, over the dark avenues of the past. I have been of late increasingly aware of being like a dried fruit; my rind hardens and reveals a hollow space with only a few seeds rattling in it. Or a ping-pong ball only existing by hurtling to and fro and then suddenly longing to be still and dreading the next impact with a bat. Then I suddenly thought for some reason of Frankie Birrell's great enjoyment of life and exuberance and early death, and of Philip Ritchie, and others, and felt disgust for this extravagant expenditure of life.

Julia came to dinner last night. There was no ghost of her old hostility to me, quite the reverse. She even made a graceful reference to the present of money I'd given her – saying that when I'd commented on how nice her flat was looking the other day she'd foolishly replied that 'her charwoman kept it quite clean, but the truth was that a very kind friend called Frances Partridge had given her a present and she'd used it to have the flat done up and cupboards put everywhere.' This was completely unexpected and touched me very much. Money preoccupies her – I think she feels it may purchase her some sort of happiness; and various plans float through her head – selling Lambourn, getting help from Christopher.[1]

August 3rd

I wrote to Gerald, trying to put in a good word for Julian. What I said I do most truly believe; that it's much more comfortable to delight in the good qualities of one's friends than rage at their bad ones. (Otherwise, who, including oneself, should escape whipping?) Julian has so many good qualities too that it ought to be easy; not being able

---

[1] Strachey, her half brother.

to face up to disagreeable realities (in this case cause an admired friend pain) really springs from his delightful sensitivity. All I said about the novel itself was that 'it was the *only* one of his books I didn't think first-rate.' True if ambiguous. Today I opened his reply with nervous fingers and read with relief: 'You show your usual kindness and sympathy in writing me such a very charming letter.' And he says he has begun writing again and that he 'will stop being angry with Julian'.

Last night came Bunny, Henrietta and Julian to spend a very pleasant evening. Everyone seemed to appreciate everyone else, though no one had a good word for poor Gerald's book.

Bunny and Julian amused each other. Bunny gave a stunning account of a Buñuel film, and also described a row with Nerissa at lunch that day. In an attempt to improve her manners he told her she must ring up Harold Hobson[1] if she wanted a lift (along with Bunny) to London in his Bentley. How easy for all three listeners to realize that Bunny's desire for his children to have good manners was the only thing that had been all right – otherwise he had 'turned purple' (Henrietta), 'blown up' (himself), and shown not the slightest tact or forbearance. When the two young had gone, Bunny blew off a little more steam to me: he is terribly upset because Amaryllis has sold his mother's house, the Cearne, which he gave her, in order to buy another little house in Islington. Islington is now Bunny's idea of hell; he says the word with a sour look of distaste, and obviously can't accept the fact that a present belongs to the receiver and the giver has no more control over it. Then he 'is beginning to hate music'. What with Fanny practising scales deafeningly on her horn, William on his oboe, Nerissa carrying her transistor all over the house, and Angelica scraping on her violin, there's no peace or quiet, and how can he possibly write his American lectures? And he can't understand why Angelica hasn't painted for a whole year, when she's a very good painter and not a good violinist. Nothing is done about cooking lunch and if he goes into the kitchen and starts on it she's angry with him. Not a very harmonious picture, but I heard him telling Henrietta that Sophie was 'simply marvellous. She comes *rippling* and chattering into the room in the mornings.'

---

[1] An old friend and neighbour at Hilton.

August 6th

I dined a few nights ago with Eardley, Jim Lees-Milne, Mattei and his French friend Roger on the top of the Post Office Tower. It was the most exciting thing I've done for ages. Luckily it was a brilliant evening, pure clean skies, washed of all but a few dramatic clouds. Before ascending we looked up at the great glistening object in awe. I've always admired it, but said to myself, 'I'll never go up *that* thing,' and I half-expected to feel afraid, and almost queasy should it sway slightly in the wind. But nothing of the sort. Favoured beings with our dinner tickets, we jumped the long queue waiting to go up for a four-shillings look at the view, and were swept swiftly up thirty and more floors and decanted at the top. The restaurant is just beneath the windblown observation terrace and gets just as good a view; it revolves slowly, sometimes one gets the feeling that it has stopped, then it seems to go quite fast. A waiter warned me away from standing on a place where one of my feet was being carried in the opposite direction from the other. We looked all the time at London spread beneath – St Paul's and Big Ben were tiny pimples, Tower Bridge a little toy with the river winding away beyond, Regent's Park a huge domain of noble trees and velvet lawns with long slanting evening shadows. There was no sense of vertigo even I think for Jim who had dreaded it. As the daylight faded, twinkling lights of all colours came out and I felt I *adored* London.

August 8th

The best part of yesterday was going to the Prom at the Albert Hall with Desmond, and giving him supper after. What a fantastic great chasm it is, and how strange to look up through the vast emptiness and see behind remote twinkling lights pale faces glimmering down from under looped curtains like a Pollock toy theatre. The music was all strange to me – Britten and Mahler. Yet without ever being carried away I was unfailingly interested and absorbed, and Desmond's intelligence and special knowledge was a delight and refreshment.

August 10th

I was well-prepared for Sonia: calm, with the soft pedal down and my tempo deliberately slowed. And my word, a good job too! She's really a monster. She arrived looking blooming and tidy and braced, noisy but fairly level. I was in a mood of cool observation by this time, my 'wool' absolutely glued to my head, and so it was with surprise but almost no emotion that I noted that she launched at once on an attack on Janetta's way of life — her passion for Spain, the pointless life she led there, the futility of her friends (Jaime[1] and the Davises), the gloom of La Cónsula, the beastliness of Spanish food, even the site of her new house was all wrong and was sure to be eventually ruined. Then over dinner the subject of Julia began, and now I was suddenly being addressed as if I were a public meeting, in a loud continuous roar, with the gaps filled with prolonged fortissimo 'ERs' so that I shouldn't get a word in edgeways. She kept repeating, 'Well now, let's see. ER. We must get this straight . . . ER. We agree something must be done about getting Julia out of Percy Street?' I had of course quite a lot to say on the subject but I really had no desire to impart it to her, so my problem was easy. I did, I think, attempt to say that I didn't consider Lawrence had really behaved badly although he had caused Julia such pain. ('Oh, I've no patience with Lawrence. Anyway, I don't know him. So that's that.') Nor was it the least use saying that I firmly believe that it is the greatest mistake to deal with these painful and delicate human imbroglios in terms of praise and blame; one should rather look at them as impersonal cataclysms. Or that with Julia of all people it's a lifelong delusion that some material change will make her happy ('If I had a servant for four hours a day' or 'If I could do up my flat'). They are mere assuagements and alleviations. No need to set them aside on that account, but it's useless to expect too much of them. Or that I didn't hold with relentless interference in other people's lives. I literally never got a sentence finished before she began shouting at the full pitch of her lungs. I began to suggest that I might talk to Craig, since Julia was consulting him. 'Oh, CRAIG's absolutely useless. He was so *cruel* over my divorce. He had no conception how painful it was.' When I said I thought he was too gentlemanly for a divorce lawyer she said, 'Gentleman my foot! He's no gentleman. Julia likes him because he thinks he's an intellectual.' Craig! The most modest and unassuming of men. And so it went on. I've never been so browbeaten, bossed and bullyragged in my life. I suppose Lady Reading marshalling her assistants for some local government campaign *might* go on so — but an acquaintance whom I'd asked to dinner! I can only think she hadn't a clue about what I feel about her,

[1] Parladé, whom Janetta married later.

that I really despise her pretentiousness, and now had added to my picture of her a full awareness of her crude, raw, arrogant, insensitive bossyness. I was pretty well given instructions to ask James for money (which I eeled out of), go and see Christopher (which I declined), and talk to Lawrence, which I said I was prepared to do, and so I've long been. But I refuse to carry out her 'instructions' and *tell* Lawrence that he has to cough up £750 a year for Julia at least. I said I was anxious to contribute financially myself, but I'm blessed if I'll consent to be on Sonia's committee.

I then plied her with more drink and deliberately switched the conversation. When I said something or other seemed rather illogical she burst out about this 'awful Bloomsbury logic'. There were several aggressive attacks on Bloomsbury, and she returned to 'her best friend Janetta' to tell me that she had 'deeply offended Mary MacCarthy[1] by making a pass at her husband' and that she 'ought to have her head examined'. I've heard Janetta's account of this episode, which is anyway ancient history to be so treasured and brought out now.

It was really far worse than I'd expected, but *so* awful as to be almost funny. I shall never have any more to do with Sonia than I can possibly help. And I shall conduct my relations with Julia, who has been my friend since she was eight, according to my lights, not Sonia's.

August 12th

I had Sophie to myself yesterday for longer than I have for some time. Angelica brought her to Henrietta's flat, from there she came with me to lunch at Magouche's and thence back here till evening. The result has been something like falling in love. She has tugged so violently at my heart-strings that when I sat alone last night thinking about her I was aware with amazement that the tears were running down my cheeks. She is a touchingly responsive little creature and her delight in a small suitcase I gave her full of tiny wrapped objects gave me delight also. She wouldn't let go of it all day and when I said it was her 'suitcase' to take in the train she wanted to go in the train at once. Such an effusion of love for her arose in me that I couldn't resist giving her an enormous hug and saying, 'I *love* you, Sophie' and she looked at me with a little smiling face which I thought showed

[1] The American writer.

258

she didn't dislike the idea. Indeed, when I left her at Angelica's house there was an almost embarrassing moment of not wanting to go in. 'No. I don't *want*.' And even inside the house she raised her arms and face to me imploringly. What made me cry? Her vulnerability, my longing to make her happy, and my impotence. To love someone in a protective way is agonizing.

August 23rd

A week in the Lakes with the Marshalls is the first of a series of summer visits made available to me by kind friends. There was one magnificent, never-to-be-forgotten day when we retraced the mountain walk taken two years ago, but in the opposite direction. It was a brilliant blazing morning when we started to climb the side of the mountain ridge above Newlands village, Mark[1] and I ahead; I felt strong, and excited by the prospect of hoisting myself a few thousand feet. What a strange but intoxicating pleasure. I never cease to marvel at the immense change in the surrounding scene wrought by each step of my puny legs. Up, up we went and great heads of unseen mountains arose to look at us over nearer ridges. At the same time as enjoying the distant view I was revelling in what was underfoot or within reach of my hand – cushions of yellowish moss squelching with boggy water, glistening stones, short rabbit- and sheep-bitten turf with the tiny faces of purple and yellow flowers. We had meant to get to the top and eat our picnic lunch looking down on Derwentwater, but poor Munia Postan,[2] who wheezes all the time with asthma, was overcome by the steepness of the climb, or (as he said, valiantly ignoring the effort) the heat and pollen of the grasses, and stood coughing and fighting for breath, with his face as crimson as what's left of his bright red hair. We stopped for him to rest, and had our lunch.

Other walks were shorter, beautiful, but not with this special obsessional excitement of mastering a peak, which gives one a glimpse of what real mountaineers must feel.

Munia's Russian voice is exactly like Boris's; he is clever, kind, egotistical and full of prejudices which I instinctively didn't want to arouse. That is, I knew it would be disastrous to express socialist or pacifist views but not anti-God ones, and that he liked to be amused

[1] My nephew.
[2] Professor of Economics at Cambridge.

but not to listen nor yet to argue much. He has enormous charm and is a real character. Tom says Munia is more of a snob than his aristocratic wife Cynthia is. She too has charm and confidence, and is obviously wholeheartedly devoted to her rather plain husband, who depends on her as a child on its mother and yet talks often and enthusiastically about his first wife, Eileen Power.

August 28th: *Celia's house at Cambridge*

Last night's dinner-party guests were the Master and Mistress of Jesus, and the Master and Mistress of Peterhouse. The Master of Peterhouse, a historian called Butterfield – 'brilliantly clever' says Celia – had a flavour of unfrocked priest about him which I found slightly upsetting. He is in fact a Methodist and touches no alcohol; also he had a faint north country, Wilfred Pickles, Jolly Jack Priestley quality, and burst into frequent cackles of healthy laughter. His plump comfortable wife was the only one who attempted to put out feelers in my direction. But it's the first time in my life I've actually experienced what I've often been told about – the provincialism of High Table conversation – the gossip about professorships and who was likely to get them, the technique of being a Master, and how they had acquired these dignities; even the old story of the election of a Warden of All Souls (characters: Isaiah Berlin, John Sparrow, Trevor-Roper) was hauled from its coffin. There was no interest in what was afloat in the great world of London, politics, books. Yet these are very clever and attractive people, no doubt of it. Is it a good thing to subject the young to such an intensely limited outlook? I was really surprised, and sat silent for about an hour in the corner of my sofa while local politics about which I knew nothing and cared less were feverishly discussed.

September 5th

I'm aloft in a Vanguard, gliding towards Cork – one stage in my unaccustomedly rapid change of situation these six holiday weeks. Yesterday's violent rainstorms, in which I drove Julia up from Lambourn, have temporarily died down and we float in the usual sandwich fillings between palest blue and blobs of cotton wool.

My weekend alone with Julia was, I really think, a great success. If I had to choose a life companion would she be the one? Yes, from the point of view of mental communication; there's no one more stimulating or constantly enjoyable. But how in the world could one arrange the physical basis of life? Am I being blind in thinking we got on without friction? Could she have been keeping a tight hold on herself? She arrived in my flat soon after ten on Friday morning, pale, distraught, and reeling, exuding the sense that an enormous effort had been made. Calling for a glass of water she swallowed a 'purple heart'[1] and very soon came to life.

Talk of her writing. She wondered if it were the least use going on. She could only write under the influence of purple hearts and then often badly. I asked her to let me see some and she did. Only two hundred pages and certainly too rough and careless to seem like the fruit of five years or so mashing over – but the essentials were all there. Though as she says it is about herself and her life, it is thoroughly transformed by her personal vision and now and then from the stream of observations about bus stops, tea-shops and suburban housewives she builds up a mountain of symbolic implications.

September 6th: *Ireland*

Oh, the magic, how quickly it takes effect. Arrived at Cork, I crossed the great grey river and went into a pub for a drink. An orange-haired barwoman was cracking jokes with a talkative regular, who at once included me in the conversation. It was at this moment I knew I was glad I'd come. Then the long bus ride, over two hours, wrapped in a kindly lethargic co-consciousness presided over by the conductor, with schoolchildren getting in and out and sitting touchingly grasping their tickets with satchels strapped to their backs, smelly schoolboys talking Gaelic. Outside green, green, green under a low canopy of soft grey clouds, often raining, sometimes grey like a grey pearl. Surprised again by the brilliant colour-sense of the Irish who are adding new colours to the old blood-red, egg, and darkish green of their houses – forget-me-not and strawberry ice, and striking combinations that made me think of Leningrad. Bantry in the rain and Robert, who drove me in his little battered car about five miles towards Glengariff and down a long tree-lined drive to the 'Irish Tudor' house they've rented.

September 10th: *Kings Land*[2]

Perfect, ripe summer weather and the delightful company of Julian and Magouche. But I must return to Ireland. It was only when I was

1 Amphetamine.
2 Formerly the home of Hilaire Belloc, Julian's grandfather, in Sussex.

describing my stay to Julian and Magouche last night that I fully realized how I loved that green country. The bromidic soothingness of the climate; its variety. Stormy and wet when I arrived, the wind dropped, all nature stood still and the sea in the inlets turned to glass. From the terrace of the grey stone house the lawn sloped down through huge clumps of hydrangea, red-hot pokers and montbretia to the rocky shore. Indoors there were enormously long baths full of brown water, the smell of peat fires in the evening and an 1890 decor – heads of animals shot in Africa, an elephant's foot mounted as a stool, assegais and old faded military groups on the walls. The General to whom it belonged, now eighty-eight but elegant, debonair and completely on the spot, lived next door, in sin or ex-sin with his handsome sister-in-law. A charming bespectacled Sheilah Murphy came to help most days. There was even supposed to be a cook but the very first day she went with Cynthia to Bantry to 'show her the shops', she borrowed a pound, bought half a bottle of Paddy and got completely plastered. She then started on the Kees' stout and took to the floor of the kitchen lavatory where she spent the whole afternoon redfaced and happy except for cooking two disgusting meals, and went home taking all the coffee, most of the tomatoes and a good many other things bought that morning. It was too like Somerville and Ross to produce anything but hilarity, and next day Cynthia sacked her.

I shan't forget Robert's kindness to the children and me, his fascinating talk about Irish history, philosophy and ideas.

September 14th: Churriana, Spain

There was Gerald at Málaga airport, and off we went to Churriana. An almost painful familiarity of sights and smells, but a huge new block of flats has reared itself at the corner of the Coin road. The substitute for Teresita, Little Mari, ran forward and kissed me on both cheeks. Antonio,[1] slightly more toothless, shook me by the hand and we sat down in wicker chairs in the patio by the familiar sound of the trickling fountain. Gamel is terribly bent from the waist

---

[1] The gardener.

upwards and feels her way along on tottering legs. Gerald says, 'Gamel's very well, really.' I don't think she is. But their life is calm; there is only one resident cat and the house smells less than it did, and looks lovely.

September 16th: The Beach House, Marbella[1]

The night I spent with the Brenans a colossal thunderstorm exploded, rain streamed into the patio and grand pianos fell out of the sky. Everyone is delighted; it was badly needed and has laid the dust, but it left a grey morning swathed in damp veils. Gerald didn't speak of his novel and though I gave him a letter from Julian about it, no word was said. When we walked up the hillside (without Gamel, 'she walks so slowly'), he told me about his visit from a girl who arrived out of the blue and went to bed with him. 'She was madly exciting. I've never known such a girl. The trouble is that as one gets older an orgasm is a very mild affair. When one was young it was like reading *Paradise Lost* for the first time, now it's as dry as *Paradise Regained*.'

Soon after six o'clock Janetta arrived having just seen someone off at the airport. Gerald had told me she was looking marvellously well and young, but the golden brown of her sunburnt skin doesn't conceal the fact that she's too thin and strained, and when I asked her how she was she said, 'Desperate'. (These two days have been for me packed full with impressions, but they lie jumbled like drawers of ransacked underclothes and I don't know when I shall be able to sort them out.)

Not till yesterday therefore did I begin to take stock of this lotus-land in which so many questions arise and there is never 'time', concentration or application to answer them. There's something frighteningly dreamlike about being surrounded by what Julia calls the playboy life. I don't mean Janetta and Jaime of course. Jaime goes off with his briefcase to work every morning on his new hotel La Fonda, and I've not seen Janetta so domestic for years. They both seem happy. Yet the surrounding waters that wash around them are full of lost souls – people who under a smiling guise live under the sway of the death instinct – who kill time, let their minds rot, chatter, have another drink and wait for something to happen.

[1] A small house rented by Jaime during the bathing season.

September 18th

Mark Culme-Seymour[1] has just driven up and asked if he could have 'one quick drink to give him courage before going off to the Windsors to lunch'. Otherwise the morning has begun much like others. It is one o'clock and we have breakfasted and Jaime has driven off in his car. Lunch will be somewhere about four, dinner between eleven and twelve; sleeping hours from two or three until eleven or twelve. I have tried to adjust to these times but it's a physical effort, such as crossing the Atlantic causes (so I imagine) and I can only begin to do it by pinning myself down to sleeping on late which I dislike. Last night I went to bed to the loud thumping of Beatles on the gramophone and voices next door, feeling, like Janetta, 'desperate'.

Two days ago, one golden evening, when the crested mountain was softened to velvet by the fading light, Janetta, Rose and I drove up the valley to the land she has bought at Tramores. We forded a river and at the last turn of the track where her property began a horseman was drawn up in a dramatic attitude. Her land is a rich and fertile triangle of orange trees, olives, persimmons, grapes, bananas, in a deep basin of mountains whose edges cut cleanly against the pale evening sky. It is a beautiful place, a very peaceful and secluded one; the ruined Moorish tower is very grand and beside it stands the original farmhouse, now empty and waiting to be rebuilt for Janetta. Beneath, in a sort of cleft, is the new little house where her tenant farmer Miguel, his wife and three children live. They hurried out to meet her, and out also came a young man who is making baskets from palmettos – they were lying out drying on the threshing-floor. An old crone, younger than me no doubt but bent over more sharply even than Gamel, looked at me out of bright brown eyes, snatched my hand and kissed it. Some turkeys were gobbling in a shed and almost at once Maria, Miguel's wife, with little Salvador her youngest child in her arms, began to gobble too, partly with hospitable invitations to visit her *casita*, partly with complaints of stopped drains and things that didn't work, all in thick Andaluz. I couldn't understand half of it and was amazed by Janetta's courage in embarking on this new adventure and taking the responsibility for so many souls.

September 20th

How has my adjustment to Beach-House life happened? How have I shaken off desperation? The day before yesterday I spent several hours

[1] Janetta's half-brother.

264

alone here while the others were in Marbella moving furniture in the new *fonda*. I picked flowers and read, and gradually some restlessly revolving mechanism within me found its proper balance and stabilized, so that I could think and orientate myself. This inability to stabilize is much like seasickness and equally detestable – it's from that moment that I date my adaptation.

4.30 p.m. Some rain and uncertain weather yesterday. Today a very rough sea. I let myself be battered by its huge waves for a while. Yesterday Janetta, Georgia and I went to lunch at the Brenans'. Gerald had given me *The Story of Poor Robinson* to read, a Candide-like account of his affair with Carrington, telling me that it gave a merciless account of everyone, particularly himself and Carrington. In fact he himself is the one figure sympathetically drawn, the poet, the innocent, the high-minded among a set of grotesque monsters. Ralph (Parrywag) is described as an absurd doltish but handsome womanizer. I find it infuriating that Gerald has launched this myth of Ralph as a lumbering carthorse, only faintly civilized by Lytton.

September 30th

A few days in Madrid, chez Nicko and Mary Henderson.

October 3rd: West Halkin Street

London life closes around me and drags me along with it. My mind is beset with grumbling boring questions, consonant with the pelting, pouring rain that never stops.

I've been remembering my extraordinary dinner party (along with the Hendersons and Anthony and Tanya Hobson) at the house of a very rich young Spanish banker and his wife out in the country a good many miles from Madrid. It was like a scene in a Russian novel. We arrived through uninhabited hills dotted with holm oaks, up a rough track and were suddenly confronted by a huge luxurious house. About four men-servants ran to open our car doors; every sort of drink and delicacy was spread to receive us; our young pregnant hostess was expensively dressed and completely assured, the soft music of Vivaldi and Mozart was swooning from an inner room. Mary told me afterwards I'd 'done extremely well' with our young host Jaime at dinner. He certainly wasn't easy to talk to, though his English was perfect with a slight north country accent, for I felt he wasn't really interested in anything but money – what an astonishingly all-absorbing topic that can be! We talked though somehow or other, and then I suddenly felt my blood simmering at the obsequiousness with which one of his servants was handing him cigars, cutters and lighters on a tray, and the fact that he took them with a gesture implying that the man did not belong to the same order of human being as he did at all. I spoke of it to Nicko and Mary afterwards and they said, 'Oh, all rich Spaniards are like that. They're hundreds of years behind the times. They never thank servants for anything, like we do. Jaime and Pirou are exceptionally enlightened.'

The only people I've seen since my return are the denizens of Montpelier Square with whom I lunched on Saturday. In the evening Julian came to dinner, supposedly to go to the opera with me, but with real kindness persuaded me I wasn't well enough to go and sat talking to me for a few hours. He says Georgie has seemed grown-up, and interested in her work at her tutor's, but she doesn't want to go back to Spain for Christmas.

October 4th

At first on returning from abroad there is solitude and silence all round, a vacuum in which one has no place. Now all sorts of mosquitoes buzz in my ears. I awoke at six this morning and finished reading, for a report to Gollancz, an extraordinarily gloomy but powerful French novel which has affected me a good deal as *Cañas y Barro*[1] did long ago. Julia came to dinner, and I can't say I feel easier in my mind about her. She had 'touched bottom' soon after I went to Spain, couldn't go to the London Library, couldn't eat, and lay on her bed feeling frightfully ill. She realized it was the purple hearts (now up to four or five a day) and by sheer will-power she has reduced them now to one or even none. 'The thing is, I was really frightened.' Her present *modus vivendi* is the wildly impractical one of drawing on her small capital to employ a typist to whom she dictates her current work. 'I can't write any more. I must get it straightened out. As I lay on my bed I felt this was the one thing I must do, the one thing of importance, before I die.' She admitted the

[1] By Blasco Ibañez.

task would be endless, for it would only be a first draft and all to do again. So at present she is spending £1,200 a year out of an income that is much less, *only* on getting this story finished – and how good is it? Of course that's not the way to think of it. It's her lifeline at the moment. Oh, the struggle of it all! I can't get over the fact that such misery can be produced by love alone if it assumes unlucky combinations. No hate at all, no 'desire to cause pain' is necessary.

October 5th

Grey, grey, I do not love you grey. The sun hasn't shone once since I touched down in Bird's Custard Island.[1] But I'm not too grey myself. Many friends have rung up, and I am dining out every day this week and going away every weekend this month except the next when I'm due to go to a Freudian banquet. Yesterday the orchestra began and on the way I visited Sophie and Henrietta and gave Sophie her Spanish dolly, which I think caused pleasure. Henrietta was extraordinarily sweet to me and as she said, 'calm'.

October 6th

Henrietta and Sophie have come to lunch with me and Henrietta has gone out to shop for a grand ball tonight, while Sophie sleeps contentedly in my bed – that is, she went off to rest most happily.

Last night I dined with Raymond to meet Lord and Lady Snow (Pamela Hansford-Johnson). It was a dull evening. Once people have become public figures they seem to be pretty well doomed. All they want to do on social occasions is to show off, and secure to themselves admiration, which is hardly necessary in view of their own tremendous opinion of themselves. Lady Snow is a solid, noisy, avid little woman, her plump form balanced on spindle heels. She held the floor continuously and confidently, far from stupidly but expressing herself tritely in such phrases as 'and the lot'. Another give-away expression is, when speaking of a third person, not 'so and-so is nice, clever or charming,' but 'I SIMPLY adore', or 'am terribly fond of so-and-so', subtly turning the limelight once again on the desired spot. She said she had been a correspondent in the Moors case,[2] as a result of which she had come round to the view that such

[1] Gerald's name for England.
[2] Child-murders by Myra Hindley and her boyfriend.

books as de Sade's should not be available to the young, and was writing a book to this effect. There would be 'terrible screams from intellectual quarters about free speech and so on'. 'It's not that I mind sex,' she said rather oddly, 'but I can't stand sex combined with cruelty and violence.' I said I was against cruelty and violence as such, regardless of what it was combined with, but she had no interest in anything an unknown elderly female had to say, and I only bothered to speak to either Snow throughout the evening 'to keep my end up' and because I knew Raymond wouldn't like it if I didn't. I can do it after a fashion, but I consider such contacts completely pointless. One is a mere claque, and I soon got tired of compulsive clapping. Lord Snow does look very like a snowman and as he drank steadily all through the evening, helping himself liberally to slugs of Raymond's whisky after dinner, he began to dissolve slowly in its golden rays. His wife kept a sharp eye on him and I drove them home, but he was virtually asleep and I expected his large head to subside any moment on my shoulder.

What incredible conceit it is for such people to think they are conferring a favour – as I felt they did – on Raymond by coming to dinner and drinking half a bottle or more of his whisky, and boasting. Raymond rang me up this morning to apologize.

October 8th

A very different evening last night, with James and Alix in their hotel next to the BBC. It is brand new, with an express lift that swirls you upwards to a restaurant providing tasteless synthetic food and drink. I think they are being treated to their stay as part of the celebrations of the completion of James's translation of Freud's *Complete Works*, which ends with a banquet tonight to which I am going in my capacity as indexer. I found them in the cocktail lounge – Alix looked splendidly distinguished, so did James but also rather disquietingly aged, pink and tottery. They were touchingly enjoying their splendour. We discussed what 'cocktails' we should have. It's a long time since anyone has offered me such a thing, and we ended with three 'bronxes' made of orange juice very dimly laced with something. James was naturally agitated at the thought of the dinner and the speech he must make at it, yet enjoying the idea of being the hero of the evening. During dinner there was some talk of Holroyd's book. Not a good word for it. Holroyd told Raymond that James could not bear the faintest criticism of Lytton to be made. James has written an immense letter of complaints to Holroyd which he says he took surprisingly mildly. Then Alix and I got going on the Labour Party. I see that, as with James in the case of Lytton or Freud, she has her heroes who can do no wrong and must not be criticized. She admitted she was getting persecution mania over the attacks on Mr Wilson and his policy. I wish I'd asked her if she didn't think criticism should always be allowed of any party. The trouble is she reads only the left-wing *Sun* which is far more critical than *The Times*. She wouldn't agree that even the Conservative press was quite enthusiastic about Mr Wilson when he first came to power. (However, this morning a large red self-satisfied man came into the greengrocer's where I was buying a cabbage and said in answer to the question, 'What would you like, Sir?' 'There's only one thing I want – for Mr Wilson to drop dead tomorrow.') I said I deplored unemployment being an even temporary aim of the Labour Government and also their setting more stress on things than services. Alix said this was the only means to an end which was in itself good and right. We also talked of crime and whether Lady Snow's notion of suppressing the pornography of sadism had any sense in it. I was fascinated to note that Alix so strongly holds the Freudian belief that human beings have a given content of aggressive violence, and that if you stop up one exit you will only find another being used, that she clearly didn't feel anything could alter the amount of violent crime and was indeed amazed to hear that it had increased threefold.

October 10th

The old refrain from one of my translations, 'nightmare, nightmare, endless nightmare', haunted me today as I walked through the grey glistening streets, with rain sousing my unprotected head, thinking of all the anguish endured by suffering human beings. Yet the people whose profession is supported on this human anguish – the psychoanalysts in fact, four hundred of them collected together in the Connaught Rooms for dinner two nights ago – looked a remarkably glossy, stylish, confident lot: women bronzed from their summer holidays, wearing exotic evening dress and with clever Jewish faces, men also with clever Jewish faces and eyes flashing through their spectacles. I expected the intelligence watermark to be high, but was surprised by the dash and self-confidence displayed.

October 12th

Woken at about one o'clock last night by a cramp-like pain in my chest. I looked for a while into an abyss of fear, and then into a bleak stony avenue of 'curtailed activities', 'going gently', having to give up my precious nippyness, and for a moment sympathized with Munia Postan for 'wanting to die on a mountain'. For of course, in any case, activities must be dropped as one ages. Poor Ralph, during those long years of restriction, of finding people walked too fast for him, and of wanting but not being allowed to carry suitcases! Did I ever show him enough sympathy and consideration? Or did my own fearful anxiety on his behalf make me nag him too much? Well, no use thinking along these lines.

Detachment is the most difficult of all positions to take up. When love-affairs and marriages explode, other people quickly line up as if for prisoner's base, and wave the flags of those they've decided to champion. How or why should one blame either party, is my commonest reaction. Yet I see my attempts at remaining uncommitted sometimes strike a chill on those partially inclined. Today I went to have a cardiogram and Dr Hensman has just rung up to say that it showed certain warning symptoms – a sign that I must be careful. I hear this at present with apathetic resignation. 'I must take things very quietly for the next fortnight' and will 'for the rest of my life have an excuse for not doing anything I don't want to do'. Heigh ho. I have the feeling that one can get used to *anything*.

October 13th

Julia came last night and talked to me delightfully about all sorts of things till about ten o'clock. I could see she took my health news almost too seriously, and I find she has already rung up my doctor and Julian about me, reminding me a little and with the same slightly irritable gratitude of my mother's fussing over illness. A familiar sense of 'trudge' has come over my attitude to living – or perhaps it might be said that I am deliberately and with an effort not thinking, as I did when my aeroplane from Madrid couldn't land. Anyway, I think of health as the drains of life and do not want to let them dominate it.

October 15th: Stokke

Mary drove me down here yesterday. We talked all the way. On arrival at Stokke we found Mary's half-crazed mother Lady Rosslyn, and a pile of letters for Mary including a long one from Charlie.

Lady R: (greeting me) I *am* so sorry about your husband.
F: It's me that's supposed to be ill. I'm afraid my husband has been dead for some years. You do recognize me? Frances Partridge?
Lady R: Oh yes, of course. How stupid of me. How lovely for him! I shouldn't say that but you know it's so awful being old, one's in everybody's way. No one wants one.

She is in her odd way rather delightful, quite a character, fumbles for her thoughts and words, and comes out with something at an odd and original angle from what she wanted to say. But she *cannot* stop talking for a single minute. Even when Mary was busy telephoning an order for animal food her mother kept going up to her, with a sort of jealousy, waving a clock at her and asking questions. It is farcical but also tragic. We were alone for quite a long time and I couldn't read — even the newspaper, or even do a crossword, she kept breaking in on me with a slow quiet ceaseless stream of prattle, in which an occasional wrong name would cause me to rack my brains furiously.

Last night Julia arrived and was brilliant with Mary's mother. 'I remember so well your telling me about welcoming some large wild animal — a tiger or a lion perhaps? — on some rain-swept quay or other,' she began. 'I don't know where it was.' Lady Rosslyn looked totally blank and incredulous but Mary coming in said, 'Oh yes, it was a leopard, and in Caracas.' She whispered to Julia and me that her mother had been drunk as a lord at the time and gone on caressing the leopard though it clawed her dreadfully. She was once an alcoholic, then became a fervent Catholic (or perhaps always was) and was cured. She has just recently at eighty or more started tippling again, and who shall blame her? She's to go into a new convent next week and is as afraid as if she had to embark on a new school. Poor old thing. And she talks of having been in 'the mental home' with a look of pale distress. Indeed, she wrings my heart and I like her; but my God, she's exhausting.

October 16th

Attracted out by the soft glow of a lovely autumn day, to wander in the garden, picking roses and spinach. Then a shift of reassuring Mary's mum, as if she were a child. Julia is in her most helpful mood, washing up, springing to help Lady Rosslyn on any of her wild projects like finding the telephone number of the Catholic priest at Marlborough. She compensates for this with a certain return to her old snubbing ways towards Mary and me. When the subject of opera came up at dinner last night she said she didn't like the human singing voice in a way that held an implication: nor should you like it.

Lady Rosslyn's malapropisms produced comic relief, and so, quietly and pleasantly but on a fairly low level, we crept through the day. I have woken to a grey interior landscape and a drizzling garden. Met Mary in the kitchen hurriedly collecting her mother's breakfast as 'she must eat it an hour and a half before Mass.' Goodness!

October 17th

This house has been all weekend the container of various dramas, like poor Lady Rosslyn's dread of facing her new school (convent) and attempts to get the hang of what is going on around her. Mary dashes about in scarlet stockings, being charming to everyone, arranging about a stopped drain in the farm (cows up to their bellies in water), about the cowman crisis, writing letters to Charlie. Julia started too well, insisting on washing up unaided, leaping up every few minutes to get Lady Rosslyn's spectacles – and then of course becoming 'completely exhausted', 'the trouble is I can't *stick* Mary's Mum,' she told me. Barley Allison[1] and David Erskine[2] came to lunch and Julia questioned Barley about her hero Saul Bellow in a rather hectoring way and came away hopping mad. But she has at least and at whatever cost seemed to keep her spirits from rocketing into the abyss.

Back to London today.

October 24th

Just back from a weekend at Wivenhoe, and not feeling altogether gruntled. Dicky went off early this morning having said, according to

[1] Publisher and friend of the Erskines.
[2] Mary's brother.

Denis, that the 'weekend had been a failure'. Would I ring him up at the college? Of course I will, but I think perhaps it *was* a failure. And why? Because poor Dicky was in a state of manifest, head-hanging gloom after an American rejection of his new book.

As for Denis, he flew through the house like a whirlwind doing nothing in particular, boasted of having been reading Nietzsche and Wittgenstein and his 'excellent' French and Spanish, and bossed Dicky unmercifully. 'Why don't you learn the aorist pluperfect, Dicky?' 'Why SHOULD I, Denis? I don't in the least want to. I've got lots of better things to do.'

Denis went fairly often to the pub, and came back in a state of euphoria saying, 'I've just won another five shillings on the fruit machine.' On Sunday evening he started an argument about 'inequality' and Nietzsche in a slow but loud voice. I did my best by comparing our acceptance of inequality in looks, health, intelligence, talent but rejection of it socially. However he began all over again, largissimo: 'I BELIEVE IN INEQUALITY.' On Monday morning Dicky went off early to teach in his art school. Meanwhile Francis Bacon rang Denis up, and the Great Painter and his friend had an endless conversation about cookery of all things. 'Well, I take my veal and flour it, add a few mushrooms cooked in butter . . . there's nothing like a good *pot-au-feu*,' etc.

October 26th: London

After my orchestra, went to Montpelier Square and watched Julian interviewing John Bayley on the telly. John Bayley was exactly as in life, though Julian said he was dreadfully nervous, and jumping up and down on his seat with the interest and surprise caused by his own thoughts. He reminds me in this of Desmond, and both have this remarkable and touching desire to pursue a train of thought with absolute honesty. I found Georgie, looking beautiful and dispensing friendly smiles, and Tim Behrens sprawling bonily on the floor and exploding into a stammering lava of thoughts. After the telly, an interesting conversation began about Tolstoy. Then Julian confessed he felt he was doing badly as Janetta's stand-in, and was glad that she's coming back at the end of this week. He looked pretty exhausted.

This morning I posted off the proofs I have been busy correcting for the last week. My first attempt to catch a new book – from the World University Library – seems to have got a bite; a history book, but not for four to six weeks, which suits me fine. I shall enjoy being lazy if I have something lined up for me.

October 27th

Julia last night described her present attitude which amounts to kicking away all the ladders that kind friends or her own efforts have propped up to her loft – she won't go to stay with Mary at Stokke, nor with Magouche in Athens, she can't go to the London Library, she has dismissed her secretary because there is nothing more to be typed. She varies between saying 'her book doesn't exist,' and there are 'chests of drawers' full of papers which would have to be sorted out, and read one by one. (This was one of the reasons she couldn't go to Athens.) I fear it is the death-wish in full operation. She wants to die – it's a case of: 'Witness then how fain I die.' Her house is on fire and she won't let the firemen in.

I think a great deal about death and the manner of dying. I dread other people's morbid gloating over it, such as is being spilt lavishly over a ghastly tragedy in a Welsh village[1] killing over a hundred schoolchildren. Yet one can only come to terms with death by pressing forward, opening the door and looking all round its room. So I read carefully Edmund de Goncourt's fanatical accounts of the deaths of friends. On the other hand I'm aware that there's much to be said against the pornography of horror. In the case of this Welsh disaster does it matter if a lot of people are revoltingly gloating over the poor little crushed children? No, for it probably won't induce one of them to commit violence, whereas a hullabaloo on the wireless might prevent other coal-tips from collapsing.

November 2nd

Janetta is back. The sun has come out. I feel a renewal of vigour. She came to have a bacon-and-egg supper with me on her first evening in England and we had a good long talk about very many things, but 'there are a lot more' she says. I think she'll stay about a month, pacify her children and dependents, convince them they're 'all right' and then be off again. I did say what I could in praise of the splendid way Julian has held the fort of Montpelier Square during her absence, cooked fish pies and worn an apron.

[1] Abervan.

November 4th

A remark by Erich Fromm has given me food for thought. He rates indignation low among human emotions – 'one of the worst – a morally rationalized form of hate'. I'm aware there are moments, perhaps because of finding no other emotion at hand, when I positively enjoy a little warming bout of indignation, so I feel touchée. What's more I think he's right. But whence comes all this steam? It seems such a purposeless emotion. Useful I suppose when it was necessary to fight for life or food. Or is it merely a reaction to frustrated desires? I like various other things he says, for example that 'responsibility' is 'really a beautiful word', implying care and concern, 'responding as a human being to what is before one, quite different from duty which implies paying a debt'. Also that a child's tie to its mother is deep but not merely sexual – 'it is certainty, protection, the total experience a child has of being safe.' I must find out more about Fromm.

November 6th

I try to savour what is enjoyable about a weekend in London: waking to silence more profound than that of a Sunday morning in the country, there being no one for me to bother about just as there is no one to bother about me, hence indulgence in selfishness. Out of my window a pale blue uncertain sky, the Sunday papers all over my bed. Yesterday I lunched at Montpelier Square and go again I think today. Janetta was looking tired, and when after lunch Julian and Andrew Murray-Thripland arrived flushed with wine and talk, her face suddenly became pink and crumpled and she retired to sleep on her bed. Nothing is more exhausting than being endlessly at the mercy of people squatting like toads, drinking and talking. I felt she had a lot on her mind, and she told me briefly that she 'had wanted to get back to Spain by the end of the month, but was wondering whether she could leave them all'. Her present note is very different from her arrival one (of universal 'all-rightness'). Nicky and Georgie having vanished as well, I felt bound to stay and talk to Julian and Andrew – but not only that, I enjoyed it. We talked of the desire for power in human beings, especially as it appeared in 'making a pile'. They were both apparently dazzled by it, to me it is an entirely worthless passion. Julian repeated that it was anyhow 'interesting'. 'Only clinically, as case history', I said. Does one say what one really thinks in these arguments? Andrew is thoughtful but rather inarticulate. I think Julian has fallen for him, because the whole shape of his face has altered. We talked and talked till four-thirty, when we all three plus Georgie got into Andrew's sports car and shot off through the streets. His lack of knowledge of where he was going, and Julian's protests and attempts to hush me when I said the best way to Halkin Street from Montpelier was not via Hyde Park Corner, and then our running out of petrol in Wilton Crescent, built up the composition of youthful wildness and afternoon abandon in whose bowl I was a pretty odd goldfish. (Later) Back from another excursion to Montpelier Square. What is to be done about the erosion and dissipation of Janetta's vital spark by so many people, of whom I'm one? Arrived to find the girls helping handsomely in the kitchen with lunch preparations, and a large crowd in the back room. Some went off, but we were at once refuelled by the arrival of Harriet [Behrens] and her two children. Human currents between these individuals were all friendly and appreciative and there is, I suppose, a warming effect of sheer company, like a hot bath, or a brisk walk, though I felt more enlivened by a prisoner's tramp round Belgrave Square gardens, where I was the only person but a sort of physical *bien-être* was engendered by the exercise, the suddenly gentler air on my face.

A desire for privacy came over me, and here in my flat, silent except for the ticking clock, I have it.

November 8th

Music at the A. P. Herberts' this morning wasn't a great success. Gwen Herbert had an appalling cold and played as usual with small sense of rhythm. Margaret had ceaseless trouble with her strings, crying aloud to high heaven that they were slipping, that she could 'hear them ticking', that 'she couldn't think why, it had never happened before – but perhaps it was because she'd coated the pegs in candlegrease'. As a matter of fact it happens to some extent or other almost every time we play, and is quite exasperating, as it interrupts everything and is not our fault though her tone of voice implies it. 'You must take your 'cello to a 'cello doctor,' I said at last, 'or a 'cello psychoanalyst.' She usually backs up her complaints of the strings by saying, 'THAT's why I'm making such an awful noise.' Take it all round it was no pleasure, and I suggested an early stop on grounds of Gwen Herbert not being well. Margaret came to an egg lunch with me afterwards and we had a delightful talk on all sorts of subjects. I felt full of affection for this good, clever, kind, warmhearted interesting person. Which shows that irritation at someone's neurotic behaviour can be quite separate and not a fringe on one's feelings for them. She said she hadn't enjoyed playing 'because of Gwen's hopeless lack of time sense.' Perhaps she unconsciously used the slipping strings to put a stop to our efforts.

Yesterday with Janetta to see the Rouaults at the Tate. A painter I've never cared much for, nor do I still, but I respect and understand him better and found him deeply interesting. His philosophy of life, his vision of the universe in all its dark rich limited emotional colour stares out at one from all the pictures. His constriction is to me almost repellent, so is the way the forms are crammed into the canvas and chained inside their thick black stained-glass outlines, nor is his view of man as tragic clown sympathetic to me.

November 10th

Yesterday was the sort of day I enjoy. Julian came to lunch and we had rich conversation for several hours, finally going into the important question of Love. He says he has been afraid of falling in love with Andrew and is putting on the brakes hard. He himself has nothing but painful scars from his one experience of love; nor was being loved by someone whom he didn't love an experience he's eager to repeat. So poor dear fellow, he tries to keep the whole emotion at bay. Rather to my own surprise I began defending love as an irradiator of the whole of life, and also saying that he hadn't yet known mutual love which was the most marvellous thing in the world, and mustn't try to escape it. And also, something that I've always felt about Julian, that he has so many qualifications for a long-term relationship that it would be sad if he refused to let himself have one. Asked him about his feeling for girls, as he seems to like them so much; he said he did, but not in the least sexually, and laid claim to low-powered sexuality. Earlier, ranging hither and thither, we had laughed over Raymond and Desmond's anxiety for him to 'wear frills' at Michael Pitt-Rivers' dinner party tomorrow.

Mary came to see me after gruelling visits to her divorce lawyer and her accountant. She went off to see Janetta, worn out and determined not to go with her to a champagne-drinking private view but collapse early to bed. Julian tells me that Janetta exerted her powers of persuasion and succeeded in taking Mary with her to the party, 'for her own good'.

The saddest news I've had lately is that poor little Charlotte[1] is

---

[1] Jenkins, née Strachey, later diagnosed as having leukemia.

seriously ill with some as yet undiagnosed blood trouble in Bart's hospital.

November 12th: Crichel

In bed in Eddy's room, crucifix to right of me, crucifix to left of me. Raymond hasn't come and probably won't; he telephoned us all separately and told us in ringing tones that he had lost his voice and had laryngitis.

Music last night – records of Rossini's *Semiramide*. I'm impressed by Julian's quickness to get the hang of a piece of music and produce a confident yet always modest reaction.

I had Adrian Daintrey to dinner on Friday night and by a happy inspiration added Isobel. He's all right in company, amusing even. Alone with me, he's inclined to become sentimental.

November 14th

I'm on my way back to London from Crichel on a brilliant morning, after a lovely drive over the plain in the local taxi. I feel rather jaded and forlorn from sleep shortage, twice waking at five-thirty. But loved the quietness and simplicity of the weekend alone with Julian and Desmond. Raymond never came, so we didn't have to go to the Pitt-Rivers party. There is a subtle change in that Moses and the yellow cat are much more with us in the drawing-room, sprawling on the hearthrug – the cat in sumptuous soft abandon, Moses a picture of affability and slightly ruffled dignity. He followed me everywhere, even to the lavatory, and came twice to whine and scratch at my bedroom door last night. The animal life occupied an important central position, like the fountains in the Piazza Navona, otherwise it was reading, damp walks on thin mud, and lots of music and conversation – the latter becoming more relaxed and enjoyable as the weekend went on. On Sunday Julian and I drove to Bryanston to fetch out Jonathan Ross, son of Alan and Jenifer, for the afternoon. An attractive, elegant, self-possessed boy of thirteen, with thick straight brown hair and very long eyelashes. We had a lot of school lore from him, including that the bus which takes boys to the Girls' School at Wardour Castle is known as the 'Passion Wagon'. I thought Julian a little sad yesterday, but he denied the impeachment. All the same I caught him staring moodily into space more than once. We listened to the whole of *Dido*, and Desmond and I to the end of

Semiramide. Poetry was read aloud and discussed, points looked up in books, there was gossip. I stare at the days ahead with a certain amount of angst.

November 19th

On the foot of my bed lies a packet of close-typed stodge – a French book about Charlemagne which is my latest job to translate. Why am I doing it? I don't need the money. I should like to know something of the period – but I suppose the real reason is I want to 'keep going' as a translator.

Julia came last night in such a broken, tremulous state that it was a fearful strain being with her. Things get no better for her, and I do fear they may get worse. When I asked her if she would almost rather not see Lawrence if she had other engagements she said, 'Yes'.

Janetta asked her to lunch the other day and told me how charming she had been to her children. When I asked Julia about them, she hadn't a good word for them. The Campbells have asked her for Christmas, at which I was relieved. But there's no gratitude really, it's just 'I couldn't think how to get out of it.' It's all part of her turning her face to the wall. I feel very much shaken by her. She hardly seemed 'there' much of the time last night, but was saying, 'No!', 'Really?' or 'Is that so?' in total unawareness of what I – or Eardley, who came for a drink – had said. It is torture being with her, poor creature, at the moment.

November 21st

Winter is here, and in an attempt not to fug and fossilize, especially now I'm on a steady 'job' again, I tend to walk about a mile round Belgrave Square gardens in the afternoon. As usual today not a soul was there (sometimes there's a dear little talkative boy) except the grouchy old gardener moving like a Niebelung through the blue fog of his bonfire of leaves. The trees are nearly bare; I looked up and saw a single motionless grey pigeon perched high aloft. The pale sun lit the top storeys of the stuccoed embassies and flashed brilliant signals from the attic windows. I barely got warm in my brisk encirclement, but felt a glow of blood in my limbs and cheeks.

This morning I drove back from the Cecils at Oxford with Clare Sheppard. Sydney[1] was also staying at the Cecils' for one ghostly

[1] Clare was Rachel's first cousin. Both she and Sydney were sculptors.

night, spreading an effluvium of endearing melancholy. Rachel gets kinder and more understanding and outgoing; she is a 'good' character, where David is rather amoral, and has few ethical responses, though many affectionate and aesthetic ones. People came in and out; Hugh, with whom I had a long interesting talk. (Research into the First World War and the League of Nations has made him almost a pacifist.) I didn't take to a friend of his called Bertie Bell — Irish, pinkish, ebullient, though David says he's 'romantic and dashing': the romance has made him marry a spoilt Persian beauty; the dash caused him to drive round Belgrave Square three times at 70 m.p.h. showing off to a girl, for which I'm glad to say he was fined £200 and his licence taken away for three years (he boasted of this). Then the delightful Bayleys and Laura, pale and mini-skirted, in her first term at St Hugh's. I went to lunch with Frances Phipps in her extraordinary hotel just up the road. She's in the seventh heaven, and has entirely altered the course of her life, from being an anxious mother and grandmother to an eternal student. She is now in some way a registered undergraduate and goes regularly to read her essays to a tutor. After lunch in the fumed oak dining-hall, she took me up to her room, upholstered in throat-pastille and sage greens, and read me one of her essays — a vivid account of the Battle of Sedan. Very good and lively. She would I'm sure have liked to go on and read me them all, but happy as I was to see her so obsessed, and dearly as I love her, I had found two hours of listening to her non-stop lecture on Foch, Clemenceau, the League of Nations, and the Fourteen Points as much as I could take. She barely ate any lunch for talking. I tried sometimes to ask an appropriate question, but she galloped at least four times round the entire landscape before I ever got an answer. How strange it was to be sitting in this unsympathetic hotel room with a person I love, counting the minutes and taking sly glances at my watch to see when I could decently go. Yet a lot that she had to say was fascinating — it was the inchoate nature of it, the inability to divert her on to *any* other theme, or even aspect of her own subject, that made my visit to her — yes, alas, boring. But I respect what she's doing and am touched by the way it has all gone to her head. She means to get rid of her London flat, and is quite content to go on living in this hotel — 'So nice to have no housekeeping'. If only Julia could live in some such way!

Frances spoke enthusiastically of Rachel, less so of David. She feels he's 'cold', and that he doesn't care about ideas! Had we talked

280

about them? A lot about books and writers (Ruskin we'd both been reading about) and people; but he wasn't in a mood this weekend to descend into the depths of first principles and value judgements.

The subject of Desmond's letters wasn't once mentioned, so last night I brought it up myself – the result confirming me that I at least will have nothing more to do with it. I couldn't get much out of David; he showed no signs of wanting to use them as the basis for a life of Desmond, and has quite different ideas from mine as to what makes a good book of letters. Again they said, 'It would be so nice to combine some of Molly's letters.' Again I said what a lot of work this would involve as she never dated them, again they exclaimed, 'Oh, yes, I see!' Here and now I rule a line under that episode, and shall try to devote no more thought to it.

Talk and company as delightful as ever, discomfort as great. Wine and biscuits ran out yesterday. 'Well, I'm afraid there's no wine left,' David said cheerfully. 'It just can't be helped.'

But it could have been, and other people, everyone else I know down to those with only a fraction of their income, always do help it, I couldn't refrain from reflecting.

November 29th: West Halkin Street

I dined very pleasantly with Eardley and Duncan (magnificently amusing, lively and interesting about his trip to America), and gained a sidelight on the Gowings' affairs. Duncan said, and we agreed, that Lawrence and Jenny had a right to their happiness and Julia ought to accept the fact.

I went to Snape for the weekend and basked in the delightful company of Anne and Heywood. Eddie was there in an unusually benign and gracious mood, and actually took me out to lunch at a grand two-star restaurant in the vicinity and on a round of church-crawling. He is much more considerate than before to his poor old mum, who is sinking sadly into decrepitude at eighty-seven, forgetful and sometimes tearful. Anne and Heywood have converted a sort of shed, accessible only by going out of the front door in all weathers, into a sitting-cum-dining-room with a slit of kitchen off it. Here, in a space about fourteen feet square, they (and if necessary Harriet and Tim Behrens and their four children) humbly congregate, while Lady Cranbrook and Eddie sit in state in the large drawing-room. I was very much touched by Anne's good-humoured way of caring for her mother and slowly pegging through household tasks, an uncomplaining philosopher (or at least blue-stocking) at the kitchen stove.

A young tart from Edinburgh had been looking after them all most successfully, nursing Anne's mother and cracking jokes with her, saucing Eddie and being loved by everyone. All she needed was an occasional lover from the local American air station to keep her happy – one of them had left her a small curly-headed boy who calls Heywood 'Lady Hill', as he told me with his delightful self-mocking smile. Anne sometimes gets carried away on slightly exaggerated crusades on behalf of her relations, and lay awake all one night writing a letter in her head to the publisher of Eddie's little pamphlet of inadvertent literary obscenities, because she heard he wasn't going to reprint more than a second edition. It seems to be going like hot cakes and has sold 15,000 copies already. She brought me a draft of her letter to read. I told her I thought most of it would do no harm though probably no good, but to say how hard up Eddie was would cut no ice at all with the publisher. 'That's just what Heywood said,' she said, and in the end she didn't send it.

A lovely walk over the fields towards an inlet of the sea lying pale between beds of *café-au-lait* mud; boats, the small ramshackle houses typical of such situations, into which the imagination projects itself; eerie cry of sea birds. It's the longest walk I've had for some time and I greatly enjoyed it.

December 1st

Dinner last night for Iris Murdoch, the Kees, Janetta and Julian. It went off very well; everyone liked Iris – how could they help it? Her magnificent realism, her Joan-of-Arc-like quality, her way of attending to what everyone said, weighing it (to the accompaniment of a very Oxford 'Yes, yes, yes') and then bringing out her response, her evident enjoyment and sense of fun. She arrived in a splendid antique military coat made of the finest black face cloth with gilt buttons; she tucked in and drank plentifully (how she must suffer at the Cecils'!), she talked. Everyone was at their best, particularly Janetta, who gave a wonderful description of sobbing real tears over a book in Harrods' book department, and was also very amusing about how she viewed the universe in terms of 'me, them and IT'. Apart from the constant tugging at one's watchfulness involved in hospitality I enjoyed the evening very much. Talk was general, right round the dinner table, and also individual; they stayed till nearly one o'clock.

As Janetta was leaving she said that she was tempted to postpone her flight to Spain next Tuesday, and stay and go out with Rose ten days later. 'Oh, do', I said. 'It would be so nice for all of us.' 'Well, I think I might. Of course Rose is quite all right. She doesn't worry. But I do.' And then, suddenly veering like a sailing ship tacking she said, 'The only thing is I do want to help him', (Jaime, though she didn't say so) 'with the preparations for opening his hotel.[1] It would be real work, and I'd like to do it, and I think he wants me to.'

Lord, Lord, Lord, how the rain comes thundering down. I've taken the bit of Charlemagne between my teeth and on I go. Now that I've made the decision I don't mind so much. Not at all, in fact. Rather enjoying it.

A story of Janetta's about returning from Paris in a crowded uncomfortable train with Diana Cooper, after all flights had been stopped for fog. Janetta fell asleep and then woke to see Diana's blue eyes staring fixedly at her. She gave a slight smile. No response, and she realized the face had been so often lifted that her eyelids wouldn't close over her eyes, and she was asleep.

Mary's news is quite extraordinary. Charlie arrived suddenly at Stokke, changed the locks on all the doors and wouldn't let anyone in, not even Ron the farm worker to collect the milk-check books and the milk itself from the fridge. He has a detective with him, so is sparing no expense to be aggressive. He has got all his things back from store. Ron comes over to the Tycoonery to report to Mary and tells her that Charlie sits at her desk, which she hates. Who washes up, I wonder? Ron also reported that the detective came and said, 'Couldn't you let me have a drop of milk? I'm sick of eating my cornflakes dry.' What can Charlie hope to achieve? He must be quite mad.

December 9th

Dinner alone with Janetta last night. Why has it left me a little sad? When we sat down to a most delicious meal of watercress soup and roast pheasant she commented that I was sitting on the very edge of my chair and that it was characteristic of me. F: 'I suppose I feel I must be ready to dash off at a moment's notice.' J: 'Yes, and I think it's that lack of calm that produces your physical troubles.' F: 'I'm sure it does – except that I'm not quite sure which is cause and which

---

[1] La Fonda, at Marbella.

effect. Do you find it hard to be calm?' J: 'No, not in the very least, but then I've got the opposite physical temperament.'

I woke this morning very early and thought that all this was true, but is calm what I want from life? I don't feel it's my chief aim, which still is (I think) intensity of consciousness and realism. But one must relax so as to defeat anxiety and wipe the slate for awareness. Yet there's something to me a little dull in calmness as an aim.

Talked about thinking. Diana Cooper had said almost indignantly to Janetta — 'Think? I never think. I just respond quickly along lines acquired long ago.' Janetta says this is true on the whole, but I think such a remark is proof she does think, something of course lots of people never do.

December 10th

Yet calm is curiously enough what I feel as I sit in a comfortable train speeding through pouring rain to Cambridge (Tom and Nadine this time). How is it that at times the effort of living from day to day seems unsurmountable, at others it can be done with the left hand, while 'thinking' of something else. But the mind is like some extraordinary sort of sponge. Last night, waking in the small hours, it turned out to have soaked up almost the whole of the music of *Dido and Aeneas* (seen last week with the Penroses) and relayed it out again, air by air, the Sorceress, the witches' chorus, the sailor's song and all the rest. As 'ho, ho, ho' rang through my tired head lying surrounded by the tousled confusion of my bedroom, I thought what queer contrasts life produces.

December 17th: Crichel

'It's extraordinary that a professional literary critic should have no idea of writing at all. I mean he writes like a computer, without any pulse of life, any sense of the rhythm or flow of language.' Thus Raymond at breakfast this morning about some book he's reviewing, and oh, alas, every word is applicable to his own productions. However, I must admit that I have not for ages found him such a delightful, easy yet stimulating person to be with as he was this weekend. One day last week he rang me up in a voice grey and shaking with despair, and told me that Simon Fleet had died. (He pitched down a steep staircase after drinking too much brandy and broke his skull. He was not, it seems, a heavy drinker but had no

284

other cure for the despair which he's been suffering from.) Could I, would I, come down to Crichel and keep him company, Raymond asked. He was alone with a servant problem to tackle and feeling depressed. I'd promised myself a quiet, industrious weekend in London and made several dates and arrangements. But after first saying I was afraid I couldn't, I thought better of it and rang back and said I would. At first I didn't take in how much he minded about Simon Fleet – I thought he was a mere acquaintance. But I'm very glad I did go. I couldn't think what to take to cheer him up and then on an impulse took my Turkish diary, edited it most carefully in the train and read it aloud to him. Wild success! I felt a little guilty about the bits I was *not* reading. (Oh guilt, guilt.)

December 19th

Getting on so well with Raymond gave me enormous pleasure. Why should one carp at and criticize one's friends, as I fear I sometimes did in Turkey? Yet I do believe he gets obfuscated by some curious cloud when he's on his travels. We had delightful conversations about the way a literary critic should approach a poem. I do hope Crichel may, somehow or other, be kept afloat, and it almost seemed as if the will and vitality to do so does exist. Raymond and I didn't see a lot of each other – breakfast, lunch and the evenings only – work for us both in the mornings, snooze for him while I walked after lunch, and once I found him in bed again (blankets to chin) not long before dinner. Much sighing of course, groaning it might also be called, over the typewriter, and sometimes as we both sat reading, his heavy breathing would fill the drawing-room, seeming to declare with each loud and laboured inhalation: 'Continuing to live is a burden, and I do it under protest.'

What else did we talk about? Some personal subjects like his reaction to the death of Simon as of other friends – first a sort of numbed uncomprehending apathy, followed after a few days by deep shattered shaky despair.

Then Shakespeare's sonnets, an endlessly profitable subject. Two were quoted in the book Raymond was reviewing, along with some critics' comments. These missed the point to a degree which astounded me. One took great trouble to prove that Shakespeare was not a Metaphysical poet – but whoever said he was? Yet he was 'speculative' in the sense of soaring from the particular to the general even if his soarings are never built into a coherent system; another critic said that his 'imagery had no tension'. Heaven help us – why do such insensitive brutes bother to read him? Both the quoted sonnets were on the theme that I find so moving – starting from the sadness of age, 'parallel lines' in the brows, and ending with a sudden magnificent leap to his superb confidence in the immortality of his own verse. How I hate these dry niggling modern critics who tease away factually at poetry, wondering which month robins nest in, or whether Wordsworth and the 'Solitary Reaper' were really alone in their field.

Social life in plenty: dinner at Michael Pitt-Rivers' on Friday night, with William Davis and an insipid pansified pianist, with an oversweet smile and voice. Quite a jolly evening, though Michael attached himself to my side and subjected me to a barrage of hammering and repetitive badinage. The subject Russia: William brought out his album of Turkish photos; turning the page, I saw they had afterwards been to Russia, but both told me with knotted features how 'they had loathed it, hated the people, who never smiled'. They had gone with closed minds, failed to be bowled over by the beauty of Leningrad ('you can see much greater beauties in Austria, and after all the architects were Italian and Scotch and Catherine the Great was a German'). This latter point gave the show away completely. Who said they weren't and what difference does it make anyway? I was praising Leningrad; the silly fellows thought that by saying it was not a Russian achievement they were countering my praise. I think I was fairly guarded, for I felt Raymond looking at me anxiously and he said afterwards he feared Michael was being a bore. But I do really despise people who go round the world too shut off by the black spectacles of their own prejudices to enjoy anything, and who with the coloured splendour of Leningrad's architecture all round them take trouble to photograph queues and shop windows full of tins. You could create the same effect with a grey-faced London bus queue and the inside of a supermarket. Do they really go abroad to look at and buy tins of baked beans? They even perpetrated the 'no bath plug' illusion.

December 21st

More than a week ago I went to a lunch party at Adrian Daintrey's, where were Joe Ackerley,[1] Diana Cooper and three others I didn't

---

[1] Literary editor of the *Listener*, and writer.

place. I never had a good look at Diana Cooper before and thought her still quite beautiful, rather to my surprise. The great blind blue eyes gazed out under the becoming shadow of a busby, the line of her chin and neck were (even if as a result of surgery) pure and clean, her figure trim. 'A triumph for face-lifting,' I said to Mary on the telephone. 'Perhaps we all ought to do it?' she giggled. Then two nights ago she confided in me that she thought of having it done, and has booked her bed for soon after Christmas.

December 28th

Christmas is over and soon the year will be done also. I look back on its disappearing surface like a featureless road rolling away from the back of a car, and don't know what I can set on the credit and debit sides. Turkey was a credit, certainly. On Christmas Eve in the middle of the day I drove quietly down to Eardley's new house, the Slade near Alton, and yesterday back again into London's intense holiday silence. Never have more people been killed on the road than this Christmas and I saw driving that was savage and horrible.

When I reached the Slade at three of a mild winter's afternoon, I wondered if this could really be it. A square box facing north and built of dark red brick, with a steep slate roof. But Eardley and Mattei are so touchingly excited and happy with their new toy that I soon began to see it with their eyes. No difficulty with their famous view, which composes itself beautifully – a line of elms (one fallen, improving the design) running down a wide waterless valley with a copse beyond. Inside, the house is warm and cheerful, excellent central heating, pretty paint and papers. We spent a quiet time, hanging curtains, cooking and washing-up, going for walks, and I sat at a table in front of a sunny window translating. Drinks one evening with John Fowler in a house full of fantastically pretty things and from what I saw of its architecture fantastically pretty itself. Fowler is like a fruit that has gone soft and squelchy ('*sweet* of you' etc.) but has a hard go-getting core. Mattei says he's very kind. We sat in a tiny room in which everything was elegant and tasteful, drinking whiskies, and I talked to a charming young man about Gibraltar. There was an American with one of the silliest faces I ever saw (but handsome), who kept making noises like a cow or sheep with some little gadget and then tilting back his face and going into a peal of foolish laughter.

The local farmer and his family, all radiant with goodwill, came up to the Slade for a drink and a look at their old home in new hands. I can't imagine what they made of our strange trio. I think Eardley, Mattei and I were all at ease together. Mattei is becoming a splendid cook and liked to tackle it alone. I wonder why Eardley has such strange reserves about Crichel? When I told him Raymond was anxious that he and Mattei should go down as visitors he said, 'I don't think I want to go to Crichel any more,' looking indignant and red-faced. But surely it's unkind of him, and unfriendly to Raymond and Desmond not to go ever? Has he some grudge against them or merely guilt?

London is dreadfully cold and has a terrible silence hanging about it. I have spent long hours alone yesterday and today and there are more to come.

December 31st

Today, the last day of the year has inevitably a dreglike quality. I'm spending it without human contact, and in London. Now, at 6 p.m., I confess I've not felt lonely at all, and have been busy all day, reading late in bed, shopping, and all this afternoon at the London Library, checking up on Charlemagne. As its familiar smell engulfed me pleasurably I looked round at the large number of other inhabitants – some old, some industrious, some sleeping, some reading *Punch*, John Julius Norwich hard at work on his book; and saw this scholarly activity as a form of rather crazy self-indulgence, an escape from the anguish of the world into this womb of paper and dust. Several queerish figures, talking to themselves, hobbling or 'toddling', a large handsome almost young man who made a disturbing impression of not being all there. He arrived when I did, walking with very long legs but tiny steps, I saw him later gazing blankly at some photographs of ancient boats.

So ends 1966, a year – I think – of some degree of moral convalescence.

Index

Sub-headings are arranged, as far as practicable, in chronological/diary order.